ACTS
an exposition

BOOKS BY DR. CRISWELL . . .

Expository Sermons on Revelation — 5 Vols. in 1
Expository Notes on the Gospel of Matthew
Expository Sermons on the Book of Daniel, 4 Vols. in 1
The Bible for Today's World
The Holy Spirit in Today's World
In Defense of the Faith
The Baptism, Filling and Gifts of the Holy Spirit
Expository Sermons on Galatians
Ephesians: An Exposition
Expository Sermons on James
Expository Sermons on the Epistles of Peter
Isaiah: An Exposition
Acts: An Exposition, Volume 1

ACTS
an exposition
Volume II Chapters 9-18

—————————

W.A. Criswell

ZONDERVAN
PUBLISHING HOUSE   OF THE ZONDERVAN CORPORATION
GRAND RAPIDS, MICHIGAN 49506

Acts: An Exposition, Volume 2
Copyright © 1979 by The Zondervan Corporation
Grand Rapids, Michigan

Library of Congress Cataloging in Publication Data

Criswell, Wallie A
    Acts, an exposition.

    CONTENTS: [etc.] v. 2. Chapters 9-18.
    1. Bible.   N.T.   Acts—Criticism, interpretation, etc.   I. Title.
BS2625.2.C74   226'.6'06   78-13525
ISBN 0-310-22890-5

Printed in the United States of America

To the
Music Ministry
of our dear First Baptist Church in Dallas,
whose contributions to the work of our Lord
reach untold thousands of appreciative
listeners, both in our services each Sunday,
and throughout the world.

Contents

1	Drama on the Damascus Road	13
2	The Glory of That Light	19
3	Paul's Persuasion of the Deity of Christ	25
4	We Go to Church With Paul	33
5	Walking in the Fear of the Lord	41
6	Harbingers of Hope	48
7	The Drag of the Old Carnal Nature	56
8	The Gospel to the Gentiles	64
9	The Reward of the Righteous	72
10	These Amazing Converts	78
11	Peter's Defense of the Faith	85
12	A New People	93
13	The Christians of Antioch	100
14	The Touch of an Angel's Hand	108
15	The Smiting of God's Angel	115
16	The Work Whereunto God Has Called Us	122
17	Facing the Pagan World	129
18	The Forgiveness of Sin	136
19	The Word of the Lord	144
20	The Doctrine of Election	153
21	Apostolic Christianity	161
22	Tribulation and Triumph	170
23	The All-Sufficient Savior	178
24	James, The Lord's Brother	187

25 The Compassionate Sovereignty of God 195
26 The Holy Spirit As One of Us 203
27 What God Can Do Through A Woman 211
28 The Man of Macedonia 218
29 The Preaching at Philippi 225
30 The Doctrine of Salvation 234
31 Saving Faith 240
32 The New Life in Jesus 248
33 How Can I Know That I Am Saved? 254
34 The Pulpit Preacher 261
35 What the Scriptures Say 267
36 To the Unknown God 274
37 Just Passing By 280
38 Commanded Repentance 287
39 The Fixed Day of Judgment 294
40 It Is Reasonable to Be a Christian 301
41 God's Tentmakers 308
42 The City Church 315
43 Apollos, Brilliant Alexandrian 322
44 Lettering In 331

Foreword

This series of expository sermons on Acts will be published by Zondervan in three large volumes, each containing more than forty chapters, sermons delivered by me in the pulpit of the First Baptist Church in Dallas. This is the second volume. They are manifestly *preached* messages, not written out and read before the people. All of the characteristics of spoken language are found in the expositions—repetition, starting over again, groping for the right words, change of direction in the middle of paragraphs, mixed-up metaphors and similes, and a thousand other like disorders. I preach without notes, extemporaneously, looking my congregation in the eye, and the language and thought-development in the sermons evidently reflect that type of speaking. That is God's way for me to preach, and He marvelously and wondrously blesses me in that type of delivery. We have just passed, in the days of the preaching of the sermons in this second volume of Acts, our twenty-thousandth church member and a total budget program of more than $7,000,000 a year.

The Bible, and the Book of Acts in particular, seems like a vast, illimitable ocean in breadth, length, and depth. To speak of the richness of the revelation of God in words and chapters is like dipping out the ocean with a bucket—the task is immeasurable. As many as these sermons on Acts are, ten times as many could well be preached if only there were time to deliver them. God's Word is like God Himself—infinite—and especially is this true in following the Acts of the Holy Spirit.

Acts: An Exposition

The Holy Spirit of God, the blessed Spirit of Jesus, is with us always. He works with us today. That is the reason the verses and chapters of the Book of Acts are so full of meaning for the church through the centuries. The Spirit moves; the Spirit works; the Spirit converts; the Spirit saves; the Spirit inspires; the Spirit directs; the Spirit leads. The man of God who is full of the Spirit is the man who of all others is most blessed. The church that is full of the moving Spirit of God is the church that is like a heaven on earth. All of this makes the Book of Acts as fresh and as pertinent today as it was when Luke wrote it almost 2,000 years ago.

May God bring the fullness and the filling of the Spirit into your heart and life as you read these spoken sermons. They are sent to you on wings of prayer and with the devout persuasion that they will be blessed of the Lord to you who read them as they were blessed of the Lord to those who heard them.

W. A. *Criswell*
First Baptist Church
Dallas, Texas

1

Drama on the Damascus Road

And Saul, yet breathing out threatenings and slaughter against the disciples of the Lord, went unto the high priest,

And desired of him letters to Damascus to the synagogues, that if he found any of this way, whether they were men or women, he might bring them bound unto Jerusalem.

And as he journeyed, he came near Damascus: and suddenly there shined round about him a light from heaven:

And he fell to the earth, and heard a voice saying unto him, Saul, Saul, why persecutest thou me?

And he said, Who art thou, Lord? And the Lord said, I am Jesus whom thou persecutest: it is hard for thee to kick against the pricks.

And he trembling and astonished said, Lord, what wilt thou have me to do? And the Lord said unto him, Arise, and go into the city, and it shall be told thee what thou must do.

And the men which journeyed with him stood speechless, hearing a voice, but seeing no man.

And Saul arose from the earth; and when his eyes were opened, he saw no man: but they led him by the hand, and brought him into Damascus.

And he was three days without sight, and neither did eat nor drink. (Acts 9:1-9)

We begin our study with the conversion of Saul of Tarsus which is built around three acts and seven scenes.

THE CILICIAN SYNAGOGUE IN JERUSALEM

Act 1, Scene 1. We are standing in the midst of the synagogue of the Cilicians in Jerusalem. As we stand in that crowded synagogue, we hear someone presenting the faith of the Lord Christ. He is not a

13

Palestinian, Aramaic-speaking Jew. He is a foreign-born, Greek-speaking Jew, a Hellenist; but he knows the Scriptures like an Alexandrian theologian and he uses them with the grasp and insight of a philosopher.

This deacon named Stephen speaks with tremendous conviction and with great spiritual power, for the Christian faith is among other things dogmatic. It is also doctrinal, assertive, exclusive, and unique. There are those who pride themselves upon their philosophical cynicism, upon their broad eclecticism. They look with superior intelligence upon feeble minds who conclude and believe anything, but the Christian faith is a mandate and a revelation from heaven. As such, it is an exact religion. It can brook no other. Poetry can hold parley with fiction, but not the science of numbers. Poetry is malleable and can be shaped in all kinds of fanciful expressions and delightful figures, but not arithmetic. The Christian faith cannot be changed, either. It is not poetic fancy. It is a voice from God. It is not supposition. It is a revelation. It is not a guess. It is an oracle from heaven.

So, Stephen is in the Cilician synagogue presenting the faith once for all delivered to the saints, and he is doing it with great majesty of thought and tremendous spiritual power. He must be answered, this layman who is witnessing to the faith of the Lord Christ. So the Cilician synagogue presents in refutation to Stephen their brightest star. His name is Saul. He is from Tarsus, the capital city of the Roman province of Cilicia. Educated in the universities of Tarsus and in the rabbinical school of Gamaliel in Jerusalem, this brilliant and capable Saul comes forward to answer that deacon. But he fails miserably. He sits down before the power of the witness of Stephen in humiliation. It is then that the Cilicians gather together paid false witnesses who are suborned to swear that Stephen blasphemed God, Moses, and the holy temple. End of Act 1, Scene 1.

THE SANHEDRIN IN JERUSALEM

Act 1, Scene 2. We are now standing in the midst of the Sanhedrin, the highest court of the Jewish nation. Before that august body of seventy men, presided over by the high priest, stands Stephen. He is being accused by suborned witnesses: "We heard this man blaspheme God, blaspheme Moses, and blaspheme this sacred place." The high priest turns to the deacon and says, "Are these things so?"

Then follows the apology of the deacon. The longest chapter in the book of Acts is chapter 7, and the longest defense of the gospel recorded in the New Testament is the apology of Stephen. Written here word for word, syllable by syllable, it sounds like a verbatim report. Who recorded those words? Who remembered that address?

Listening to Stephen was that young, brilliant rabbi from Cilicia named Saul of Tarsus. Every word that Stephen said burned like a flaming fire in his soul. He never forgot Stephen's address and recounted it to the beloved physician, Dr. Luke, who wrote the Book of Acts.

What is it Stephen is saying in his defense and in his apology? He is speaking of the new dispensation, the new age of grace, the new approach to God through the Son in heaven. He is saying that now there is no such thing as God being worshiped in one place only. He speaks of Abraham who worshiped God with altars which he built throughout thê land of promise. He speaks of Moses, who, on the back side of the land of Midian, stood in a place that God said was holy ground, listening to the voice of the Lord. Stephen in his apology speaks of David who worshiped in the tabernacle, not in Jerusalem. And finally, when Solomon built the sacred house of God, he said, "The heaven of heavens cannot contain the great, mighty, Jehovah Lord."

Then he speaks of the exclusiveness of their selfish sacerdotalism in Jerusalem, cutting at the very heart of private privilege on the part of priestcraft. Any penitent anywhere is acceptable to God when he comes by faith through Jesus, the same Lord Christ, who parted the veil and who welcomes us boldly to lay before the Lord our petitions of need.

When the angry Jews heard those words, they gnashed on him with their teeth, and in a rage they dragged Stephen outside their city walls to stone him to death. End of Act 1, Scene 2.

The Stoning of Stephen

Act 2, Scene 1. Outside the city wall, at the base of Mount Moriah in the valley of the Brook Kidron, they stoned this young deacon to death. His execution is being presided over by the brilliant young rabbi, Saul of Tarsus. He would not deign to soil his hands with those rocks. But presiding over the execution with infinite satisfaction, Saul watches Stephen being beaten to the ground. The executioners lay their garments at Saul's feet. Answer Stephen by reason or by word?

They are unable to. Answer him by stones of death? Yes, and with total pleasure and satisfaction Saul watches the blood of Stephen pour out on the ground.

But that face! Stephen had a face like that of an angel. That vision! Stephen saw heaven opening and the Son of man standing on the right hand of God. That prayer! Kneeling beneath the hail of murderous stones, Stephen prayed for those who took his life. Saul never saw a man die as Stephen died. If a prophet had stood by the side of the young rabbinical student and had prophesied, saying, "Saul, the day will come when you will be stoned for the same faith and you will lay down your life as a martyr for the same name," he would have been highly indignant and insulted.

You see, the young man must rave awhile. He must be furious awhile. He must try to find an answer in his madness. But God makes the wrath of man to praise Him. End of Act 2, Scene 1.

THEY MADE GREAT LAMENTATION

Act 2, Scene 2. "And devout men carried Stephen to his burial, and made great lamentation over him" (Acts 8:2). It was as though a gallant general in an army going into battle had been cut down.

I remember reading a quotation from Robert E. Lee. His mighty general, Stonewall Jackson, had been accidentally killed by his own soldiers. Lee said after the Battle of Gettysburg, "If I had had General Stonewall Jackson, I would have not lost the war."

Watching Stephen die, burying him with great lamentation, was like looking into the face of the sky and seeing the sun turn to ashes and plunge into the darkness of the abyss. End Act 2, Scene 2.

IN THE HOMES OF THE CHRISTIANS

Act 3, Scene 1. We are now in the homes of the Christian disciples of the lowly Jesus. They are confronted with a terrible and implacable foe. Saul is like a wolf ravaging the flock. He has seized with both hands the destruction of the church of the living God, and he strikes as he has never struck before. He persecutes with an intense activity. It is as though he felt himself called of God to destroy this "heresy" from the face of the earth. He hails men, women, and children into prison and puts them to death. Having received the keys to the prison, he crowds it with disciples. Having seen the opening to the dungeon, he fills it with the faithful followers of the blessed Jesus. He compels these

Christians to blaspheme and he sees them scourged until the floor is covered with their blood. When they are sent to death, he casts his vote against them. This persecuting wolf, Saul of Tarsus, breathes out threatening and slaughter against the people of God.

AT NIGHT IN THE RABBINICAL STUDENT'S ROOM

Act 3, Scene 2. We are now in the room of a student in the school of Gamaliel. A young man is seated at the desk pouring over the Mishnah and Gemara. As he seeks to study the endless traditions of the Jewish elders, he sees on every page the face of Stephen. When he shuts his eyes, he hears the voice of the martyr Stephen. When he kneels to pray before his God, he hears the prayer of Stephen ringing in his soul. When he goes to sleep at night, he sees Stephen's face.

It is often true that when a great conviction is forming in the heart and soul of a man, he violently opposes the conviction. The young rabbi is in his student room warring violently against the faith he saw in the apology, the face, and the prayer of God's first martyr, Stephen.

THE DAMASCUS ROAD

Act 3, Scene 3. On the Damascus Road nearing the city, travels this violent persecutor, breathing out threatening and slaughter against the disciples of the Lord. Suddenly a bright light, brilliant above the glory of a mid-day, Syrian sun, shines upon him and encircles him. There, on the way, appears the immortalized, resurrected, glorified Lord Jesus, who says, "Saul, Saul, why do you persecute me? It is hard for you to kick against the pricks. All the convictions that are forming in your heart and soul are impossible for you to drown. You cannot forget the testimony of My martyr, Stephen. You could not answer his witness. You cannot drown the face of that godly, dedicated layman. Saul, Saul, it is hard for you to kick against the pricks."

The arch persecutor, falling in deepest humility, contrition, and penance, cried, "Lord, Lord, what wouldst thou have me to do?" In Acts 22 there is added, "Lord, in the same place that Stephen died, let me die, and let the same ground that drank up his blood drink up the crimson of my life." But the Lord replied: "No, Saul. Pick up the torch which was laid down by the stricken hand of Stephen. Raise it up, and bear it to the Gentile world. Saul, Saul, I will show you how great things you can suffer for My name's sake." What an astonishing development!

I'm sure that Stephen never would have dreamed that his death could be the cause of the conversion of that young rabbi-zealot, Saul of Tarsus. The conversion of Saul changed the whole course of Christianity and the world. It was like winning an army. It was like converting a nation. And God used the sweet spirit of Stephen to convert that flaming and violent persecutor, Saul.

So often this word is found in ecclesiastical literature: "Had Stephen not prayed, Paul had not preached." The witness and the death of that first martyr was beyond what Saul could ever answer or forget.

And it is so with us. There is no tear ever shed on behalf of our Lord, there is no drop of blood ever poured out in His name, and there is no sacrifice ever made but that God sees and blesses it. It never falls in vanity and in emptiness to the ground. God blesses and uses it mightily.

One time I visited a young man at Baylor Hospital. He was a member of JAARS, the aviation wing of Wycliffe Bible Translators and was stationed in the Amazon Jungle in Peru. I owe my life to that young man. Had he not been a skilled pilot, I would not be alive. I baptized his three boys in our church.

One of them, fourteen years of age, became a friend of another lad fourteen years of age, whose family was without Christ, agnostic and unbelieving. The unbelief of the family poured over into the life of that fourteen-year-old boy. But Nathan witnessed to them, though he was just a boy, and he talked to his friend. In a tragic plane crash, Nathan was killed in the Amazon jungle.

But God saw it, and out of the sweet memory of that boy, the entire agnostic family confessed their faith in the Lord, became devoted and consecrated Christians, and the friend of Nathan is now a senior in Southwestern Baptist Theological Seminary, soon to begin his ministry as a preacher of the gospel of the grace of the Son of God. Nathan's little brother is going to live two lives for Jesus—one for him, and one for his brother who died.

The Lord never lets a testimony, a sacrifice, or a witness fall futile to the ground even though we may be in heaven when God brings it to pass.

You never know and maybe shall only be apprised of what God has done with you when you open the Book of Life in heaven. Here was a word of testimony. There was a tear of concern. This was the witness that changed a man's life. That is God!

2

The Glory of That Light

And as he journeyed, he came near Damascus: and suddenly there shined
round about him a light from heaven. (Acts 9:3)

Do you ever wonder why this young man in our text, Saul of Tarsus,
should have been so bitter against the Christian faith? Was he elected
for that purpose? Was he a member of the ruling temple guard? Was
he a captain? Was he an appointed leader in the preservation of that
place of worship? There is no intimation of it in the Bible. Some say
that because Paul avows that when the Christians were put to death, he
cast his vote against them, that he was a member of the Sanhedrin.
That is a supposition, for the Sanhedrin had no choice of death. That
right had been removed from the hands of the Jewish leaders and was
now vested in the Roman procurator. Why then was it that this young
rabbinical student in the school of Gamaliel took upon himself the
bitter onslaught against the Christian faith? I do not know. Sometimes
the more a man gives himself to what he is doing and sometimes the
greater pride he takes in his work, the more viciously he responds and
replies to something that humiliates him, that makes him less than
what he thinks he is, or that destroys the work and the foundation upon
which he stands.

The only thing I know from reading the Bible is this: The provinces
of the Roman empire had synagogues in the holy city of Jerusalem,
and when people from the various provinces visited Jerusalem, they
gathered in the synagogues that were dedicated to their people, possibly
because they spoke the language of the nation in that particular

synagogue. In the synagogue of the Cilicians, Stephen, in the power of the Spirit, crushed and shamed those who sought to speak against the faith that Stephen presented in the power of the Lord. Of course, one could easily imagine the reaction that Saul, a brilliant rabbinical student from the school of Gamaliel, had when he was unable to stand up before the wisdom of that young deacon. Stephen was not a rabbinical student. He was not someone who had prepared to give his life in synagogue service. Saul was. He was trained for that in one of the greatest schools the rabbis had ever created. So the background of the conflict reached a dramatic climax in this confrontation between Stephen and Saul of Tarsus in the synagogue of the Cilicians in Jerusalem.

The Glory of That Light Changed the Life of the Bitterest Enemy Christianity Ever Had

When Saul was a little fellow up to about five years of age, he most likely was taught Judaism by his mother. Having been brought up in the pagan city of Tarsus, the capital of Cilicia, the little boy, from the beginning of his consciousness, became sensitive to the truth of God, Judaism, and the false gods that were worshiped all around him. From the age of about five to about thirteen he would have been taught by the rabbi in the synagogue in Tarsus. Later Saul went to Jerusalem and became a student of Gamaliel. When the angry Jews bought and paid men to lie against Stephen, they dragged him outside the city and stoned him to death. The young fellow who presided over the stoning of Stephen was this young rabbi, Saul of Tarsus.

Let us see what Saul did to the church in Jerusalem. When we read the story in English, we can somewhat see what is meant. But the awfulness of it is largely lost to us, so we shall look at the words in the Bible as Luke wrote them down and see what Saul did to the church in Jerusalem.

One must remember that the Jerusalem church was a large congregation. When Saul began to strike that church in Jerusalem it had approximately 50,000 members. When he succeeded in crushing the church in Jerusalem, he persecuted the disciples of the Lord in many cities.

The story begins with Saul's satisfaction in the stoning of Stephen: "And Saul was consenting unto his death." That is rather a lame English word that haltingly describes how Saul felt when he saw

Stephen die. He was pre-eminently lifted up in triumph over the
slaughter of that godly man. Then we read in the same verse: "At that
time there was a great persecution against the church at Jerusalem, and
they were all scattered abroad." When Saul hit the church, he struck it
hard. He dealt the church a death blow.

Now let us look in verse 3. "As for Saul, he made havoc of the
church, entering into every house, and haling men and women committed them to prison." Let us look at the word "havoc." The Greek
word *lume* means "outrage" and the verbal form of that Greek word,
lumainomai, means "to outrage" or "to violently mistreat." Paul made
"havoc" of the church; he "violently mistreated" the church.

Now look at Acts 9. It begins the same way. "And Saul, yet breathing out threatenings and slaughter against the disciples of the
Lord. . . ." The word "threatenings" in Greek is *apeile*. If one saw a
man who was damning and cursing with all the harshness of human
language, he would be issuing "threatenings," *apeile*. The word means
"harshness of language," or "menacing." That is the word that is used
here. Saul was breathing out curses, violent language.

Look at the next word, "slaughter." One would translate that word
"murder." *Phonos* is the Greek word for murder. *Phoneus* is the Greek
word meaning "to commit murder." That is the word that is used in
Acts. "Saul, breathing out threatenings, curses, harshness of language,
and murder against the disciples of the Lord." There are no stronger
words in the Greek language than those words that are used to describe
Saul at this time.

Now look at verse 21. "But all that heard him were amazed, and
said; Is not this he that destroyed them which called on this name in
Jerusalem?" Look at the word "destroyed." The Greek word is *portheo*
which means "to ravage." If one were describing the rampaging army
of Genghis Khan or some other bloodthirsty tyrant, he would use the
word *portheo*, which means literally "to sack, to destroy by blood, by
fire, and by murder." That is the word that is used here. "Is this not he
that *portheo* them which called upon the name of the Lord in Jerusalem?"

Now let us turn to the first chapter of Galatians where Paul uses
this same word and he adds one to it. "For ye have heard of my
conversation in time past in the Jews' religion, how that beyond
measure I persecuted the church of God, and wasted it" (v. 13).
Look at the word "persecute," *dioko*. *Dioko* literally means "to place

in rapid motion," "to follow furiously." Then as it was used in the Greek language, it came to mean "to pursue with a vicious and malicious intent." That is the word that the apostle uses as he writes of himself in the Book of Galatians. He followed the Christians with malicious intent. He did not just strike and oppose the church in one area, but he followed and hounded the Christian cause everywhere. Wherever Christians lived, Saul and his men were at the door knocking. Wherever the Christians sought refuge or escape, Saul was there haling them out, presenting them before the authorities, beating them, compelling them to blaspheme, and rejoicing in their blood. When they were put to death, he cast his vote against them. Saul of Tarsus took it upon himself to destroy and remove from the earth this Galilean heresy. He was the most openly hateful and despicable opponent the Christian faith has ever had.

OH, THE GLORY OF THAT LIGHT

A free reading of our text would be, "And as he came near Damascus, the capital city of another nation, to hale into Jerusalem those found calling upon the name of the blessed Jesus, threatening murder and harshness of language, Saul met Jesus along the way." This is without a doubt the most dramatic confrontation in the history of the human race. Saul met Jesus. The Lord said: "I am Jesus, whom thou persecutest." He did not say, "I am the resurrected, glorified, and coming Judge and Lord of the earth." He cut across the bitterness, the hatred, and the harshness of Saul's persecuting soul. "I am Jesus, whom thou persecutest." Saul met Jesus on the way, and the light of the glory of God shone from the face of the Lord. I think Paul wrote these words from that experience: "For God, who commanded the light to shine out of darkness, hath shined in our hearts, to give the light of the knowledge of the glory of God in the face of Jesus Christ" (2 Cor. 4:6). Above the brilliance and glory of the Syrian midday sun, shone the light from the face of the Son of God. And Saul fell down, blinded. This is how he describes it in Acts 22, "blinded by the glory of that light." When Saul sought to rise and walk, he had to be led by the hand and now as a humble penitent, he gave himself to the blessed Jesus. Thereafter, as vigorously and as violently as he had opposed and persecuted the Christian faith, just as triumphantly and as zealously he now defends and preaches that faith. Do you suppose that Stephen in heaven looked down to see Paul pick up that torch that fell from his hands and bear it to the Gentile world?

John Calvin had on his coat of arms a hand lifting up a blazing, burning heart to God. That is what Saul of Tarsus did before the Lord. And as Paul stood before Herod Agrippa II and recounted his conversion, he said to King Agrippa, "I was not disobedient unto the heavenly vision, but showed first unto them of Damascus, then at Jerusalem, then through all Judaea, and then to the Gentile world that they should repent and turn to God and do works meet for repentance." Is it not unbelievable what God is able to do!

THE LORD CAN CHANGE ANY MAN'S LIFE

We do not know the power of God and His ability to convert anyone, no matter how hard or how harsh that one may be. The Lord has the power to convert and to change and to remake the human soul and the human life, however steeped in sin, however bitter in rejection, however violent in opposition that one may be to God.

When as a young man I visited the Bowery in New York City, I learned that the brilliant preacher and leader guiding that Christian work in New York City had once been a drunkard in the gutter, but was now raised up by the power of the glory of that light.

There is not a more beautiful story in American legend than the train ride of infidel Bob Ingersol and infidel General Lew Wallace. Ingersol said to his friend and fellow infidel, General Wallace, "Why do not you study the New Testament and write a book ridiculing the faith of these Christians who believe in Jesus?" General Wallace, who was Governor of New Mexico, replied, "I think I will." He went to his mansion in New Mexico to write that book. When he finished reading the New Testament, he couldn't help but write the book which is entitled, *Ben Hur, The Story of the Christ.*

Every preacher ought to read B. H. Carroll's sermon, "My Infidelity and What Became of It." He was a blatant infidel and God marvelously changed him. Oh, the glory of that light!

When George Truett went to Baylor, he lived in the home of B. H. Carroll. Now Carroll was a giant of a man, six feet six inches tall, with a heavy beard. He would come to the First Baptist Church and tell George W. Truett, "I have come over here to preach." It was the day before any kind of air conditioning, and when it was 110 degrees in the auditorium, Carroll would preach for an hour and a half. He became the founder of the Southwestern Baptist Theological Seminary in Fo

Worth. God is able to reach and convert any man, no matter what he has done in the past.

In a testimony meeting a man stood up and described his bitterness against God. He was a blatant Christ-rejector, a man in the world with no use for the church, for Christ, for the people of the Lord, for the preacher, and for religion. He was a prospering young man, a man whom God seemingly blessed. He had a wife and a son who was a teen-ager. Then in the providence of life a baby girl was born into the home. One can imagine the love the father lavished upon that little girl. She grew up to be four or five years of age, the darling of the home.

One day the little girl became ill and died suddenly. As the custom was in those days, the casket was brought to the home and the little girl lay as though sweetly asleep in a bed. In the room just beyond, the father sat cursing and hating God, recounting everything vile that could rise in a man's heart in reaction to the death of his precious little girl. The teen-age boy came into the room and said, "Dad, let us go into the next room so I can look at my little sister one more time." So they walked together into the room and stood there, looking down into the sweet, sleeping face of that little girl. The boy began to cry, and putting his arm around his father, he said: "Dad, let us pray." The father in his heart said, "Pray? Pray! I hate God!" But the boy stood by his side with his arm around him, saying, "Dad, let us pray." And the man said: "I never intended to kneel. My knees just bent. I found myself down on my knees by the side of that casket and I began to think 'Dear God in heaven, what about this boy with his arm around me, his head on my shoulder, and his tears falling like rain, who has asked his dad to pray. What shall I do?'" And there came to his memory the prayer he had learned from his mother, and so he began, "Our Father who art in heaven, hallowed by thy name. Thy kingdom come, thy . . ." and he stopped. How could he say, "Thy will be done"? Then the big man said, "In a burst of tears and confession I prayed, 'O God, thy will be done'." The father said: "When I rose to my feet I was a changed man. I was a saved man. I had found the Lord."

You never know. The most bitter of the blasphemers against Jesus is the man who may be the greatest exponent and champion of the faith. That is the wonder and power of God to save. We are never to limit the ability and power of God to change the human heart, for just as He changed Saul of Tarsus, so he has done for us.

3

Paul's Persuasion of the Deity of Christ

> And straightway he preached Christ in the synagogues, that he is the Son of God.
> But all that heard him were amazed, and said; Is not this he that destroyed them which called on this name in Jerusalem, and came hither for that intent, that he might bring them bound unto the chief priests?
> But Saul increased the more in strength, and confounded the Jews which dwelt at Damascus, proving that this is very Christ. (Acts 9:20–22)

The master miracle of the church age and the most wonderful triumph the Christian faith has ever seen is the conversion of Saul of Tarsus. It is almost unbelievable how Saul turned to accept the deity of Christ. When the people in Damascus, whom Saul had come to arrest and deliver into imprisonment and to death heard him, they were amazed and said, "Is not he that destroyed us?" Then we read further in Acts 9:

> And when Saul was come to Jerusalem, he assayed to join himself to the disciples: but they were all afraid of him, and believed not that he was a disciple.
> But Barnabas took him, and brought him to the apostles, and declared unto them how he had seen the Lord in the way, and that he had spoken to him, and how he had preached boldly at Damascus in the name of Jesus (vv. 26-27).

In the kindness of Barnabas, Saul was received as a brother in the faith, but it was hard to accept and realize that the greatest antagonist, the most destructive persecutor that the church has ever known, could turn and now preach the faith that he once destroyed.

That same amazement at the conversion of Saul is something that amazes us today. For example, an article in a local newspaper stated that at a large convention in Dallas, a pseudo-scientist, a doctor, read a paper before a great convocation. In the paper he explained Paul's conversion by saying that Paul's blindness occurred when the corneas of his eyes were burned by a flash of lightning. The doctor stated that he recently treated a patient involved in a house explosion who experienced the same conditions described in Paul's experience. He said that being struck by lightning may have affected the musculature around the throat which would explain Paul's inability to eat for days. He said that a digitalis poisoning, a poison derived from fried toad skins and other plants and related compounds, that have been used since antiquity, would explain the blindness, the seeing, and the conversion of the apostle Paul. Those statements were made in the name of modern science!

OUR OWN AMAZEMENT AT SAUL'S CONVERSION

There are some things about Saul that make his conversion unbelievable. One factor is that he was a Jew and the basic tenet of the Jewish faith is this: God is invisible and without form, and to think of Him assuming any kind of form, much less the form of a man, would be beyond what is thought recognizable in the Jewish faith.

Second, Saul was a theologian. He was not just a member of the tribe of Benjamin, but he was trained in the Scriptures and taught in all the Talmudic traditions of the elders. He was a young rabbi sitting at the feet of Gamaliel, who, in the Talmud, is one of the seven great rabbans of the Jewish faith.

Third, Saul was a Pharisee of the strictest sect. To us a Pharisee is congruent with hypocrite. That is because of the attitude of the Pharisees toward the Lord. The Pharisees were the portion of the family of Israel who were dedicated beyond all others to the truth of the Scriptures, and Saul of Tarsus was a fanatical, zealous Pharisee. He was not indifferent; he was committed.

A fourth thing about Saul of Tarsus is that he was a great Hellenist. He was a Greek scholar. He was a citizen of the Roman empire and he had been taught all the knowledge and culture of his day. One would suppose that he was a graduate of the University of Tarsus when he stood in the midst of the Supreme Court of the Athenians. He was perfectly at home speaking to the university group, the very center of the intellectual life of both the Greek and the Roman empires. He quoted their poets. When he wrote the greatest theological treatise that has ever been written, namely, the letter to the church at Rome, he wrote it in Greek. Saul was no ordinary man; rather he was one of the most extraordinary men who has ever lived, having been the most vigorous and bitter of all the opponents of the Christian faith. When he struck the church, he struck it as it had never been struck before. This is the man who had turned about. He had been converted and he declared that Jesus is the Son of God.

Thinking through all the letters of Paul, I chose out of them seven great dogmas or truths, that persuaded Paul that Jesus is the Christ, the Son of God.

JESUS' VIRGIN BIRTH

First, Paul believed that Jesus was born of a virgin. In Galatians 4:4 he says: "When the fulness of the time was come, God sent forth his Son, made of a woman." What does he mean? He is referring to Genesis 3:15, called the Protevangelium. This is the first announcement of the Christian faith, namely that He who is promised to be the Savior of our souls should be born of a woman. It is the seed of the woman who shall crush Satan's head. Not the seed of Adam, not the seed of a man, but the seed of a woman. Paul believed in the virgin birth of Jesus Christ. The extent of it can be found in the Gospel written by his friend, traveling companion, and personal physician, Dr. Luke. When one reads Luke 1 and 2, he has before him in beautiful form and presentation what Paul believed about the birth of Jesus Christ. When unbelievers scoff at the virgin birth of the Lord and tell you of the miraculous virgin birth of Hercules, or of Alexander the Great, or of Augustus Caesar, folly wide the mark! Read those accounts. They are manifestly fictitious and highly immoral. But when we read what Paul believed in Luke 1 and 2, the beautiful story of the heavenly visit from God when Gabriel announced that a virgin Jewess would be the mother of the foretold, foreordained child, we are elevated into another and heavenly world.

JESUS' RISE OUT OF OBSCURITY

Second, Paul was persuaded of the deity of Christ because He arose out of obscurity, that is, the Lord cannot be explained by His environment. Paul wrote in 2 Corinthians 5:16: "Yea, though we have known Christ after the flesh, yet now henceforth know we him no more."

There is no accounting for Christ as knowing Him in the days of His growing up and His carpentership in Nazareth. The Lord cannot be explained by the environment around Him. Isaiah 53:2 says that same thing: "For he shall grow up before him as a tender plant, and as a root out of a dry ground." Out of a sterile and barren desert came forth this marvelous, glorious creation of God. It is unthinkable, it is unbelievable that the Son of God, Christ, should have arisen out of the background that He did.

Have you ever been to Nazareth? The guide will show you a place and say that inside that cave is where Jesus lived. Then he will show you a grotto that tradition says was His carpenter shop. That is tradition, I know, but it emphasizes the great truth that the Son of God arose out of peasantry and poverty. He cannot be explained by His environment.

Let me illustrate that. In the Gospel of Mark, which is Peter's writing of the Gospel, we read:

> And he went out from thence, and came into his own country; and his disciples follow him.
>
> And when the sabbath day was come, he began to teach in the synagogue: and many hearing him were astonished, saying, From whence hath this man these things? and what wisdom is this which is given unto him, that even such mighty works are wrought by his hands?
>
> Is not this the carpenter, the son of Mary, the brother of James, and Joses, and of Juda, and Simon? and are not his sisters here with us? And they were offended at him (Mark 6:1-3).

The Lord had lived for thirty years (as just one of the citizens) in a despised town called Nazareth. When the Lord, anointed by the Spirit of God, came before the people speaking these words and doing these deeds, they were offended. "This man is the lowly carpenter." "These are His brothers and sisters." One cannot explain Christ by any environment in which He grew up. He is separate and apart.

The apostle John says that while Christ was doing a great work in Capernaum, His mother and brothers came to take Him home, saying: "He is mad. He has lost His mind. He is beside Himself." They never realized, growing up with Him in Nazareth, who He was.

One time a member of my church asked me, "Where is that story in the Bible about Jesus making little mud birds, and then by clapping His hands, they come to life and fly away?" I answered: "My brother, you will not find anything like that in the Bible. That is in an apocryphal story of Jesus trying to make Him what He was not." He became obedient to the life of a slave. Paul tells us in Philippians that Jesus humbled himself in the fashion of a man; He became a slave, as low as it is possible for a man to become.

JESUS' FULFILLMENT OF PROPHECY

Third, Paul was persuaded of the deity of Christ because He fulfilled the Scriptures concerning the coming of the Messiah. We read in Acts 17 that when he left Thessalonica and came to Berea, "they received the word with all readiness of mind, and searched the scriptures daily, whether those things were so" (v. 11). They poured over the Word of God and found under the teaching of Paul that Christ fulfilled all the prophecies of the coming Messiah in the Old Testament.

In the back of some Bibles you can find many pages of the prophecies concerning Christ. Those found in the Old Testament are printed on one side, and on the other side are written the fulfillment in the New Testament. Paul preached these prophecies and the people searched the Scriptures to see whether those things were so or not.

For example, in Micah 5:2 we read that the Messiah would be born in Bethlehem. That was written 700 years before the Lord was born.

Isaiah said in the fifty-third chapter that the Messiah would be numbered with the transgressors, but by His stripes we would be healed, and that He would make His grave with the rich.

One would have thought that David, 1,000 years before, and that Isaiah 750 years before, were standing at the cross watching Jesus die, so meticulously do they describe His death and His burial. He fulfilled those Scriptures, and Paul was persuaded of the deity of Christ because He fulfilled the prophecies of the Old Testament.

JESUS' OWN PROPHETIC WORDS

Fourth, Paul believed in Jesus as the Lord Christ because He Himself was able to prophesy the future. For example, in 1 Thessalonians 4:15 Paul describes the tremendous promise of our Lord that we shall be raptured up to meet the descending Christ from heaven. When he describes the coming rapture of the church, he says: "For this we say unto you *by the word of the Lord.*" That is, the prophecy is not a speculation on his part. It is not even a revelation given unto him, such as the Lord's Supper where he writes in 1 Corinthians 11:23, "I have received of the Lord [by revelation]." Paul says that this revelation the Lord Christ has avowed by His own word, that the dead shall be raised, and all of us who are alive at His coming shall be caught up with them to meet Him in the air.

He believed in the deity of Christ because Christ knew the future. The Lord said of Capernaum, Chorazin, and Bethsaida that they would be destroyed forever. Have you ever been in northern Galilee? Have you been on the site of those three cities? There is nothing remaining.

When the disciples said to the Lord, "Look at the stones in this temple," the Lord said, "There is a time coming when not one of these stones will rest upon the other." Have you been to Mt. Moriah? The temple is so destroyed that there is now a Mohammedan mosque there called the Mosque of Omar.

The Lord prophesied the dispersion of the Jews to the ends of the earth among all the nations of the world.

Jesus the Christ knows the future: "This we say unto you by the word of the Lord." He is Deity and it is the prerogative of the Deity alone to know the future.

JESUS' SINLESS LIFE

Fifth, Paul believed in the deity of Christ because He was the only sinless One who ever lived. As a Lamb without blemish, He was offered an expiation for our iniquities. In 2 Corinthians 5:21 Paul wrote: "For he hath made him to be sin for us, who knew no sin; that we might be made the righteousness of God in him." The reason we die is because we are sinners, all of us. If a man did not sin, he would never die. It is because we are sinners that we die. In our estimation one of us may be a bigger sinner than another, but in God's sight we are all lost, we are all sinners. The only One who was never accused or convicted of wrong or sin is Jesus the Christ. Because He was sinless, the perfect man, He did not have to die. He would live forever, but He gave His life an atonement, an expiation for us, for God made Him to be sin in our behalf, Him who knew no sin, that we might be made the righteousness of God in Him. The Lamb must be perfect without blemish, spotless. He was offered to God the sacrifice for our sins that we might be saved. Paul believed in the deity of Christ because He was sinless, and as a sinless Lamb of God, He made atonement for our sins.

JESUS' RESURRECTION AND VICTORY OVER DEATH

Sixth, Peter believed in the deity of Christ because He was raised from the dead. I do not know of a more powerful verse in the Bible than Romans 1:4. Talking about Jesus, the Son of God our Lord, Paul writes that He is "declared to be the Son of God . . . by the resurrection from the dead." When one reads it in the King James Version he does not see the exact meaning, so let me explain the Greek word and when I do, you will immediately see it. Paul says that Jesus Christ, our Lord is *horizo*, "marked out," to be the Son of God from the resurrection from the dead. *Horizo* is the word from which our English word "horizon" is derived and refers to the line "marked out" where the earth meets the sky. It is a designation, a pointing out that this is the place where the earth meets the sky. The actual word *horizo* means "to point out," "to separate," "to designate," and that is the word Paul used here. He says that Jesus Christ our Lord is designated, He is pointed out, He is set apart, as the Son of God by the resurrection from the dead. Lazarus was merely resuscitated, but he died again. The son of the widow of Nain was resuscitated, only raised up to die again. The only One who had fallen into the grave and who was immortalized, glorified, and resurrected in glory is Jesus of Nazareth, the Son of God. It is in that resurrection that the Lord is declared to be the Son of God with power by the Holy Spirit. Christ Jesus wrestled with our last great enemy, death, and overcame him triumphantly. He is thus declared the Son of God by the resurrection from the dead. Scholars say that the high water mark of all revelation is 1 Corinthians 15 in which Paul avows that because Jesus lives, we shall live also. Because He is raised, we are going to be raised from the dead, too. The apostle says: "But every man in his own order: Christ the firstfruits; afterward they that are Christ's at his coming" (1 Cor. 15:23).

PAUL'S PERSONAL EXPERIENCES WITH THE LIVING CHRIST

Seventh, Paul believed in the deity of Jesus Christ because of His personal experience with Him. In 1 Corinthians 15:8 Paul says, "Last of all he was seen of me also, as of one born out of due time." Three times in this short Book of Acts is this encounter with Jesus presented.

But that experience of Paul is not just a one-time thing that happened to a person two thousand years ago. It is not just a story in the

Bible, nor is it only the experience of those who lived in other generations and in other centuries. To meet Jesus in the way is a present
experience. You can meet the Savior today.

One time I preached to a convocation of Baptists, the North American section of the Baptist World Alliance convening in the Bahamas in
Freeport. The first day of that convocation was given to the Bahamian
government. The meeting was presided over by the president of their
Senate, a dynamic Christian. Then five ministers of state stood up to
address us. One of them was their Governor General. In the United
States he would be called the President. In Great Britain he would be
called the Prime Minister. In the Bahamas he is called the Governor
General. That man stood up and said: "This is a dark world and our
only hope lies in Jesus Christ, in the love and grace of our Lord. This is
a Christian nation and we are committed to keeping it so." One of the
ministers of the government described his personal confrontation with
Jesus and said that all of us must be born anew. Then in the course of
the meeting, a scientist stood up and said, "It was drilled and drilled
into me that all one sees in this manifestation of life is an empty,
endless cycle of nothingness. Out of the dust we are born, we live our
brief life, and then we turn back to the dust. I was taught that life had
no meaning or purpose and that we were here by accident without
reason. We came out of the ground and we are going back to the
ground. There is no ultimate meaning in life. And in those days of
purposeless sterility, of no reason, of no goal, I met the Lord." Then
the scientist used the illustration of Saul of Tarsus as he met Jesus on
the road to Damascus. "I, also, met the Lord and found in Him the
Savior of my soul, and now I have meaning and purpose in my life
today as it was when Paul met the Lord in the way."

Meeting Jesus in the way is not just something that ancient people
knew or something about which they wrote in the days of the Bible. All
who have met the Lord could write a little chapter ourselves. In the
world there are millions of people who know what it is to have fellowship with God through Christ, a living and glorious faith. And Paul
"preached that Jesus is the Son of God."

have I succoured thee: behold, now is the accepted time; behold, now is the day of salvation) (2 Cor. 5:20; 6:1-2).

In all that Paul did we can feel the tug of that seeking, searching, soul-winning note. The same concern for the lost ought to be present in everything that we do in the church—in the songs we sing, in the lessons we teach, in the sermons that the pastor preaches.

Another fire that burned in Paul's soul was the refusal to be discouraged. If any man lived whose life was seemingly fraught with endless disaster it was the apostle Paul. We do not realize that in the ministry of Paul, which extended for many years, he spent much of it in prison behind stone walls and iron bars. He lived a life of apparent defeat and desperation. He was stoned at Lystra and dragged out for dead. He was beaten in Philippi and thrust into the inner dungeon. He found time and again an absolute rejection and refusal of his message. When he spoke to the Athenians in the university city he was mocked, ridiculed, and laughed at. In most of the other cities where he spoke, he created a riot of opposition and had to be taken secretly out of town. Paul's whole life seemingly was one of defeat and frustration, rejection and refusal, but he was never discouraged.

Let me read the following about another man:

> He failed in business in 1831.
> He was defeated for the legislature in 1832.
> He again failed in business in 1833.
> His chosen bride died in 1835.
> He had a nervous breakdown in 1836.
> He was defeated for speaker in 1838.
> He was defeated for elector in 1840.
> He was defeated for Congress in 1843.
> He was defeated for the Senate in 1855.
> He was defeated for Vice President in 1856.
> He was defeated again for the Senate in 1858.
> But he was elected President in 1860!
> What was his name? Abraham Lincoln.

What a life of sorrow, sadness, and defeat. But President Abraham Lincoln never lost faith and he never lost hope. His eyes were always fixed upon some greater and better tomorrow. That is exactly the way the apostle Paul lived. It was out of a Roman dungeon that he wrote in the Philippian epistle, "Rejoice in the Lord always: and again I say, Rejoice." For years he was chained to a Roman soldier. The guard changed every six hours. Paul wrote that the whole Praetorian guard,

the personal army of the Roman Caesar, had become acquainted with
the Gospel. I have thought of how good it would have been to have
been chained to the apostle Paul day after day. There was no defeat in
the heart of this man. He claimed nothing but victory, triumph, and a
glorious and heavenly tomorrow. He preached that way. He wrote his
letters with that spirit of triumph. He lived in that manner of a glorious
victory.

A MESSAGE FOR US TO REMEMBER

Paul has a wonderful message for us to remember today. God is
always for us. He is always with us. He is never against us. God the
Father answers our prayers. God the divine Son has sent us out, and
He has promised to be with us to the ends of the age. God the Holy
Spirit works in convicting power. When a man speaks for Jesus, he can
always know that in the heart of the man to whom he is addressing his
appeal, the Holy Spirit is working, giving evidence of the truth of the
revelation of God. The Lord is always for us. He is always with us. He
is always working by our side. With God the Almighty, how could we
ultimately fail?

The Word of the Lord is always blessed. God says, "My word . . .
shall not return unto me void, but it shall accomplish that which I
please" (Isa. 55:11b). Again, we read in Hebrews:

> For the word of God is quick, and powerful, and sharper than any two-edged
> sword, piercing even to the dividing asunder of soul and spirit, and of the joints
> and marrow, and is a discerner of the thoughts and intents of the heart.
> Neither is there any creature that is not manifest in his sight: but all things are
> naked and opened unto the eyes of him with whom we have to do" (Heb.
> 4:12-13).

We read also in Jeremiah:

> Is not my word like as a fire? saith the LORD; and like a hammer that breaketh
> the rock in pieces? (Jer. 23:29).

THE MESSAGE MUST ARISE OUT OF THE WORD OF GOD

God will always bless His Word. We may not see nor understand,
but God never fails to bless His Word. Maybe He will not bless us, but
He will always bless His Word.

In my reading I ran across a quotation from a preacher telling how
he put together his sermon. I quote:

The preacher passed a little cottage where one man was saying, "Guess there will be a lot of women miserable when I marry." The other let that rest for a moment, then responded: "Oh, I don't know. How many women are you planning to marry anyhow?" So as the preacher walked along, he said, "That's my first point, humility."

Then the preacher passed the auction barn where he sees a sweet young wife gently calming a rather upset husband. "What can be wrong here?" he wondered. Then he heard her say to her husband: "Of course, I spend more than you make, dear! I have confidence in you." The pastor almost jumped for joy as he said, "Perfect for point two, namely, optimism."

The preacher then came upon the farmer plowing with one mule, but who was calling, "Giddap, Pete! Giddap, Barney! Giddap, Johnny." Stopping in amazement, the preacher asked, "How many names does that mule have?" "Just one," says the farmer. "His name is Pete. But he does not know his own strength so I put blinders on the rascal, yell a lot of names at him, and he thinks that two other mules are helping. Amazing what we can get done that way."

Our pastor leaps for joy and he says, "Does not know his own strength . . . amazing what we can get done. Eureka! That is my third point, power!"

The preacher had all three points for his sermon. That is the way most sermons are made. They arise out of the peripherals of the day, out of the adventitious events that the preacher watched during the days of the week. Tell me, would it not be a wonderful thing if the young preachers were taught: "Let your sermon arise out of the immutable, inerrant, eternal Word of God. Expound the Scriptures, and in that way you will touch every human life at each needed point. Let the sermon arise out of the holy Word."

That is how Paul preached and that is how all the apostles preached. "To Him give all the prophets witness." When a man opens God's Book and expounds the inspired, infallible Word of the Lord, there is immediately a repercussion in the hearts of the people. This is the authority of God Himself: "Thus saith the Lord."

We should remember one more thing. The Lord God who saved then in the preaching of the apostle Paul is the same Lord God who saves today under the witness and testimony of the blessed Jesus, doing it just as miraculously, just as gloriously, and just as wondrously as He did during Paul's ministry. When we turn to Acts 16, we read the marvelous conversion of the Philippian jailer. This man was rough and tough, brutal and cruel, and he beat Paul and Silas. He placed them in an inner dungeon and put their feet in stocks. He was brutal far above the call of duty of the law or of necessity, and yet that night that cruel Philippian jailer was wondrously saved. We read that and say, "How marvelous, how glorious!" But the same Lord Christ who saved the Philippian jailer saves today in the same wondrous and miraculous way.

I remember when I received word that the Stone Age Indian tribe called the Aucas, in the Amazon Valley, had slain five white missionaries who had gone to tell them about the saving grace of the Lord. Then I learned that the wife of one of the missionaries and the sister of another of the missionaries who had been slain had made their way to that awesome tribe and had won them to the Lord. I said in my heart, "I want to see that with my own eyes." So I went down to the Amazon jungle where the Aucas lived and I conducted church services with that tribe of Stone Age Indians who were used to dipping their hands in human blood. Later, at my invitation, three of the Aucas who had slain those five missionaries sat in three chairs on the platform of the First Baptist Church of Dallas and stood up to witness to what Christ had done for them. The Lord is still in the saving business— miraculously, gloriously, and wondrously, just as He spoke to you and you found the Lord and were saved.

We read of the Asian ministry of Saul of Tarsus when the whole nation came to the Lord, when the seven churches were founded, when all of the people knew of the saving grace of Christ, and we say, "What a marvelous outpouring of the saving Spirit of Jesus." My brother, in our modern times, He is just the same.

In the ministry of Charles Haddon Spurgeon and with the young men he trained in Spurgeon's College, 265,000 souls were won to Jesus and baptized into the fellowship of the churches. The same Lord God is still saving His people.

When we read in the Bible of this ministry of Saul of Tarsus in the school of Tyrannus, a place where throngs could come and Saul could teach them the Word of the Lord, we can know that the same Lord God gathers with His people in Bible-believing churches. When we preach the Word of the Lord, people continue to respond to the Lord's call. The power of God in His witness on the sacred page is a miracle and a wonder of heaven. He is the same Lord with the same power. He has the same presence and the same saving grace. It is the same Jesus. To stand in that line of those who have followed the Savior, who have given their lives in trust to Him, to pilgrimage with the disciples who call upon His name, finally to lift up our faces to the great and wonderful consummation is the life that God intended for us when He created us and we were born into this world!

5

Walking in the Fear of the Lord

Then had the churches rest throughout all Judaea and Galilee and Samaria,
and were edified; and walking in the fear of the Lord, and in the comfort of the
Holy Ghost, were multiplied. (Acts 9:31)

Could a more typical characterization using Bible words, imagery,
and thought be found than in the phrase, "walking in the fear of the
Lord"? The phrase "fear of the Lord" is one the Bible loves and uses
frequently. For example, there are more than 300 instances in the Old
Testament where the phrase "fear of the Lord" can be found. The
wisest man who ever lived closed the Book of Ecclesiastes with that
phrase: "Let us hear the conclusion of the whole matter: Fear God,
and keep his commandments: for this is the whole duty of man"
(12:13). All the relationships of this earth with God are said in that
brief word. "Fear God, and keep his commandments: this is the whole
duty of man."

The phrase is also found in the New Testament. For example, in
Acts 10 Cornelius, the worthy centurion in Caesarea, the capital of the
Roman province of Judaea, is described as a man who feared the Lord
with all his house and that commended Him to the grace and mercy of
God.

THE MEANING

What does "the fear of the Lord" mean? One can see its meaning in
Psalm 139 when the psalmist says, "I am fearfully and wonderfully
made" (v. 14b). That is, it is awesome how God has constructed this

human frame. There is no miracle seen in the stars above or in the earth below like the miracle of the framing of the human life. All of those little engineers, carpenters, and bodies are working day and night in the unseen womb of a mother, building a new frame, a new life, an anatomical miracle. It is an "awesome" wonder; "I am fearfully and wonderfully made." The more we think of it, the more miraculous and wondrous it seems.

Look again at the use of that word in the Book of Hebrews. Speaking of the atoning death of Jesus, the author writes of our Lord, "Who in the days of his flesh . . . offered up prayers and supplications with strong crying and tears unto him that was able to save him from death, and was heard in that he feared" (5:7). That is, when the Savior, who learned obedience by the things which He suffered, offered Himself to God, He did so in the reverent awe of God the Father who is able to save Him out of death. Jesus gave Himself on the cross and committed Himself to the Lord God in heaven who raised Him from the grave to elevate Him to glory. The Lord's awesome reverence before God was accepted in the presence of the Almighty as a gift of love, praise, and obedience.

THE BEGINNING OF WISDOM

According to the Word of the Lord, "The fear of the LORD is the beginning of wisdom" (Ps. 111:10), and that is the text of the Book of Proverbs. What does the Lord mean by that? It is something that is most apparent and beautiful. What is the difference between wisdom, knowledge, and science? Knowledge is merely a collection of facts. Science is the arrangement of those facts. The facts are in one position or another. That is science. But wisdom is in a different category altogether. Wisdom comes from God. It is the sensitivity to the hand of God in all the phenomena and all the facts that we observed in human life and in the world of nature around us, below us, and above us. Without God, there is no purpose, no meaning, and no ultimate in any fact that we know in the universe. It is God, and the hand of the Lord that gives pertinency and purpose to fact.

When one stands in the presence of the almighty God and looks at His hand in history, in human life, and in the universe, he stands in reverential awe. For example, by the word of His mouth, God can destroy an entire civilization. The author speaks of that in the eleventh chapter of the Book of Hebrews. "Noah, being warned of God of things not seen as yet, moved with fear, prepared an ark to the saving of his house" (v. 7). With just a word from God, a whole civilization was destroyed.

With a word from God, cities are destroyed. When Lot came to his sons-in-law and pleaded with them in Sodom to escape the judgment of God, we read that "Lot . . . seemed as one that mocked. . ." (Gen. 19:14). Lot seemed to be jesting. Surely He could not be serious. Who is this God who is going to destroy Sodom and Gomorrah? But in verse 24 of that same nineteenth chapter of Genesis we read, "Then the LORD rained upon Sodom and upon Gomorrah brimstone and fire from the LORD out of heaven." It is a fearful thing to fall into the hands of the living God.

The Lord in a word can destroy a great army. We read in Isaiah 37 that in one night only one angel passed over the Assyrian army that was encompassing Jerusalem, and the next morning 185,000 dead corpses lay in those forsaken and judgmental tents. Ah, the awesomeness of God!

With just one word of the Lord, a whole nation can be destroyed. The little book of Nahum is a description of God's destruction of Assyria. What God is able to do!

God's wrath is no less seen in the life of a king and queen. Jehovah God sent Elijah to confront Ahab and Jezebel in the stoning to death of Naboth. The Lord through Elijah said to Ahab, "In the place where dogs licked the blood of Naboth shall dogs lick thy blood, even thine" (1 Kings 21:19). Turning to Jezebel, Elijah said, "The dogs shall eat Jezebel by the wall of Jezreel" (1 Kings 21:23). The terror of the omnipotent judgment of almighty God!

We may wonder why men do not tremble before the judgments of God. Listen to the word of the Lord and you will see why:

> Because sentence against an evil work is not executed speedily, therefore the heart of the sons of men is fully set in them to do evil.
> Though a sinner do evil an hundred times, and his days be prolonged, yet surely I know that it shall be well with them that fear God, which fear before him:
> But it shall not be well with the wicked, neither shall he prolong his days, which are as a shadow; because he feareth not before God (Eccl. 8:11-13).

Does God allow time and delay to temper that ultimate judgment? No. He said to Adam, "In the day that you eat thereof, thou shalt surely die" (Gen 3:17). That day his soul died and 930 years later Adam died. The judgments of God inevitably fall. Though maybe not now, yet some day they inevitably fall. Nahum delivered his prophecy against Assyria but it was a whole generation before it came to pass. When Elijah told Jezebel that dogs would eat her flesh at the entrance of the gate of Jezreel, that prophecy did not come to pass until twenty years later, but it came to pass. That is the fear of the Lord. That is the beginning of wisdom. The beginning of wisdom is the fear of the almightiness of God; it is reverential awe as we stand in the presence of Him who holds our life and breath in His hands.

To Hate Evil

The fear of the Lord is to hate evil. Is that not an unusual word? One will find that thought much elaborated in the Bible. Listen to the psalmist as he says:

> Do not I hate them, O LORD, that hate thee?
> I hate them with perfect hatred: I count them mine enemies (Ps. 139:21a, 22).

The fear of the Lord is to hate evil. How does one interpret that?

Let me illustrate. Never can I forget the first time I saw a child with polio. It was in my first pastorate out of the seminary, and polio was a disease to which I had never been introduced. In the congregation there was a precious family who had a boy fourteen years of age. I went to see the boy in his home, and as I stood there and looked down into his face I could see he was nearing death. When I looked upon him, he was a living skeleton. His suffering and the length of his illness was terrible to me. As I knelt by the side of the boy and prayed, I felt in my heart a hatred toward evil and sin and Satan and the devil that brings such sorrow, such tragedy, and such suffering upon the human race! God never intended that. God never planned for death. He never planned for disease, wasting, and corruption. He made us to live forever, but Satan has deceived us. For it is Satan who has brought sin, sickness, sorrow, suffering, and death into the world. To fear God is to hate evil.

In Kentucky, where numerous distilleries are located in the limestone hills, I had a man in my little congregation who hated the liquor traffic. He did not just hate liquor traffic casually, or indifferently. He hated it with a vengeance. One day in visiting with him I asked him why he was so vehement about the liquor traffic. He told me he had a friend who was an alcoholic, and late one cold Saturday night, when he had spent all his money, he was kicked out of a saloon. That drunk staggered down the road and finally fell face down in the ditch on the side of the road. When he did not appear the next morning, they sought to find him. They found him lying face down in the ditch, frozen to death. The man in my congregation described to me how his friend looked as they pried him up and stood him up in the mud. When he saw the mud-covered face of the image of God in his friend, he said, "I hate the liquor traffic!" The fear of the Lord is to hate evil. When men compromise with evil, they affront God. When Christians play games with iniquity, they disgrace the name of the Lord. When we live compromised lives, we do dishonor to the name of the blessed Jesus. The fear of the Lord is to hate evil.

NO WANT

Look again at the beautiful way the Lord presents the fear of God. The psalmist writes in Psalm 34:9, "O fear the LORD, ye his saints: for there is no want to them that fear him." Continuing in the thirty-seventh psalm, we read:

> The steps of a good man are ordered by the LORD: and he delighteth in his way.
> Though he fall, he shall not be utterly cast down: for the LORD upholdeth him with his hand.
> I have been young, and now am old; yet have I not seen the righteous forsaken, nor his seed begging bread (vv. 23-25).

God will take care of those who love and fear Him.

There is a reason why a man who loves God prospers in this life. There are thousands of evil habits to which he never gives himself. God prospers those who walk in the fear of the Lord, who give one tenth of what they have to Jesus, who give an offering above that to the Lord. His way is known to Jesus. There is no want with those who walk in the fear of the Lord.

An elderly gray-headed woman, a widow of many years, entered my study. She had come to tell me of the want and need in her life. She said: "My sole support is my only daughter who takes in sewing to support me, and now my daughter is sick in the hospital and we have no money to pay our bills, and we are in want. I do not know what to do." I told her about her rich Father and that she should ask Him but she remonstrated: "Pastor, no, my father has been dead for years and he died a poor man." Then I told her: "Your Father is rich in houses and lands. The cattle on a thousand hills are His. All the gold and silver are His." She said, "Oh, you mean God?" I said, "Yes, I mean God. Our Father is rich. Why do not you ask Him for your need?" She said, "I never thought to do so." I said, "Let us bow our heads and ask the Father to take care of all your want and need." So the gray-headed widow bowed her face before the Lord and told God all about it. The next Sunday morning I told our people about that dear old woman and I said, "I am going to stand back there at the door, and I want all of you when you go by me to take a $1 bill and put it in my pocket." When I got through shaking hands with all those people, I looked like a decorated Christmas tree! They placed bills in my collar, down my neck, in my shirt, in my pockets, in my shoes, in my belt . . . they covered me, they showered me with those sweet, kind remembrances. I put them all together and gave them as a beginning of a remembrance of love for that old gray-headed mother.

> God will take care of you,
> Through every day,
> O'er all the way,
> God will take care of you.

Trust God for your needs; ask Him for everything. There is no want to them who fear the Lord. "I have been young, and now am old; yet have I not seen the righteous forsaken, nor his seed begging bread" (Ps. 37:25).

One of the most beautiful and precious passages in the Bible is found in Malachi:

> Then they that feared the LORD spake often one to another: and the LORD hearkened, and heard it, and a book of remembrance was written before him for them that feared the LORD, and that thought upon his name.
> And they shall be mine, saith the LORD of hosts, in that day when I make up my jewels; and I will spare them, as a man spareth his own son that serveth him (Mal. 3:16-17).

They who feared the Lord often spoke one to another. It is a part of that inwardness of the Christian life itself that makes us want to be together and to talk about the rich mercies of the blessed Jesus.

A little boy goes through many things in growing up. When I was a boy my family went to church all the time. We went to Sunday school, we went to B.Y.P.U., we went to church Sunday morning, Sunday night, and Wednesday night. I even went with my father to the choir on Thursday night. Every time the church was open, my family went to church. I came to the rich conclusion as a growing young man that going to church was idiocy and foolishness. So when the next Wednesday night came, I said, "I am not going." Our home was across the street from the church, so my father, mother, and brother went to prayer meeting, but not I. I was going to stay at home. So I stayed home and tried to read a boring book. In a little town there was nothing else to do but read a book. And while I was trying to read that boring book, I heard the people begin to sing. As you might have guessed, I couldn't concentrate. That was the last time I ever tried that. I closed that book, stood up, walked out the door, and went into the house of the Lord.

I do not attend church because I have to. I love it. I love to mingle with Christian people. I am most awkward and most ill at ease where people are taking God's name in vain, where they live worldly lives, but I love being with God's saints—to pray, to sing, to listen to the expounding of the Word of the Lord, just to be in God's house. O Lord, how happy and how precious have You cast my life and lot that I can be with You!

6

Harbingers of Hope

And it came to pass, as Peter passed throughout all quarters, he came down also to the saints which dwelt at Lydda.

And there he found a certain man named Aeneas, which he had kept his bed eight years, and was sick of the palsy.

And Peter said unto him, Aeneas, Jesus Christ maketh thee whole: arise, and make thy bed. And he arose immediately.

And all that dwelt at Lydda and Saron saw him, and turned to the Lord.

Now there was at Joppa a certain disciple named Tabitha, which by interpretation is called Dorcas: this woman was full of good works and almsdeeds which she did.

And it came to pass in those days, that she was sick, and died: whom when they had washed, they laid her in an upper chamber.

And forasmuch as Lydda was nigh to Joppa, and the disciples had heard that Peter was there, they sent unto him two men, desiring him that he would not delay to come to them.

Then Peter arose and went with them. When he was come, they brought him into the upper chamber: and all the widows stood by him weeping, and shewing the coats and garments which Dorcas made, while she was with them.

But Peter put them all forth, and kneeled down, and prayed; and turning him to the body said, Tabitha, arise. And she opened her eyes: and when she saw Peter, she sat up.

And he gave her his hand, and lifted her up, and when he had called the saints and widows, presented her alive.

And it was known throughout all Joppa; and many believed in the Lord.

And it came to pass, that he tarried many days in Joppa with one Simon a tanner. (Acts 9:32-43)

We begin an exposition of the passage with the text, "And it came to pass, as Peter passed throughout all quarters, he came down also to the saints which dwelt at Lydda" (v. 32). I have never heard about saints in Lydda, have you? I did not know there were any saints there, and yet the passage in Acts states that Peter met with the saints in Lydda. There are saints in the most unexpected places.

When I was a younger man a tragic plane crash in Alaska shocked the world. Riding in that plane were Wiley Post, the famous American aviator, and Will Rogers, his famous companion. The whole world was overwhelmed by the death of those two distinguished and gifted Americans. But do you know who advertised it to the world? A Presbyterian mission in Point Barrow, on the other side of the Arctic tundra of Alaska. We did not even know they were there. Yet when that plane fell bearing to death Wiley Post and Will Rogers, the saints were already in Alaska.

One time I was with a physician, a Christian doctor-missionary inside the west African continent. We were driving in his little English car in the remote bush country. Through those mud huts and villages in the interior of dark Africa, there suddenly appeared on the side of the road a little cottage with a white picket fence around a beautifully trimmed front yard. Out of the door came an English missionary who greeted us and invited us into his house for tea and crumpets.

There are saints all over the world just like that, in the most unexpected places. Is it not a marvelous thing that when Peter came to Lydda, he found saints? Simon Peter, God's chief apostle, and the saints at Lydda, were drawn together by a heavenly magnetism.

But did you know that all mankind is like that? No matter where you go or whatever city you enter, you will meet yourself. You are already there. If you are a drunkard and go into a strange city, you will find your fellow drunks. They will meet you at the bar and you will drink you life away together. If you are a whoremonger and go into a strange city, you will find yourself in a bawdy house or in a hotel room. If you are a gambler and you enter a strange city, there you will find yourself with your fellow gamblers. You will be at the table with dice, with cards, or at the roulette wheel. If you are a member of the underworld and you go into a strange city, there you will meet yourself. Out of the sewer they will come to welcome you. On the dark, seamy sides of the city there you will be plotting some of the dark travesties on human nature. Wherever you are, there you will see yourself.

How precious and beautiful if you are a Christian and if you love God, for wherever in the world you go, there you will meet yourself.

There will be fellow Christians with arms outstretched to welcome you.

One of the most unusual things I ever experienced took place many years ago. I was coming into Istanbul for the first time. It was in the days when they pulled up ramps to the plane for the passengers to deplane. At the bottom of the ramp, holding an umbrella above his head because it was raining, stood a tall, young Greek. He asked everyone who stepped off the plane, "Are you the two missionaries from America?" I turned to my companion, Dr. Duke McCall, and said, "I wonder if he knows about us." So when we finally got to the bottom of the ramp, he asked us, "Are you the two missionaries from America?" I replied to him, "Young man, we are not missionaries, but we are Christians and we are from America." He said, "Then it must be you whom I want to welcome." We crossed the Hellespont with that young man and that night for the first time I put my foot down on the continent of Asia. We immediately went to a home for a prayer meeting and a praising of the blessed Jesus together.

All over this world I can illustrate that truth. The first time I was in Calcutta, that vast, illimitable, poverty-stricken and heathen city, I was in a home on my knees before God's open Book praying to Jesus and praising His blessed name. You see, you find yourself wherever you go, and thus it was with Peter. He is now in Lydda and he has found himself with the saints.

HUMAN NEED

Notice that Peter arrived in answer to great human need. In Lydda there was a man who was sick and needed the hand of the Great Physician. When Peter came to Joppa, he found that a godly woman by the name of Dorcas had become ill and died. Dorcas must have been a most affluent woman. She gave what she had to the Lord and did many good works. Not only did she give what she had to the Lord, but she also worked with her needle making coats and garments which she gave to the poor. One would think that a woman like that would live forever. But the Bible says that she became ill and died.

That is one of the most inexplicable things that I see in human life. When a good woman like Dorcas dies, we wonder why a thousand prostitutes can walk up and down the streets. When a good man dies, we think about the shiftless bums standing on every corner. They are a reproach to the name of God. And they seem to continue to live.

Consider the butcher of Uganda named Idi Amin. If there was ever a reproach to the human race, he is one. Uganda was once our brightest mission field. When I once preached in that nation, I met a young black pastor, who in nine months or less, had baptized more than 1,000 converts into his Baptist church! But after that Uganda had a wretch reigning over it. It's hard to understand those things. At the same time the people of God, the Lord's saints, sicken and die.

How many people have you known in your life who were taken away and all your world seemed sad and dreary. Sometimes the home is no longer a home because one of the members has been taken away. Sometimes in despair we only wait for the grave. How bleak the world is without these whom we have loved and lost!

But God is not done yet. The Book is not yet closed. The last chapter is not written yet. God purposes some better thing for us. That is why we are given these marvelous narratives written on the sacred page. You see, these narratives are harbingers and promises of what God is yet to do in the ultimate and final triumph of the Christian faith.

THE NARRATIVE IS A HARBINGER OF THE CHRISTIAN TRIUMPH THAT LIES AHEAD

One of the most remarkable things I find in the Word of God is this: that whatever God intends at the consummation, He does it in miniature before our eyes. There are no surprises at the consummation of the age. God has laid it all out before us. When He comes to the end of the age and He does what He has planned, it is just something that he has already told us.

For example, at the end of the age there is coming the great Judgment Day, but God has already seen to it that we understand what He means by that awesome and final visitation from heaven. It was a judgment day when God destroyed this world by flood and the antediluvians perished in the breaking up of the deep and the rising of the waters. It was a judgment of God upon Sodom and Gomorrah when the cities of the plain were destroyed by fire and brimstone. It was a judgment of God upon Jerusalem, when in 70 A.D., Titus and his Roman legions destroyed the city and scattered the nation to the ends of the earth. God speaks of a great judgment. These judgments that we read about in the Bible are but harbingers of what God is going to do.

We read of the tribulation at the end of time. We know what tribulation is because we have already seen it. In the days of the judges when the children of Israel departed from God, they were sold to their enemies, and they went through agony and tribulation. During the 430 years that Israel was in Egypt, they groaned under the taskmasters, the tribulation, and the fiery furnace. In the days of the Babylonian captivity, when they hanged their harps upon the willow trees and wept because they were asked to sing by the rivers of Babylon, that is a tribulation. God has sent harbingers of what is to come.

All that God is going to do at the consummation, He has already demonstrated to us. Enoch walked with God, and suddenly he was taken away. Elijah, in a whirlwind, was carried up to heaven in a chariot of fire. This is a harbinger of the rapture. God has already done these things that we might know and see.

The resuscitations that we read about in the Bible are announcements beforehand of the power of God to raise us from among the dead. In the days of Elijah He brought back to life the son of the widow of Zarephath. In the days of Elisha, He brought back to life the son of the Shunamite woman. In the days of Jesus, the Lord spoke to Lazarus and he was raised from the dead.

What adumbration could there be of the return of our Lord? Is there anything in the Word of God that beforehand would present the clouds bearing down the glorious coming of the Lord, the shekinah glory of God, when the heavens are rolled back like a scroll and Jesus personally appears? Yes, there is. The sixteenth chapter of the Gospel of Matthew closes, "Verily I say unto you, There be some standing here, which shall not taste of death, till they see the Son of man coming in his kingdom" (v. 28). Then immediately follows the incomparable story of the transfiguration of our Lord upon the mount.

Peter wrote of that glorious experience in the first chapter of his second letter. He said, "We made known unto you the *parousia*." What is the *parousia*? It is the personal coming of our Lord in glory and power. Then Peter described it. "We were eyewitnesses of His majesty and we heard that voice from glory which said, This is my beloved Son, hear ye him." He was describing the Mount of Transfiguration. What the disciples saw and what they experienced on the Mount of Transfiguration was a harbinger of the glorious day of the Lord when Christ will come down and His face will shine like the brightness of the sun and His garments will be as white as snow, and the Lord Jesus will appear personally, visibly, bodily. Whatever God is going to do, He has given us a preview before the day comes to pass.

So it is also in the day of the recreation of the heavens and the earth. The apostle John writes in Revelation 21: "And I saw a new heaven and a new earth: for the first heaven and the first earth were passed away" (v. 1). The Bible begins the same way it ends. The first verse of Genesis begins, "In the beginning God created the heavens and the earth." If God made it, it was perfect. It would be unthinkable and inconceivable that God would make anything imperfect, chaotic, or dark, for God is light. Then the second verse says, "And the earth was void and dark and chaotic." The whole creation was destroyed because of sin. Satan, Lucifer, introduced sin into God's world. Wherever there is sin, it hurts and destroys. Sin tears apart. So God's perfect universe fell into chaos and into darkness. Then we read in the first chapter of Genesis of the recreation. God makes it anew on the first day and the second day and the third and the fourth day. God remade His world.

That is exactly what God is going to do at the end of the age. He is going to rejuvenate, He is going to remake this world. I do not think that He will destroy the world and then create it again, but He says, "Behold, I make all things new." The word "new" is exactly as it is used in 2 Corinthians 5:17: "If any man be in Christ, he is a *new* creation." God is going to take this world and make it new. He is going to take this burned-out universe, and He is going to remake it all, regenerate it all. The harbinger of what God did in the beginning is that we might know what He is going to do at the end.

OUR RAISING FROM THE DEAD

As it is with this story we just read in the ninth chapter of Acts, so there is going to be a resurrection and a healing at the great consummation of the Lord. The Lord Jesus said in John 5:25: "Verily, verily, I say unto you, The hour is coming, and now is, when the dead shall hear the voice of the Son of God: and they that hear shall live." The Lord's message has two meanings. One, He is speaking to those of us who are dead spiritually, to those who are dead in trespasses and in sin. The body, which ought to be a holy temple of God, is then nothing but a sepulcher with dead men's bones. The whole world is a vast cemetery of dead people. But those who listen to the voice of God (souls who are spiritually dead), are brought to life, they are regenerated and recreated. "They that hear the voice of the Son of God shall be raised."

Second, He is also speaking of physical death. The day is coming, says the Lord Jesus, when people shall hear the voice of the Son of God, and hearing, shall live, shall be raised "from among the dead." O triumph, O glory, O victory!

We have an adumbration of that day also. The Lord stopped the procession from the little city of Nain when the poor widow was weeping for her only son, who had died. Putting His hand on the bier the Lord said: "Young man, I say unto thee, Arise." The boy arose and the Lord gave him back to his weeping mother.

Look at the fifth chapter of Mark. When the Lord spoke to the twelve-year-old daughter of Jairus and she came to life at the voice of the Son of God, He gave her back to her weeping father and mother. Mary and Martha were weeping over Lazarus. The Lord stood at the tomb and said, "Lazarus, come forth."

An appropriate illustration comes from the life of the infidel Bob Ingersol, who was making fun of Jesus and scoffing at His miracles. Among the contemptuous remarks Ingersol made was, "Why did Jesus say, Lazarus, come forth'?" A saint listening to that infidel rave said, "I will tell you why the Lord said, 'Lazarus, come forth.' Had the Lord not said, 'Lazarus, come forth,' the whole cemetery would have stood up and walked out to meet the Lord!" "But they shall hear the voice of the Son of God, and they that hear shall live."

Back in the days of the old south, there was a black slave who loved his master. The master died and was buried in the garden on the plantation. The old colored saint, the father of a large family, lived in north Georgia in 1833 when the notable meteoric display known as the "falling stars" occurred. Being awakened by the noise and the confusion outside, he looked out from the window of his humble home and saw what appeared to be stars falling like snowflakes from heaven. He thought that the end had come, so he quickly roused his wife and children, saying, "De day of de Lawd am at hand." Hurrying them into the street where the scene was indescribable, the old black man turned to his companion, his wife, and said: "Ole woman, de Lawd am a comin', an jes' you take de chillun along up to the de public square and stay dere till I is come. I's gwina go down in the garden an see ole massuh get up, and as soon as he do, him and me'll come along up to de square and we'll all go up to meet de Lawd together!" This faithful black man could not read or write, but he was taught by the Holy Spirit of God.

What we read in the Book of Acts is a harbinger, of what God is going to do at the end of the age. What God has prepared for those who love Him!

7

The Drag of the Old Carnal Nature

On the morrow, as they went on their journey, and drew nigh unto the city, Peter went up upon the housetop to pray about the sixth hour:

And he became very hungry, and would have eaten: but while they made ready, he fell into a trance,

And saw heaven opened, and a certain vessel descending unto him, as it had been a great sheet knit at the four corners, and let down to the earth:

Wherein were all manner of four-footed beasts of the earth, and wild beasts, and creeping things, and fowls of the air.

And there came a voice to him, Rise, Peter; kill, and eat.

But Peter said, Not so, Lord; for I have never eaten any thing that is common or unclean.

And the voice spake unto him again the second time, What God hath cleansed, that call not thou common.

This was done thrice: and the vessel was received up again into heaven.

Now while Peter doubted in himself what this vision which he had seen should mean, behold, the men which were sent from Cornelius had made inquiry for Simon's house, and stood before the gate,

And called, and asked whether Simon, which was surnamed Peter, were lodged there. (Acts 10:9-18)

God had to prepare His apostle whom He had chosen to bestow the Holy Spirit upon the world—first at Jerusalem upon the Jew, then at Samaria, upon the half-Jew, and now in Caesarea upon a full Gentile. We read of the Lord's word to Peter: "And I will give unto thee the keys of the kingdom of heaven: and whatsoever thou shalt bind on earth shall be bound in heaven: and whatsoever thou shalt loose on earth shall be loosed in heaven" (Matt. 16:19). That is, when Peter moves and acts according to the will of God, what he does has been foreordained in heaven. For Peter to be used of God, to use the keys to open the door to the Gentiles, he must be prepared for that heavenly assignment.

PETER'S TRAINING THROUGH THE YEARS

When one looks at the life of Peter, we see that all through the years the Lord was preparing him for that glorious mandate. When He called him, Peter was conscious of his unworthiness. At the miracle of the large catch of fish, he fell down on his knees before the Lord and said: "Master, I am not worthy to be in Your presence. Depart from me; I am a sinful man." The Lord said, "Simon, Simon, I have chosen you to catch fish, only you are now to become a fisher of men." Simon, with his partners, James and John, the sons of Zebedee, laid their nets aside and forsook their old business and followed Jesus.

Then in the years that followed, the Lord prepared Peter for the assignment. In Matthew 16 the Lord calls Simon "Satan." When the Lord made the announcement that He must die and the third day be raised again, that He was to be delivered into the hands of sinners, Peter replied, "Lord, Lord, that shall never happen unto Thee," seeking to dissuade and to pull the Lord away from His redemptive mission. The Lord said, "Get thee behind me, Satan . . . for thou savourest not the things that be of God, but those that be of men" (Matt. 16:23). In Matthew 17 Peter, with James and John, saw the Lord transfigured into heaven and Peter said: "Lord, let us stay here, not down there in the valley where there is sickness, disaster, drudgery, dreariness, and darkness. Let us stay up here on the mountain top." But Peter had to be taught that we cannot always remain on the mountain top, for there is work to do in the valley. Then he was led by the Lord into the valley to minister to the poor father with his demented son.

As the story continues we see that Peter was much aware of his strength. He must have been a tremendous man physically. We read in John 21 that six disciples were struggling with a great catch of fish, and John said that Peter went down and pulled up the nets by himself.

Another example of the tremendous physical prowess of Peter can be seen in Acts 3 when he took a man who had never walked (he was born without ankle bones able to sustain him), by the right hand and physically lifted him up. Peter was a natural-born leader, and whatever he did, the other disciples followed after.

When the Lord made the announcement that all the disciples would deny Him that night and forsake Him, Peter said: "All these other disciples may do that, but not I. You may be denied by others, but not by me. Lord, I will follow You unto death." That was when the Lord said, "Simon, Simon, before the cock crows before the dawning of the morning, you will thrice deny that you even know Me." Then follows the sad story of when the little maid asked Simon, "Are not you one of His disciples; you talk like Jesus." Peter replied, "You think I talk like Him, then listen to this." Then he swore vociferously, and while he was swearing and cursing, denying that he even knew the Lord, the Lord turned and looked at Peter. Peter then remembered the saying of the Master and went out and wept bitterly.

After that we read of his second calling. He announced to his friends, "I am going back to my old business and back to the old nets, back to the sea, back to the old life, back to the old world, and back to the fishing business." The other disciples said, "Simon, if you have given up, we also will go back." One day while they were fishing but catching nothing, they saw a dim figure in the gray mist of the dawn standing on the shore. The figure called out, "Have you caught anything?" They answered, "No." He then said, "Take the net and put it on the right side and you will catch fish." They moved the net only a few inches and caught a large number of fish. John, the beloved disciple, said to Simon: "Simon, do you know Who that is? That is the Lord!" Peter jumped into the sea and swam to the shore and stood before the blessed Jesus. Then the Lord gave Peter his second call: "Simon, lovest thou Me?" "Lord, You know that I do." The Lord replied, "Take care of my lambs; feed my sheep; shepherd my flock." Then the Lord prophesied how Peter would die with outstretched hands, by crucifixion. The Lord was preparing Peter for his Pentecostal opening of the kingdom of God to the Jew, to the Samaritan, the half-Jew, and, finally, in the tenth chapter of the Book of Acts, to the opening of the kingdom of heaven to the Gentile world, to you and to me. The Lord had to prepare Peter for the task, and that is the passage of our text.

Could a Gentile be saved just by trusting Jesus? Unthinkable to a Jew. Could these idolator worshipers of Juno, Jove, Neptune, Venus, Isis, Adonis, and Osiris be saved out of their idolatry and heathenism just by trusting Jesus? There was an everlastingly deep prejudice in the heart of any Jew about a Gentile. So the Lord had to prepare Peter for his assignment to open the doors of the kingdom of God to the Gentiles. We read in Acts 10:

> And [Peter] saw heaven opened, and a certain vessel descending unto him, as it had been a great sheet knit at the four corners, and let down to the earth:
> Wherein were all manner of four-footed beasts of the earth, and wild beasts, and creeping things, and fowls of the air.
> And there came a voice to him, Rise, Peter; kill, and eat.
> But Peter said, Not so, Lord; for I have never eaten any thing that is common or unclean.
> And the voice spake unto him again the second time. What God hath cleansed that call not thou common (vv. 11-15).

While Peter thought on the meaning of the vision, men from the Gentile centurion came asking for him. We continue reading in the passage:

> Now while Peter doubted in himself what this vision which he had seen should mean, behold, the men which were sent from Cornelius had made inquiry for Simon's house, and stood before the gate,
> And called, and asked whether Simon, which was surnamed Peter, were lodged there.
> While Peter thought on the vision, the Spirit said unto him, Behold, three men seek thee.
> Arise therefore, and get thee down, and go with them, doubting nothing: for I have sent them.
> Then Peter went down to the men which were sent unto him from Cornelius; and said, Behold, I am he whom ye seek: what is the cause wherefore ye are come? (vv. 17-21).

Would you not think that Peter, having gone through such a marvelous training and heavenly direction from the Lord, would have been in the hands of God the most marvelous instrument of this new freedom that one could imagine? But look at him. The old nature is still there and the old weakness of Peter comes out again and again.

SIMON PETER'S INHERENT WEAKNESS

We cannot help but identify with Peter, for all of his human weaknesses are ours, and all the problems that he had with himself we have with ourselves. Paul says in Galatians 2:

> But when Peter was come to Antioch, I withstood him to the face, because he was to be blamed.
> For before that certain came from James, he did eat with the Gentiles: but when they were come, he withdrew and separated himself, fearing them which were of the circumcision.

And the other Jews dissembled likewise with him; insomuch that Barnabas also was carried away with their dissimulation.

But when I saw that they walked not uprightly according to the truth of the gospel, I said unto Peter before them all, If thou, being a Jew, livest after the manner of Gentiles, and not as do the Jews, why compellest thou the Gentiles to live as do the Jews?

We who are Jews by nature, and not sinners of the Gentiles (vv. 11-15).

Peter had gone back into his old weaknesses and his old habits. "You can count on me," he said to the Lord. Then when the time came, he swore that he never knew the Lord. The same thing is happening again over whether or not a man who is a Gentile could be saved just be faith without first becoming a Jew.

Look at the word that Paul calls Peter and what Paul calls those who are with him. In the King James Version the word is translated "dissimulation," which sounds like a fine word. "And the other Jews dissembled likewise with him." The Greek word actually is *hypokrites*. Let me read it just as Paul writes it. "And the other Jews played the 'hypocrite' with him insomuch that Barnabas also was carried away before 'hypocrisy'," translated here "dissimulation." It may be that whoever translated the passage in 1611 was afraid to use the word that Paul used to describe Peter. What do you think about that with regard to this chiefest apostle of the blessed Jesus?

When you are converted and saved, the chances are that your old human nature will still be with you. You will still drag it along after you. When I was a boy I heard one of my preachers describe it like this. He said: "You have a pig's heart and you want to wallow in the dirt and the mire. Then you are saved and you have a lamb's heart, but you do not get rid of that pig's heart. It is still there. It is just that God has given you a lamb's heart, and those two war together, the pig's heart and the lamb's heart."

Paul words it like this: "The spirit strives against the flesh, and the flesh strives against the spirit." He again writes in Romans 7:

For that which I do I allow not: for what I would, that do I not; but what I hate, that do I.

O wretched man that I am! who shall deliver me from the body of this death? (vv. 15, 24).

You are going to experience that in your life. The chances are that however you are when you become a Christian and are saved, you will still have with you and in you that same old carnal nature warring against the things of the Lord. For example, if you are a man who has a volatile spirit and temper and you get angry easily, when you get saved, you probably will still have that old volatile spirit. You will be praying, "Dear God, deliver me from the seething that I have on the inside." You may have to fight it all the days of your life if you are made that way.

Simon Peter was that way. That is why we can so easily identify with him. He is like us. He had a certain turn to him on the inside which he carried with him to the day of his death.

God's Use of the Man

God has a way of using us even though we are weak in the flesh. Let me illustrate that out of my own experience. People have asked me, "How long do you take to prepare a sermon?" I say, "Fifty years." "What, fifty years?" "Yes. Every sermon I prepare I have been working on for fifty years. The sermons come out of my soul, out of my life, out of my relationship with God and with you." When I was a youth, I started preparing to be a preacher, even when I was a little boy in grammar school. In the fourth, fifth, and sixth grades I was studying to be a preacher. Then through high school and college I was getting ready to be a preacher. In the days of my youth, I was so idealistic. I looked upon the pastor as a representative of God Himself. I looked upon my teachers as being the epitome of God's grace and glory. I exalted all the preachers and teachers on a high pedestal. Then as time went along, and I came to know the professor and the preacher, what a disillusionment! All of them had feet of dirty clay. They all had tremendous weaknesses in their lives.

One time Dr. J. B. Gambrell, who was the architect of the Baptist General Convention of Texas in the mission work of our Southern Baptist Convention, said: "God can hit many a straight lick with a crooked stick." God can use these people who are weak and human like the rest of us. Thinking in years gone by of that word of Dr. Gambrell, I began to think about the men in the Bible such as Abraham. One of the great passages in the Book of Romans says: "If Abraham were saved by works, he would have whereof to glory but not before God." God knew him and all about him, and for Abraham to boast before God about his works would be unthinkable and a travesty. God knew a thousand things about Abraham. He could not boast about his works.

Jacob was a supplanter from the beginning. What could one say about David, the man after God's own heart?

When we come to the New Testament, we see that James and John are volatile in their spirit.

Paul is the most marvelous of all the Christian leaders who ever lived. We read in Acts 15, after the first missionary journey, about the great Jerusalem conference in which discussion took place as to whether the Gentiles could be saved just by believing in Jesus:

> And some days after Paul said unto Barnabas [he and Barnabas had gone together on the first missionary journey], Let us go again and visit our brethren in every city where we have preached the word of the Lord, and see how they do.
> And Barnabas determined to take with him John, whose surname was Mark.
> But Paul thought not good to take him with them, who departed from them from Pamphylia, and went not with them to the work.
> And the contention was so sharp between them, that they departed asunder one from the other: and so Barnabas took Mark, and sailed unto Cyprus;
> And Paul chose Silas, and departed, being recommended by the brethren unto the grace of God (vv. 36-40).

The word "contention" in Greek is *paroxusmos*, and when you translate it into English, the word is "paroxysm." The emotional, volatile confrontation was so sharp between Paul and Barnabas that they separated and Barnabas took Mark while Paul took Silas and went on his way. Did Paul regret that? He surely did. Years later Paul wrote saying, "Bring Mark to me, for he is profitable in the gospel." You see, these were men with their weaknesses, the old carnal nature. The apostle Paul, God's greatest exponent of the faith, had weaknesses with the old carnal nature. You and I have them, also.

Well then, what do we do? This is what we do. If a preacher exhibits some poor weakness, or if a great denominational leader falls into error, or if you do, we must not look at the man, but we must keep our eyes on Jesus. I am not looking to a preacher for my salvation. God bless him in whatever gifts he can command and dedicates to the Lord. If he has weaknesses, may the Lord be merciful as He was to Peter. If there are weaknesses in your life, I do not hate you for them. You see, I have them in my life also. We are all alike. Our weaknesses may not be the same, but we all have them. We are not looking to the church, we are not looking to the deacon, we are not looking to the denominational leader, we are not looking at the pastor—we are looking to Jesus. There is no fault in Him. As Pilate said, "I find in him no fault at all."

That is why we have peace with God and with one another. When we fall into error and into weakness, let us pray for one another. Let us bear each other up. Let us be the first to forgive. Let us be the last to remember, to hold a grudge. In that sympathy and brotherly encouragement, may we walk together growing in grace, our eyes fixed upon Jesus. Bless you as we pray for and love one another!

8

The Gospel to the Gentiles

There was a certain man in Caesarea called Cornelius, a centurion of the band called the Italian band,

A devout man, and one that feared God with all his house, which gave much alms to the people, and prayed to God alway.

He saw in a vision evidently about the ninth hour of the day an angel of God coming in to him, and saying unto him, Cornelius.

And when he looked on him, he was afraid, and said, What is it, Lord? And he said unto him, Thy prayers and thine alms are come up for a memorial before God.

And now send men to Joppa, and call for one Simon, whose surname is Peter:

He lodgeth with one Simon a tanner, whose house is by the sea side: he shall tell thee what thou oughtest to do.

And when the angel which spake unto Cornelius was departed, he called two of his household servants, and a devout soldier of them that waited on him continually;

And when he had declared all these things unto them, he sent them to Joppa.

On the morrow, as they went on their journey, and drew nigh unto the city, Peter went up upon the housetop to pray about the sixth hour:

And he became very hungry, and would have eaten: but while they made ready, he fell into a trance,

And the morrow after they entered into Caesarea. And Cornelius waited for them, and had called together his kinsmen and near friends.

And as Peter was coming in, Cornelius met him, and fell down at his feet, and worshipped him.

But Peter took him up, saying, Stand up; I myself also am a man.

And as he talked with him, he went in, and found many that were come together. And he said unto them, Ye know how that it is an unlawful thing for a man that is a Jew to keep company, or come unto one of another nation; but

God hath shewed me that I should not call any man common or unclean.

Therefore came I unto you without gainsaying, as soon as I was sent for: I ask therefore for what intent ye have sent for me?

And Cornelius said, Four days ago I was fasting until this hour; and at the ninth hour I prayed in my house, and, behold, a man stood before me in bright clothing,

And said, Cornelius, thy prayer is heard, and thine alms are had in remembrance in the sight of God.

Send therefore to Joppa, and call hither Simon, whose surname is Peter; he is lodged in the house of one Simon a tanner by the sea side: who, when he cometh, shall speak unto thee.

Immediately therefore I sent to thee; and thou hast well done that thou art come. Now therefore are we all here present before God, to hear all things that are commanded thee of God. (Acts 10:1-8, 24-33)

With this passage of Scripture we have come to a great continental divide, to a watershed. In the tenth chapter we see that the Lord is doing a new and wondrous thing. It includes us who are not Jews, who are not of the seed of Abraham, but who belong to the gentile families of the earth. We are following a story that is told at length and in great detail, which is not only presented in the long tenth chapter of Acts, but continues through 11:18. For centuries the Lord had been dealing with His chosen family, Israel, but now the grace of God is extended to the nations of the world. The love and mercy of our Lord is overflowing its banks and now in loving grace is bathing the feet of all the peoples of mankind.

It is as though the Holy Spirit were saying: Look at this company. It is the guiding hand of God that has brought together this audience and prepared their hearts and prepared the preacher to deliver the message. This little group is not together by accident or fortuitous circumstance. They are not adventitiously meeting in this place. They are not here by custom, by routine, or by long familiar practice. It is a gathering under the hand of God for a marvelous and heavenly purpose.

We shall follow the leading of the Holy Spirit as we look at the story in our text intently, purposively, and prayerfully, for God is saying, "This is something of the hand of the Lord."

CORNELIUS

The name of the man in the story is Cornelius, an ancient and an honorable name among the Romans. It was the name of Sulla, the great Roman general and dictator. We read that this Cornelius lived in Caesarea.

There are two Caesareas in the New Testament. There is one in the gospels which is called Caesarea Philippi. It was at the base of Mount Hermon, where the waters of the Jordan begin to flow south from the melting snows of that great Lebanese range. Philip, the son of Herod the Great, built a city there at old Dan, and named it after the Roman Caesar. To distinguish that Caesarea from the Caesarea which was the capital of Judaea, they called the Caesarea at Dan, Caesarea Philippi. We are familiar with the expression, "From Dan to Beersheba," from the far north to the extreme south. That is the Caesarea of the gospels.

The other Caesarea is the one that is often mentioned in the Book of Acts. This is Caesarea-by-the-sea, the capital of the Roman province of Judaea. It was built by Herod the Great at astronomical cost. There was no indentation, no harbor on the Mediterranean seashore in Palestine, so Herod the Great built a harbor there and with it a Greek-Roman city. The streets of Caesarea were lined with Corinthian columns which were most impressive. The city was filled with theaters and pagan temples where the gods of the Greeks and Romans were worshiped. Caesarea also had spacious amphitheaters. As a pagan, Roman-Greek city, Caesarea was an abhorrence to the Jews. The seat of the Roman government was there. The procurators Felix and Festus lived in Caesarea, not at Jerusalem. It was the home of Pontius Pilate. It was in this Roman capital of the province of Judaea that Paul was imprisoned for two years. It was here that Philip the evangelist lived with his four unmarried daughters who were prophetesses. It was in a riot in this city of Caesarea that the war of rebellion began against Rome in A.D. 66. The great Jewish historian, Josephus, describes the course of that war with power and pathos. In the midst of that rebellion Vespasian, the Roman general, was acclaimed emperor of the empire. When he went to Rome to govern the vast empire, he left the final direction of the war to his son, Titus, who carried it to a tragic conclusion, destroying Jerusalem and the Jewish nation.

Eusebius, the ecclesiastical historian, was born in Caesarea in A.D. 260. In contradistinction to the theological interpretation of the school at Alexandria, the school at Caesarea followed a historical-grammatical method of interpretation which, I think, is the true and only way to understand God's Word. This is the method I follow in all my study and preaching.

Cornelius was a soldier and an officer in the Roman army. As such, he represented a hated, tyrannical, and foreign power, an abhorrence to the Jew. But one of the most remarkable things in the New Testament is this: the soldier, and especially the centurion, seemed to have a kindly, generous attitude. Roman soldiers came to hear John the Baptist preach and were baptized by the great forerunner. It was to a Roman centurion that the Lord said, "I have never seen such faith, no, not in Israel." The centurion asked the Lord to heal his servant who was sick, but also said, "I am not worthy that you come under my roof; just speak the word, and my servant will be healed." It was a Roman centurion presiding over the execution of our Lord under the orders of Pontius Pilate, who, standing beneath the cross seeing Jesus die, exclaimed in testimony, "Surely, this was the Son of God!" It was Claudius Lysias, a Chiliarch, a man over a thousand soldiers (whereas the centurion was over one hundred soldiers), who befriended the apostle Paul. It was a centurion who took care of Paul so he would not fall into the hands of those who had plotted his murder. It was Julius, a centurion, who out of deference to the life of Paul when they were shipwrecked in Malta on the way to Rome, spared all the prisoners. Not one prisoner was executed because Julius favored the great preacher of Christ. The New Testament soldier is ever acceptable. This is the centurion of Caesarea, Cornelius.

Look at Cornelius himself. He is described as a devout man, a humble, good man who was now being introduced to the Christian faith. He is called a man who feared God with all his heart; that is, he had given up the sterility and emptiness of pagan idolatry and embraced the moral rectitude demanded in the code of Moses in the Ten Commandments. But he was still a Gentile. He had gone to the temple in Jerusalem, in the court of the Gentiles, he could have mingled with those who were present. But the heavy wall threatening death against any Gentile who would enter through the Beautiful Gate would have prohibited him from going into the inner court.

Cornelius was a typical man of the strength and power of the Roman army. There was a reason why Rome conquered the civilized world. They were a family people. They were sturdy and strong in life and character. It was only when the family life, the domestic life, the inward life of Rome decayed that Rome fell, just as America is beginning to disintegrate and to be afflicted from every side. We are decaying inwardly. And that is why Rome fell. She was corrupt in her soul, but until she was, Rome was the greatest empire and lasted far longer than any other empire that had ever conquered the civilized world.

Cornelius, even though he was a wonderful man of character and strength, an officer in the Roman army, described as a devout man, one who feared God with all his house, who gave much alms to the people and who prayed to God always—yet he was lost. What a startling revelation! Cornelius, a man of integrity and character, was a lost man. The angel told him, "Send word to Simon Peter in Joppa who will come and tell you how to be saved." When his conversion was recounted to the church at Jerusalem, they praised God, saying, "Then hath the Lord granted repentance unto life to the Gentiles."

The first foundational truth in the preaching of the gospel is this: the Christian faith presupposes that all men are lost, that all men are sinners. Isaiah, the evangelist of the Old Testament, in 53:6 says: "All we like sheep have gone astray; we have turned every one to his own way." The apostle Paul wrote in the third chapter of the Book of Romans:

> There is none righteous, no, not one.
> All have sinned, and come short of the glory of God (vv. 10, 23).

The Christian faith presupposes that all mankind is lost. We are sinners by nature and by practice. Compared to one another, we seem to be fine and good, but against the white holiness and purity of God, we are total sinners. As Isaiah says, "And our righteousnesses are as filthy rags." All of us are lost. Our nature is fallen. We call this the doctrine of total depravity. This means that we are not as vile as we can be, but that we are fallen and sinful in all our faculties. My mind does not work perfectly, my heart does not feel perfectly, and my will does not volitionally always please God. We are a fallen people.

That doctrine has come upon an evil day in our time. One of the presidents of a church-related university said, "Those who believe in total depravity have been unfortunate in their friends." We think that way because we have been led unconsciously into the false persuasion of evolution. Sin is nothing but the drag of our bestial forefathers. Life is a stumbling upward. There is inevitable progress. We are getting better and better, and finally the evolutionary process will make of us angels and maybe even archangels. That is the evolutionary persuasion of the world today. But it does not take into account that underneath the thin veneer of civilization and culture there is the awesomeness of the corruption of human nature. There is progress in the world, but there is progress also in blood and in murder. It used to be that men killed each other with an ax, then with bow and arrow, then with a gun, then with TNT, and now with hydrogen bombs. There is progress in evil as there is progress in any other area of life. God says that we are a fallen family. We are a corrupt people. We are sinners in our nature. We are all lost outside of Christ. If a man could be saved by his good works, then the atoning death of our Lord is a travesty and a disgrace to the Lord God in heaven who sent Jesus to die for our sins.

God Makes a Way for His Salvation

The Lord was preparing the way of salvation for Cornelius. He prepared an angel to come and to tell Cornelius what to do. Cornelius obeyed immediately. As Jeremiah says, "And ye shall seek me, and find me, when ye shall search for me with all your heart" (Jer. 29:13). That night Cornelius sent three men, the two servants and the Roman soldier, down to Joppa thirty miles away in order to tell Peter what the angel had bid him do. The Lord was preparing Peter. When Peter saw that great sheet lowered down, held by the four corners, and on the inside of it all kinds of creatures that to him were unclean, the Lord said, "Peter, rise, kill, and eat." Peter answered, "Lord I have never done anything like that, and I am not about to do it now."

That could be the refrain of 10,000 preachers and churches, "Lord, I never did that before, and I am not about to do it now." Bound down in some kind of an iron-clad tradition, and because it was never done before, therefore, we are not going to try it now. You know, principles never change, the gospel does not change, Jesus does not change, for He is "the same yesterday, today, and forever," but the methods of how we mediate the truth of God change every day and with every changing generation. Wherever there is a finer approach that we can use to proclaim the message of God, let us learn it and do it.

Peter said, "Lord, I have never done that and I am not about to do it now." So the Lord prepared him, "You are not to call anything common or unclean, not even these beasts." It is a new day and it is a new hour.

The Preacher's Assignment

Then the Holy Spirit prepared the audience. Cornelius described it, "Now therefore are we all here present before God, to hear all things that are commanded thee of God" (Acts 10:33b). What a marvelous thing to say about a company of gathered-together people! We are all here. The father, the mother, and the children are here. The friends and all of the family members are here. We are present before God and we are riveted in attention, so much one in heart, spirit, and anticipation until that one centurion can stand up and speak for the whole throng of the people. It takes two to make a sermon—someone to preach, to break the Bread of Life, but also someone to listen and to pray. A wonderful listener, a prayer partner, is one of God's benedictory gifts in the household of the saints.

When we worship we are all present before God. Jacob said, "This is none other than *Beth-el*, the house of God; this is none other than the gate to heaven." The Lord said to Moses at the burning bush: "Take off your shoes from your feet, for the ground whereon you stand is holy ground." That is how I feel when I stand in the pulpit. Many important people have stood in my pulpit but above all God is there and the people are assembled in prayer and in eager anticipation. For what? "Therefore we are all here before God to hear all things that are commanded thee of God." This is the great assignment of the church and of its preacher, to declare all the things that are commanded us of the Lord.

How often do we find a tendency to change that! That is the inspired description and interpretation of a service held in the name of Christ. But how often do we see that changed in the church. Jesus preached, John the Baptist preached, Peter preached, Paul preached, Apollos preached, and James preached. But today there is a tendency in many of our churches in Christendom to take the preacher out and get him out of the way. However, we must be reminded that central in our worship must be the preaching of the Word of the living God. "We are all here gathered in the presence of God to hear the things that are commanded thee of the Lord." Listen to what the Lord says: "Faith cometh by hearing, and hearing by the word of God" (Rom. 10:17). Listen again to the Word of God: "For the preaching of the cross is to them that perish foolishness; but unto us which are saved it is the power of God" (1 Cor. 1:18). We read again in 2 Timothy:

> All scripture is given by inspiration of God, and is profitable for doctrine, for reproof, for correction, for instruction in righteousness.
> I charge thee therefore before God, and the Lord Jesus Christ, who shall judge the quick and the dead at his appearing and his kingdom;
> Preach the word (3:16, 4:1-2a).

How often do I hear it said: "Protestants do not worship." These critics have a distorted definition of the approach to worship God.

When we come together according to the definition of the Holy Scriptures to hear the Word of God, we are worshiping in the highest manner. When our faculties are raised to their highest usefulness, when the thoughts of the mind, the emotions of the heart, and the volitions of the will are brought into the presence of the Spirit of God, that is worship in the loftiest definition and in its scriptural meaning.

How many times in looking over all of Christendom does one find the church departing from that scriptural admonition? When you go to church, what do you hear? You hear a book review, a lecture on positive thinking and the winning of affluence and status in the world, or a psychological dissertation upon human behavior and reaction, or something about economic amelioration, or about politics, or about human behavior and reaction, or about all of the things that pertain to the problems of the government, of the human race, war, and of a thousand welfare programs. We hear that in the church. My brother, that is what you hear every day of your life! When we read the editorial page in the newspaper, that is what we read about. When we listen to the commentator on radio or television, that is what we hear. Why come to the church to hear the same thing rehashed? Every member in the State Department knows twice as much as any ordinary preacher standing in the pulpit about the problems of the world. What we want to know when we come to church is this: Does God say anything? What can deliver our souls from hell? What can save us from damnation? What will I do in the hour of my death and at the judgment bar of almighty God? How do I find strength to live and to face all the exigencies that overwhelm me in life? That is our heavenly assignment. "We are all here present before God, to hear all things that are commanded thee of God."

I think of Spurgeon, who with a sweep of his hand, taking in the great tabernacle in London in which he preached from God's Book, said, "There is not a pew, there is not a seat in this great tabernacle but that someone has stood from it, risen from it to accept Christ as his Savior." That is life everlasting!

9

The Reward of the Righteous

But in every nation he that feareth him, and worketh righteousness, is accepted with him. (Acts 10:35)

A man cannot be saved by his good works. There is no doubt about it. That is a message from the Lord. Cornelius, the leading character in the tenth chapter of Acts, is described as a devout man, one who feared God with all his house, gave much alms to the people, prayed to God always, but was lost. As noble as he was, he was not saved. The angel told him to send for Peter who would come and tell him words whereby he and his house could be saved.

THE IMPOSSIBILITY OF GOOD WORKS TO SECURE SALVATION

The Christian faith presupposes that all mankind is lost in sin. As Titus 3 says, "Not by works of righteousness are we saved, but by the grace of God." And Ephesians tells us that we are saved by grace, the free gift of the Lord, and that not of ourselves, not of works, lest any many should boast. It is a gift of God. We are saved in the grace, mercy, and atoning sacrifice of our Lord. Our good works are like a bridge over an abyss, that however long or however short the bridge is, it never quite reaches to the other side. A man cannot be saved by being good, by attempting to do good works, in order to buy or earn himself into heaven.

There is a corollary following that. We are much impressed when men who are evil are wonderfully converted and are saved. We are moved by the conversion of that prodigal boy, who having lived in

72

harlotry and drunkenness, came to himself and returned to his father and home. That is a cause of rejoicing, and we feel it when we read the story. We are affected by the conversion of Saul of Tarsus, who turned from destroying the faith, to preaching it. One of the characteristics that we find in so many of our evangelists is that once they were wicked men, but then came to know the Lord. One evangelist had a little daughter who died. In his drunken condition he stole the shoes off her little feet as she was in the casket, and sold them that he might have money to buy liquor. The conversion of that world-famous evangelist is impressive to us.

I once listened to a convict who had been sentenced to more than 600 years in the penitentiary and then came to know the Lord. To listen to him thrilled your soul. The consequence of that is that we somehow have the impression (though we may never state it), that it must be an achievement to sin and fall into the depths of iniquity, and then to be lifted out of it and to be wonderfully saved.

But there is another side to that picture, and this is the Lord's true side. No matter when or what, it is tragic for men to fall into sin that they might be marvelously saved. Can you imagine father and mother teaching their children to fall into the depths of iniquity that they might be lifted out of it into the light of the Christian faith? Paul says, "Shall we sin that grace may abound? God forbid."

THE RIGHTEOUSNESS OF CORNELIUS WAS A MEMORIAL BEFORE GOD

So Acts 10:35 tells us that there is a reward in righteousness, and it makes no difference whether we are pagan, Gentile, or Jew. There is a nobility in righteousness that is ever true and acceptable to God. The marvelous revelation that we have of Cornelius is that he was a tremendously fine man, a devout man, a God-fearing man, a charitable man, and a man of prayerful intercession. The Bible says that he was accepted before God. The Lord heard him pray. God listened to this man, though he was lost, and He sent down an angel from heaven. Always there is wonderful reward and recompense in righteousness wherever it is found. Let us look at some of the men in the Bible whom God seemed to favor.

Abraham was a man God seemed to favor for the Lord said, "Shall I do something and not tell Abraham about it?" Joseph lived a beautiful and exemplary life, a life without a hint of error. Samuel also was a noble and a fine man all his life, acceptable to God.

When the Lord looked upon the rich young ruler kneeling at his feet, He said to him, "You know the commandments; keep the commandments and you will find life." The young man replied, "All of the commandments have I observed from my youth." The Lord beholding him, loved him. And we could not help but love him, too.

Timothy was a splendid young man. The Bible says that from the days of his childhood he had known the Holy Scriptures and was taught in the way of the Lord. His mother, Eunice, and his grandmother, Lois, did not teach Timothy to be vile and sinful and then out of a life of depravity and iniquity, to be saved. It was the strength of the lad that he grew up from childhood knowing our blessed Jesus. It is a strength in a man's life, no matter who he is, that he be righteous and upright and that his children be strong and stalwart in goodness.

The same is true for a nation. Our text says, "In every nation, these who fear God and work righteousness, are acceptable to Him." God looks upon them in acceptance as they are righteous in their life. That means that when a nation or a people turn away from righteousness, they fall into tragic and awesome judgment. Israel did that. When the people were carried captive into Babylon, Jeremiah lamented, saying: "The crown is fallen from our head. Woe unto us that we have sinned." Wherever there is righteousness, the Lord looks upon it with acceptance.

Indulgence in Sin Hardens Men's Hearts

Wherever there is iniquity, it brings with it a judgment from almighty God. That is true in America. We are living in a day of the awesome judgment of God upon our people.

One time while at a speaking engagement in Columbus, Ohio, I bought a copy of the Columbus morning paper, *The Citizen's Journal*. I also bought the current issue of *Time magazine*, which on the cover picture had a Homo sapiens sitting by an ape which had human characteristics. The article inside the magazine purported to present to us how we evolved out of the trees and how the primates called apes and simians became not only our great-great-great-grandparents, but our parents as we know them today. The article said that the ape is the origin of humanity and explains our existence on the earth. There were great crustal plates, continental masses, and the subcontinental mass that we know as India was pushed up under Africa and Asia lifting up the great Himalayan range. Once a vast forest covered the earth, but when the continents were lifted up over the molten core in the earth, the weather changed, and the great forests died and grasslands appeared. The forest-dwelling apes had to come out of the trees into the grasslands, and having come out of the forests, they had to stand up in an erect position to enable them to see over the tall grass. The article concluded that that is how our evolutionary parents came to walk upright and we became men.

After reading the *Time* article, I looked at the Columbus newspaper. I read about a Dr. Medad Schiller who is the chief surgeon at Hadassah Hospital in Jerusalem. He avows that numerous outstanding pediatric surgeons have trained in Columbus, Ohio, where is located one of the most famous children's hospital in the world. Having received his hospital training in Children's Hospital in Columbus, he returned to Israel. In this interview he discussed the Arab and the Jew in Israel and the life that he saw in America. He said:

> In Israel we do not have two problems that are big in the United States. We seldom see the battered child syndrome or the pelvic inflammatory diseases, venereal disease, in young girls. In America you see abcessed ovaries and Fallopian tubes, even gonorrhea and syphilis that is resistent to treatment in young girls because they start at six, seven, and eight years of age in prostitution. . . .
>
> This is non-existent as a social-medical problem in Israel because most Jewish and Arab girls will not have sex before marriage.
>
> Sex is not regarded as the peak of life. It does not have to be done in the streets. There is a high morality in Israel. In fact, it is unlawful to have sexual relations with a girl under sixteen and that law is strictly enforced.

I had the two articles in my hands. I read in *Time* magazine that these pseudo-scientists teaching in our universities and schools in America say that we are animals. In the newspaper I read about a great world-famous surgeon who looked at America and said that we live as animals in moral decadence. Why should we be amazed when our children act like animals if we believe that we are animals?

In a recent *Dallas Morning News* there was an editorial entitled, "The Attack on Anita Bryant." The last paragraph of that editorial said:

> Jane Fonda, who barely sidestepped the treason laws during the Vietnam War, was never treated like this. But Anita Bryant, because she stands up for what God says concerning homosexuality, is now apparently going to lose her job on television.

Anita Bryant has become persona non grata in the entertainment areas of the world. She is picketed, she is hated, and she is despised. There is hardly a cartoon, there is hardly an entertainer in Las Vegas, Broadway, or Los Angeles but who loves to tear her down. Yet while our American boys were dying by the thousands trying to stem the Red tide in southeast Asia, no one sought to destroy Jane Fonda, and as far as I am concerned she is as bad a traitor as Tokyo Rose.

The Bible says that wherever in the world there is righteousness, God looks upon it in acceptance. It commends a man and it commends a nation to live uprightly in fear of the Lord.

It Is Better for a Child Never to Know the Darkness of Sin

The Bible teaches that we cannot be saved by our own righteousness. We have to be saved by the blood of Jesus, but I am avowing to you according to the Word of God that there is a corollary that goes along with it. We do not have to be immoral and evil in order to experience the grace of God. It is better if a child can be brought into the saving grace of Jesus having never known the darkness of sin. The nation that walks in uprightness is looked upon with favor from the Lord God in heaven. Whenever there is a people who are of righteous character, there will you find the Spirit of God working in grace, love, and mercy. If we think that there is any virtue in being sinful in order that we might experience the grace of God, we have absolutely lost sight of the great purposes of God's revelation in the holy Word. The apostle Paul persecuted the church of God, but he said, "I am the least of the apostles and am not worthy to be called an apostle because I persecuted the church of God." It was a bitterness to him as long as he lived.

B. H. Carroll, who was an infidel at one time in his life, said in one of his sermons: "O, how many thousand times I myself have regretted that I ever did distrust God, that I ever was skeptical about revelation, that I ever did turn from the Bible! There never will come a time when it will be of advantage to me, when it will cease to be anything but a shame to me, that I did not from the first with a full heart receive all the truth of the Lord."

No man who ever sins can be proud of it. No nation that ever falls into moral disintegration can lift up its head in pride. God said that sin is a reproach to any people. To teach our children to walk uprightly and to know no other thing than to fear God all the days of their lives is a blessing from heaven. Sin hurts, sin damns, and sin destroys. Sin lifts its ugly head all over the world, but holiness, righteousness, and godliness commend themselves to the grace of the Lord.

How beautiful to rear our children as I was reared, knowing nothing other than to love Jesus and to walk in the way of the Lord, to attend the worship services of Christ, and to seek to obey the great commandments of God. How easy it was when I was ten years old to be introduced to the love of the Savior that washes away all our sins! But how difficult it is when one is brought up in iniquity and darkness to be led into the light! There are few who are ever saved out of a world of iniquity and darkness. You see, God says that goodness and righteousness open His heart toward us and He sends His angels to guide us into the way of true salvation, just as He did with this Roman soldier, Cornelius.

10

These Amazing Converts

While Peter yet spake these words, the Holy Ghost fell on all them which heard the word.

And they of the circumcision which believed were astonished, as many as came with Peter, because that on the Gentiles also was poured out the gift of the Holy Ghost.

For they heard them speak with tongues, and magnify God. Then answered Peter,

Can any man forbid water, that these should not be baptized, which have received the Holy Ghost as well as we?

And he commanded them to be baptized in the name of the Lord. Then prayed they him to tarry certain days. (Acts 10:44-48)

Our discussion concerns the concluding portion of the tenth chapter of the Book of Acts. God was opening the door to all of us who live in the gentile world. The chapter began with Cornelius, a Roman officer, a centurion. The success of the Roman army and its conquest of the world could be found in the astuteness of the leadership of the centurion.

Cornelius was stationed in Caesarea, the seat of the Roman government of volatile Judaea. God visited him, sent an angel to him, and told him to send to Joppa, which is thirty miles south of Caesarea, and ask for one Simon Peter who would come and tell him words whereby he and his house might be saved. Peter, in the meantime, was being prepared for that invitation by the vision of a great sheet held by its four corners, let down from heaven, and filled with all manner of non-kosher, Mosaically unclean things. They were not unclean in themselves, but they were ecclesiastically unclean. When Simon Peter was commanded to "Rise; kill, and eat," he said, "Lord, I have never done that." Then the Lord spoke, saying, "What God hath cleansed, call not thou common or unclean." While Peter was pondering the meaning of the vision, three men from Cornelius appeared and invited Peter to the house of Cornelius in Caesarea. The Holy Spirit said, "Peter, do not hesitate to go; this is of the Lord." Therefore, the next day they arrived in Caesarea and saluted the household of Cornelius. We read in verse 24:

> And the morrow after they entered into Caesarea. And Cornelius waited for them, and had called together his kinsmen and near friends.

What a blessed thing to find a man seeking God. There is nothing more rewarding or blessed in life than to visit with someone who wants to know God. The Scriptures say that Cornelius waited with a hungry heart and an eager ear, waiting to hear a message from God.

The Ethiopian eunuch in Acts 8 was reading Isaiah 53 and wanted to know of whom the prophet was speaking when he talked about this One upon whom all of our iniquities are laid. What a privilege to speak to a man like that!

One time when I was in Buenos Aires, the capital of Argentina, in one of the beautiful hotels downtown, I was invited to a dinner given by a group of local citizens. There were about 150 men and women at the dinner. I was the only "foreigner" present. The host said to me: "We do not want anyone else here. We just want you." So I said, "Why such an arrangement?" He replied, "We want you to talk to us about the Lord, about what you think God could mean to us, and about how He can bless us in our great thriving nation of Argentina." Can you imagine anything more delightful than that? "We are all gathered here waiting to hear a message from the Lord." What blessedness it is to find a man who wants to know God!

PREPARATION OF THE MESSENGER

Had the Lord not prepared Peter for his message and invitation, he would not have gone. "What? Enter into the house of a Gentile? I have never done that before! Be a guest of a man of another faith? I have never been in a situation like that! Preach the gospel to a Roman soldier? Such a thing never entered my mind nor would I ever do that. In Caesarea? Of all places! The seat of the Roman government where every building is a sign and an emphasis of our foreign oppression. Never would I do that!"

Peter was just like Jonah going to Nineveh. Had it not been for the intervention of God, Jonah would never have appeared in Nineveh. Had Peter gone to Caesarea through some turn of fortune, he would have preached Jewish ceremonialism; he would have preached circumcision, the Mosaic law, as well as the belief in Christ. But when the Lord prepared Peter, he was ready. The heart of Cornelius, likewise, was open to God's direction. God's Holy Spirit brought together the messenger and the hearer, providing the ideal situation. Peter's first announcement was:

> And he said unto them, Ye know how that it is an unlawful thing for a man that is a Jew to keep company, or come unto one of another nation; but God hath shewed me that I should not call any man common or unclean (Acts 10:28).

So Peter is there, ready with a message of the Lord.

SIMON PETER OPENED HIS MOUTH

What message did he preach? This is a magnificent portrayal of the gospel of the grace of the Son of God. "Then Peter opened his mouth." How vulgar, how common, and how unaesthetic! In our day of overrefinement and our emphasis on cultural veneer, for a man to open his mouth is considered crude. But Peter opened his mouth to preach the gospel of the Son of God.

I once heard a preacher defined as "a mild-mannered man, speaking to a mild-mannered congregation on how to be more mild-mannered." Another definition of a preacher often repeated is that he is "a dispenser of peace-of-mind soothing syrup."

If a preacher stands up, opens his mouth, and declares the Word of the Lord, the people in the congregation immediately say: "Why, I can hear! He does not have to lift up his voice, he does not have to shout, he does not have to holler at me. I can hear!"

What we do not know and realize when we have certain segments of our "worshiping" congregation say things like that is this: a preacher is not preaching syllables and sentences. A preacher, if he is a God-called preacher, is speaking fire, judgment, damnation, hell, and the fury and wrath of God upon sin. He is also preaching tears, love, sorrow, repentance, and salvation. It is most inaccurate to think of a preacher as being just a crooner who is lulling an uninterested congregation into some kind of false security. No. "Peter opened his mouth." That is the reason I love the passages in *The Messiah* which quote my favorite chapter in the Bible, Isaiah 40: "The voice of one crying in the wilderness, Prepare ye the way of the Lord." Then they sing: "O Jerusalem, get thee up into the high mountain. Be not afraid. Lift up thy voice and say, Behold your God." That is just what God has committed to the burning heart of a God-called preacher. The gospel begins in Matthew 3:1: "In those days came John the Baptist, *kerusson*." What does *kerusson* mean? *Kerusson* means "heralding," "exclaiming," "announcing." One could hear him clear to Jerusalem and over on the other side of the mountains to the Mediterranean Sea! That is exactly what the Bible says. "Then Peter opened his mouth," standing in front of his audience with a burning message in his heart, and he delivered it vigorously. What did he say?

SIMON PETER'S SERMON

First, he opened the kingdom of God to all men everywhere. What a marvelous, glorious announcement! How could one make that announcement with indifference, with a soft, uninterested voice, with his head down, and with his mouth closed! Why, it is unthinkable. Let us read the account:

> Then Peter opened his mouth, and said, Of a truth I perceive that God is no respecter of persons:
> But in every nation he that feareth him, and worketh righteousness, is accepted with him (Acts 10:34-35).

That is earthshaking! We take Peter's words for granted in some parts of Christendom today, but what a marvelous announcement that the first time was preached! God is no respecter of persons, but whosoever believes in Him shall receive remission of sins. That is glorious!

One time I was in Washington, D.C., attending a service at the Calvary Baptist Church. The auditorium was filled because our Southern Baptist Convention was meeting in the city. From where I was seated, I looked across the aisle and saw a member of the church, who, at that time, was the most distinguished man in America. His name was Charles Evans Hughes, the Chief Justice of the Supreme Court. He was the man who retired one evening thinking that he had been elected President of the United States, and only by a hair's breadth was Woodrow Wilson elected instead. Charles Evans Hughes was a distinguished jurist and one of the most impressive-looking men you could see. When he joined Calvary Baptist Church in Washington, D. C., a Chinese laundryman came right behind him, and they sat on the front row together side by side. Now that is great!

That is why, among other reasons, I love the First Baptist Church of Dallas, where seated by your side may be one of the richest men in this city, or one of the poorest. It does not made any difference, because before God, we are all alike. God is no respecter of persons. He looks down upon us, and through His name, whoever believes in Him shall receive remission of sins.

"Simon Peter, what are you doing, and do not you know better than this? Why, you are preaching to this man about sin and the remission of sins. You are taking him to the cross!" Peter preached about the Lord Jesus "whom they slew and hanged on a tree for our sins." Peter preached Jesus to Cornelius, one of the finest men in the Bible. In God's sight and in the message and deliverance of the true gospel of Jesus, all of us are sinners alike.

I well remember when I was in seminary, that a preacher, who never had spoken to a seminary group before, came to speak to us. He said to me: "I am going to speak at the chapel service in this great seminary. How shall I preach, and what shall I do?" I answered: "I can tell you exactly how to preach. You preach to us as though we were a bunch of sinners, which we are, needing to repent, and if you do, you will bring God's message."

In a recent article in a local newspaper, I read about a group of youngsters who had turned into vandals. They had taken baseball bats, guns, and rocks, and had destroyed all the automobiles which were parked in the streets in that part of the city of Dallas. When I read that, I thought that such a thing could happen in the ghetto world where all the poor people live and the kids grow up in crime. Do you know where that happened? It happened in the elite section of our city. The youngsters who grow up in fine, affluent homes are just as mean, just as devil-minded, and just as lost in sin as the youth who grow up in what are called "crime-infested" ghettos. Without Jesus, they are all lost. Without the Lord, they are all the same. They are all condemned before God. When a rich man comes to trial, he has money to buy lawyers, but when a poor man comes to trial he does not have anyone to help him, and still they are both alike. In God's sight there are just two classifications. We are either lost in our sin, or we are saved by the blood of the Savior. There is no difference.

Have you been to Jesus for the cleansing power?
Are you washed in the blood of the Lamb?
Are you fully trusting in His grace this hour?
Are you washed in the blood of the Lamb?

That is the gospel, and Peter preached it to Cornelius, a fine Roman soldier, a man lost in sins but saved in the Lord.

THE RESULTS ARE THE SAME

Look at what happened. We read:

While Peter yet spake these words, the Holy Ghost fell on all them which heard the word.

And they of the circumcision which believed were astonished, as many as came with Peter, because that on the Gentiles also was poured out the gift of the Holy Ghost.

For they heard them speak with [glossa] tongues, and magnify God (Acts 10:44-46a).

That was a demonstrable fact, a scientific fact, a fact one can see repeatedly. While the sermon was being preached, the Holy Spirit fell upon the people.

One time when I was preaching at the Cain Road Baptist Church in Hong Kong, I had an interpreter who was a professor in a university and a wonderful Christian. If I have an interpreter who has a spirit like mine, we just encourage each other. While I was preaching, the Spirit of God came down and I could feel the moving of the loving grace of our Lord. In the middle of the sermon, one of those Chinese men walked down to the front of the church and stood before me with his hands clasped and his head bowed. Then soon another came, and another, and still another, and they stood before the pulpit. Soon a large group was standing with their hands clasped and their heads bowed. Finally, I stopped and turned to my interpreter and asked, "What are these people doing down here?" He said to me, "Praise God, these are they who cannot wait until you are though with your message, but they have come and stood before the pulpit signifying that they have accepted Jesus as their Savior in open confession before men and angels." What a marvelous thing!

At another time I was preaching at Falls Creek Assembly, which once was the largest Baptist assembly in the world, having about 25,000 people in attendance. I started preaching at 11:00, and in the midst of the message something happened. Someone came down the aisle to the front. The Holy Spirit had fallen upon him. At 2:00 in the afternoon, when I had started at 11, that service was still going on. We had forgotten about lunch, we had forgotten about dinner, we had forgotten about everything. The thousands who were there were all praising God together. It was like heaven. And such an experience happens again and again. While Peter was preaching, the Holy Spirit fell upon his listeners.

"For they heard them speak with *glossa.*" Let me explain the word *glossa*. When Peter described this experience in his defense, he said that "God gave them the like gift as He gave unto us at Pentecost." If it were the like gift, then we know exactly what happened at Caesarea in the gentile Pentecost. In the Jewish Pentecost at Jerusalem in the initial outpouring of the Spirit of God upon the Jewish nation, they spoke in languages praising God. If a like thing happened here, then one can easily describe what took place in the household of Cornelius. The Roman army was composed of numerous nations from all provinces of the empire. There were Greeks, Cappadocians, Latins, Aramaeans, Scythians, and many others in the Roman army. A psychologist will tell you that if a man is frightened, he will immediately revert to his mother tongue. If he is greatly excited, he will speak in his mother tongue. That is exactly what happened in Caesarea. The Greeks, the Latins, the Cappadocians, the Aramaeans, and the Scythians began to praise God in their mother language. It was incomparable what happened, and it was a glorious hour, one that you will hear and see repeated again and again when the Holy Spirit falls upon His people.

Forbid Water?

Peter said, "Can any man forbid water, that these should not be baptized, which have received the Holy Ghost as well as we?" (Acts 10:47). Baptism was of the utmost importance in this great experience. Having believed, they were to be baptized.

There is a great doctrinal truth here. The ordinance of baptism is not invested in a man, not even in Peter, the chief apostle, but it is a shared ministry. It belongs to the people of God. It belongs to the church. When the people were converted, Peter turned to the brethren and said, "Are not these prepared to be baptized who have received the Holy Spirit, having believed on Jesus just as we?"

O the depths of the love and wisdom of God in Christ Jesus!

11

Peter's Defense of the Faith

And the apostles and brethren that were in Judaea heard that the Gentiles had also received the word of God.

And when Peter was come up to Jerusalem, they that were of the circumcision contended with him,

Saying, Thou wentest in to men uncircumcised, and didst eat with them.

But Peter rehearsed the matter from the beginning, and expounded it by order unto them, saying,

I was in the city of Joppa praying: and in a trance I saw a vision, A certain vessel descend, as it had been a great sheet, let down from heaven by four corners; and it came even to me:

Upon the which when I had fastened mine eyes, I considered, and saw fourfooted beasts of the earth, and wild beasts, and creeping things, and fowls of the air.

And I heard a voice saying unto me, Arise, Peter; slay and eat.

But I said, Not so, Lord: for nothing common or unclean hath at any time entered into my mouth.

But the voice answered me again from heaven, What God hath cleansed, that call not thou common.

And this was done three times: and all were drawn up again into heaven.

And, behold, immediately there were three men already come unto the house where I was, sent from Caesarea unto me.

And the spirit bade me go with them, nothing doubting. Moreover these six brethren accompanied me, and we entered into the man's house:

And he shewed us how he had seen an angel in his house, which stood and said unto him, Send men to Joppa, and call for Simon, whose surname is Peter;

Who shall tell thee words, whereby thou and all thy house shall be saved.

And as I began to speak, the Holy Ghost fell on them, as on us at the beginning.

Then remembered I the word of the Lord, how that he said, John indeed baptized with water; but ye shall be baptized with the Holy Ghost.

Forasmuch then as God gave them the like gift as he did unto us, who believed on the Lord Jesus Christ; what was I, that I could withstand God?

When they heard these things, they held their peace, and glorified God, saying, Then hath God also to the Gentiles granted repentance unto life. (Acts 11:1-18)

The beginning of the story of the outpouring of the Spirit of God upon the Gentiles is in Acts 10. Peter saw a vision, and in that vision God said, "Rise; kill, and eat." Peter replied, "Lord, I have never eaten ceremonially unclean things." The Lord said to the great apostle, "What God hath cleansed, call not thou common or unclean." Then came the emissaries from Caesarea, the hated and despised Roman capital of the province of Judaea, the city which was a sign of the Jews' foreign slavery and oppression. These men invited Peter to come to Caesarea, about thirty miles north of Joppa, to bring words that would bring salvation to Cornelius, the Roman officer, and his household.

So Peter arrived at the home of the Roman centurion. After the centurion recounted to him how an angel had instructed him to send for Peter, the apostle began, "I perceive that God has revealed to us that I am to call no man common or unclean and that God is no respecter of persons, but that anyone anywhere who believes in Him shall receive remission of sins." Then upon them fell the Spirit of the Lord, the Spirit of saving grace, and Peter commanded them upon the authority and vote of the brethren to be baptized. So we begin.

And the apostles and brethren that were in Judaea heard that the Gentiles had also received the word of God.

And when Peter was come up to Jerusalem, they that were of the circumcision [*diakrino*], contended with him (Acts 11:1-2).

The basic meaning of *diakrino* is "to separate" and "to sever." Finally, the word came to mean "to accost," "to confront," "to contend with," "to dispute with," "to condemn vigorously and violently." We continue the passage:

Saying, Thou wentest in to men uncircumcised, and didst eat with them (Acts 11:3).

CONTENTION IN THE CHURCH

What a marvelous revelation of human nature. Whenever there is trouble in the church, it will seldom be over any great commitment or doctrinal statement, but will be over some minutiae issue that is not worthy to be mentioned. They said to him, "You ate with a Gentile." They did not mention the marvelous salvation of grace that was extended to the gentile people. Nothing was mentioned about God's mercy for the whole world, but they condemned Peter because they said, "You visited an uncircumcised man and you ate with him!" Lest we think that was the church in Jerusalem, we can see that is exactly like the churches of today. Many of our altercations are also over little issues.

One time I was preaching at a state convention, and every time I got through preaching, the preachers would gather in little groups in one corner or another, in the basement, in the choir room, or in the attic. They were highly displeased about an unimportant matter of no consequence which the executive secretary had done!

One time I preached in a church that had a vicious split right down the middle. Some of the people left and organized another church. What they split over was whether the piano ought to be in front of the pulpit or on the side by the choir. Such are people!

These Jews accosted Peter with an unbelievable statement. This is the church that began "with one accord," as the Bible says: "And they were all with one accord, loving God, praising the Lord." Then they got into an altercation over the Hellenists and the Aramaeans, the Greek-speaking Jews and the Aramaic-speaking Jews. Now they are in conflict over the issue of eating with a Gentile.

PETER'S DEFENSE

The only way Peter could exonerate himself was to tell them what God had done. Then our story continues: "Peter rehearsed the matter from the beginning, and expounded it by order unto them, saying," then he followed through what God did. "The Lord told me to rise; kill, and eat. The Lord told me not to call any man common or unclean. The Lord God said, 'What God hath cleansed, call not thou common.' The Spirit bade me, 'Go with these men, nothing doubting.' And the Holy Ghost fell upon them while I was preaching to them. God gave them the like gift as He did to us at Pentecost. Who was I that I could withstand God?" The only way Peter could exonerate himself was to say, "God did that." The entire plan, purpose, revelation, and commandment was from heaven. God did it.

The Judaizers Are Ever Present

We have this Judaizing party in the churches and in Christendom to this day. You will stumble into them everywhere. The Judaizers followed Paul and were his bitterest enemies. In Philippians 3, Paul calls them "dogs." In Galatians 5 Paul talks about the party of the circumcision (circumcision was a sign of the Mosaic law), and says, "I would that they themselves were cut off, were mutilated, destroyed, from the Christian faith." It was an awesome thing that the Christians faced in these Judaizers in the days of Peter and Paul, in the days of the New Testament. But we have that Judaizing party with us forever. You see, the gospel is that we are saved in the Lord and in Him alone. As Ephesians 2 says, "By grace are ye saved through faith, and that not of yourselves; it is a gift of God, not of works, lest any man should say, 'I did it,' lest he boast." In Romans 10 the passage says, "Whosoever shall call upon the name of the Lord shall be saved." John 3:16 says that "Whosoever believeth in him shall have everlasting life." That is the gospel. It is a message from heaven. It is something God does. God saved us. But we still have these Judaizers who come along and say: "To believe on the Lord Jesus Christ and accept Him as your Savior is not enough. You must believe in the Lord Jesus *and* you must do all kinds of things." As for the Judaizers in our text, they avowed, "You must believe in the Lord Jesus *and* you must be circumcised, *and* you must keep the law of Moses, and you must make distinction between clean and unclean, *and* you must do a thousand other things in order to be saved." Some of them said, "You must believe in the Lord *and* be baptized. If you are not baptized, then you cannot be saved." Others say, "You must believe in the Lord *and* you must do good works." That Judaizing party is forever around us and it sometimes seems to govern Christendom.

But the gospel message is never that. The great revelation of the Lord God on the pages of the Holy Scriptures is that we are saved by the Lord Jesus Christ, by Him alone, and by nothing that a man can do or add to the atoning grace of the Son of God.

Repentance Unto Life

When they heard these words, they said, "Then hath God also to the Gentiles granted repentance unto life." Even saving repentance is a gift of God. We do not work ourselves into it. It is something that comes down from heaven. Look at the result of our human efforts toward repentance. A man can listen, and he can tremble and be moved, but that is not saving repentance. When Felix listened to Paul preach, he trembled and then said, "Go thy way; I will call you at another convenient season," and he died lost.

Look at Herod Agrippa II. He asked, "Do you want me to be a Christian?" After they had dismissed Paul and the chained soldier by his side, he said to the procurator Festus: "There is nothing that this man has done worthy of death. Had he not appealed to Caesar, he could have had his freedom." But Herod Agrippa II died lost. To be greatly impressed is not saving repentance.

To be scared to death is not saving repentance. Elijah said to Ahab, "In the place where the dogs licked up the blood of Naboth, they shall lick up thy blood." And the Lord God said to Elijah, "Look how he has humbled himself and how he walks quietly." But the prophecy came to pass. Jezebal and Ahab, her husband, never repented to the saving of their souls. Being scared to death by the threatening of God is not saving repentance.

Reformation is not saving repentance. In Matthew 12, the Lord describes a man who has an evil spirit in him, and He thrust him out. After the spirit was gone, he came back and looked into that man's heart and found it swept clean. He went to get seven spirits worse than himself and came back and lived in the heart of that man, and the last state of the man was worse than the first. We may drink, or curse, or gamble, or desecrate God's name, and decide to quit. We are going to turn over a new leaf. That is reformation, but that does not save us. Reformation is not repentance unto salvation.

Nor is remorse repentance unto salvation. Judas, when he saw what the iniquity of his traitorous betrayal had done, took the thirty pieces of silver and cast them down on the temple floor, saying, "I have betrayed the innocent blood." And he went out and hanged himself. *Metamelomai* is the Greek word for "remorse." Remorse is not saving repentance.

How the Holy Spirit Works to Bring Saving Repentance

What is saving repentance? That question is simply answered in the Bible. Saving repentance occurs when the Holy Spirit of God takes a man's heart and mind and leads him to look at Jesus. You see, in John 16 the Lord says: "The Spirit shall not speak of Himself. He never exalts Himself, He never points to Himself, but He shall take the things of mine and show them unto thee. He shall glorify Me." This is saving repentance when the Holy Spirit of God takes a man's soul and leads the man to look upon Jesus.

The first thing that will happen to a man when he looks upon Jesus is that he will have a feeling of sorrow. "My sins did that? Drove these nails into His hands? Thrust that Roman spear into His side? My sins did that?"

> Was it for crimes that I have done,
> He groaned upon the tree?
> Amazing pity, grace unknown,
> And love beyond degree.

That is the first thing that happens when a man accepts the Lord. There is a spirit of sorrow. "Lord, Lord, my sins did that?"

Second, when the Spirit takes the man in saving repentance, and He leads him to look upon Jesus, the man will be filled with a love for the Lord that is indescribable. Years ago the word "personal" was used so frequently. "Jesus, our personal Savior." Had there been no one else in the world who sinned, He yet would have died for me. If there were no hell, we would still love Him. If there were no judgment, we would still love Him. If there were no reward for the righteous, we would still love Him. Serving Jesus for the love of God, not for anything we propose or hope to get out of it—that is saving repentance.

Third, there will be a great turning. You will be someone else. You will be a new creation. You will be a new person. People will not recognize you had they known you before.

Let me illustrate that in two ways. First, I read of a missionary who, with his wife, went down to live among the lost and indigenous people of the South Pacific islands. While they were there, the islanders came and stole everything the missionary and his wife had in their house. Then, as the missionaries worked with the people, the Holy Spirit led the natives to saving repentance and to saving faith. Do you know what happened? One by one, a native would come and knock at the missionary's door and say, "Missionary, I stole this out of your house, but since I found the Lord, I am bringing it back to you," and he would set the article down. Another native would come and knock at the door and say, "Missionary, I stole this out of your house, but since I have found the Lord, I am bringing it back to you" and so on. In the grace of God, the natives who had stolen these articles, returned what they had stolen. That is saving repentance.

Second, I was once pastor of the First Baptist Church of Muskogee, Oklahoma. In Muskogee, which was the capital seat of five civilized tribes of Indians, the public library has a large room filled with the lore, literature, and history of those Indian tribes. I used to go to that library and pour over those old volumes, looking at the old newspapers and reading the stories written about the Indians. I copied down one of those poems. In the Chickasaw nation, on a dark and stormy night, the parson was speaking to ninety criminals gathered together by the United States marshall in his prison. This is what happened:

> I am going to preach and I'll try to teach
>   To the ninety men in here
> Of the words of love from the throne above
>   (And his tones were loud and clear).
>
> I preach to you of a Saviour true
>   In a happy home on high.
> Where the angels dwell, all saved from hell
>   And the righteous never die.
>
> And he prayed a prayer in the prison there
>   As the ninety bowed their heads,
> To bold Choctaw and the Chickasaw,
>   The whites, the blacks, the reds.
>
> He prayed for the chief with his unbelief,
>   For the black highwayman bold,
> For the robber, too, and his bandit crew,
>   For the criminals, young and old.
>
> Then he sang an hymn in the prison grim,
>   He sang, "Turn, Sinner, Turn.
> It is not too late to reach God's gate
>   While the lamp holds out to burn."
>
> Then from his bed 'tween the black and the red
>   Up rose an outlaw bold,
> With trembling step to the parson crept,
>   All shivering as with cold.
>
> And a vicious flash of the lightnings crash
>   Showed his features pale and stern,
> As he bowed his head and slowly said,
>   "I am resolved to turn."
>
> And it seemed to me no one shall see
>   A scene so glad, so grand
> As the white and the red on their blanket bed
>   'Round the Christian one did stand.

> While the night came down like a silvery crown
>   And a promise gave to all,
> For the ninety men in the marshall's den
>   Heard only the Saviour's call.

I would have loved to have been there to have witnessed such saving repentance, turning to the Lord Jesus.

That is God's gift to us. It is a gift of the Holy Spirit, from God's hands. It is not something that we earn ourselves, but it comes from the Lord Himself.

12

A New People

Now they which were scattered abroad upon the persecution that arose about Stephen traveled as far as Phenice, and Cyprus, and Antioch, preaching the word to none but unto the Jews only.

And some of them were men of Cyprus and Cyrene, which, when they were come to Antioch, spake unto the Grecians, preaching the Lord Jesus.

And the hand of the Lord was with them: and a great number believed, and turned unto the Lord.

Then tidings of these things came unto the ears of the church which was in Jerusalem: and they sent forth Barnabas, that he should go as far as Antioch.

Who, when he came, and had seen the grace of God, was glad, and exhorted them all, that with purpose of heart they would cleave unto the Lord.

For he was a good man, and full of the Holy Ghost and of faith: and much people was added unto the Lord.

Then departed Barnabas to Tarsus, for to seek Saul:

And when he had found him, he brought him unto Antioch. And it came to pass, that a whole year they assembled themselves with the church, and taught much people. And the disciples were called Christians first in Antioch. (Acts 11:19-26)

We have now come to one of the great passages in the Bible. We can see that the circumference of the Christian faith is constantly broadening. First, in Acts 2 we find the story of the outpouring of the Holy Spirit upon the Jews in Jerusalem. In Acts 8 we read of the preaching of the gospel to the half-breed Jews, the Samaritans. Then later in that same chapter is recorded the conversion of a proselyte of the temple, a Gentile who had become a full-fleged, temple-worshiping Jew. Then in Acts 10 we read where the gospel message is extended through the preaching of the gospel to a Gentile, a proselyte of the gate. He has embraced the moral code of Moses but he is still a Gentile.

Now in Acts 11 we come to the preaching of the gospel to people who are downright idolaters. They have no part with the Jewish faith at all. There are Romans, Greeks, Scythians, and all kinds of people in Antioch who are marvelously converted out of their idolatry and heathenism directly into the precious grace and regenerating power of Jesus Christ. Finally, in Acts 13, the gospel message out of Antioch is proclaimed to the entire world in the great missionary journeys of Paul and Barnabas.

WHY THE COINED NAME

The latter part of the eleventh chapter of Acts describes an altogether different departure. Let us look at the providence that gave rise to this new people in pagan Antioch. Heretofore, the Christian religion had been looked upon as a sect of the Jews. There were Pharisees, Sadducees, Herodians, Essenes, and Zealots. All of these were sects of the Jews. The development of the early followers of Jesus was also looked upon as a sect of the Jews. All of those sects, including the disciples of Jesus, lived as the Jews lived. They worshiped in the temple, they were circumcised, they kept all the feasts, they observed all the prayers, they followed all of the rituals and the ceremonies, and they made their pilgrimages to Jerusalem, the holy city. They were either Jews, or sects of the Jews. For many years the Christian faith was just a part of the Jewish religion.

But what happened in Antioch was something new and different. It was not like anything that had ever happened before, because these converts in Antioch were certainly not Jews. They had no Jewish background and they observed no Mosaic ceremonies or rituals. They were downright heathen, pagan, Greek idolaters. The conversion to the Christian faith of this new people was an amazing development, for in no sense were they Jews. They were a conglomerate of differing peoples. They had only one thing in common; they had given their hearts to the Lord Jesus.

THE CONSTRUCTION AND MEANING OF THE NEW NAME

The Antiochians invented a name to describe the new group of followers of Christ. The first part of the word is Greek, *Christos*, the name of the Lord Christ. The second part of the word is *ianos*, a Latin ending which was widely used in the Roman Empire. The suffix *ianos* was primarily used first to refer to a man who was a slave in a great household. For example, the word *Caesarianos* referred to a slave in the household of Caesar. *Christianos* would be one who was a slave in the household of Christ. That is the way the ending *ianos* had its primary meaning. Later on *ianos* came to refer to one who followed a certain party or who followed in the way of some great leader such as *Herodianos*, one who followed Herod; *Aristotilianos*, one who followed the philosopher, Aristotle; *Pompeianos*, one who was a member of the Pompey party in Rome, or *Augustianos*, referring to those who were followers of Nero, the last Caesar. So the word *Christianos*, "Christian," came to apply to those who were followers and slaves of the Lord Jesus.

There is an unusual designation of the word "called." "And the disciples were *called* 'Christianoi' first in Antioch." The ordinary Greek word for "called" is *kaleo*, but an altogether different word is used here.

The word used is *kramatisai*, and came to refer to people who were called after their business. A man who was a baker was called "Baker." A man who was a tailor was called "Taylor." That is the way that the word *kramatisai* came to be used to refer to *Christianoi*. *Christianoi* are people who are doing business for Christ. That is exactly how Dr. Luke writes it. "They were called '*kramatisai Christianoi*' first in Antioch."

WHO GAVE THE NAME?

Let us look at those who invented the name Christian. It was certainly not the Jews. To them Jesus was no Christ, no Messiah. The Jews bitterly opposed the idea that Jesus was the Messiah, the Christ, so the name *Christianoi* did not come from them.

The name did not come from the disciples themselves. One can read all through the New Testament and see how the Christians referred to themselves. They called themselves "brethren," "saints," "the elect," "the disciples," but they never referred to themselves as "Christians."

So if the Jews did not do it, and if the disciples, the followers of the Lord, did not do it, then who invented this new name of "Christian"?

The people of Antioch had a world-wide reputation for their sarcastic, ridiculing, sardonic, contemptuous wit. They were adept in nicknaming, or name-calling. The name for this new group came from the heathen who lived in Antioch. *Christianoi* was a heathen appelation.

Let us now look at the place where the name originated.

WHERE THE NAME ORIGINATED

Antioch was the third great city of the Roman empire. First was Rome, second was Alexandria, and third was Antioch. It was founded by Seleucus I, Seleucus Nicator in 300 B.C. The four great generals of Alexander the Great divided into four parts his vast Greek empire. Cassander took Macedonia. He had married Alexander's sister, Thessalonice, and named the capital of his part of the Greek Empire after her. Lysimachus took Asia Minor, Ptolemy took Egypt, and Seleucus took Syria, the great segment from the Euphrates down to the river of Egypt. In a beautiful location where the Orontes River flows out of the Lebanese mountains, Seleucus Nicator built his capital. The Orontes River, a clear and abundantly flowing stream, flows north, then makes a turn due west, between the Lebanese and Taurus Mountain ranges, and pours into the Mediterranean Sea. In that beautiful valley with the mountains rising on either side, there Seleucus Nicator built his capital. He named it for his father, Antiochus. Antioch was a glorious Greek city which had four walls with another enormously high wall around those four walls. It swept from the mountainside down to the Orontes River with four-and-one-half miles of Corinthian colonnaded streets. Antioch was a beautiful city whose wide boulevards were made out of solid marble.

Of course, as all Greek oriental cities, Antioch was licentious, vile in the extreme. Right beside Antioch were the groves of Daphne in which people indulged in every kind of orgy. This is the city in which Paul and Barnabas preached the gospel, in which the hand of the Lord in power was upon them, in which was gathered this new people, the first time that the world ever saw such a conglomerate congregation. "They were called *Christianoi* first in Antioch."

WHAT IS A CHRISTIAN?

What is a Christian? Three times the word is used in the Bible, twice in Acts, and once in 1 Peter. What is a Christian?

The following article appeared describing a court case in Iowa regarding how to define a Christian.

> The Supreme Court of Iowa ruled on a most unusual case. It concerned a
> trust fund a Methodist physician left in charge of four trustees, with instructions
> that the proceeds be distributed among "persons who believe in the fundamental
> principles of the Christian religion and the Bible, and who are endeavoring to
> promulgate the same."
> There was a dispute between the trustees and the nephews and nieces of the
> deceased as to what "the Christian religion" is.
> The relatives argued, "There is no common agreement as to what constitutes
> the fundamental principles of Christianity." To prove this, seven clergymen
> took the witness stand and testified that they could not define the Christian
> religion.
> Attorneys for the trustees countered by producing clergymen who testified
> that Christians can be identified as those who believe in God, in the Apostles'
> Creed, in the Holy Trinity, and who confess faith in Christ.
> The Judge of a lower court in Iowa ruled that among Christians, "there is
> widespread lack of accord in their characterizations of the man Jesus and their
> interpretations and applications of his teachings. Furthermore," the judge said,
> "it was beyond the perogative of the courts to define Christian fundamentals.
> We do not know what Christian fundamentals are," the court said. So the Judge
> ordered the trustees to hand over the fund to the nieces and nephews.
> The trustees took the case to the State Supreme Court which upheld the late
> doctor's will. The State's highest court ruled seven to two that it is possible to
> define what kind of a person can be called a Christian and decreed that the
> trustees were capable of determining from the language of the will who should
> benefit from the trust fund.

God bless those seven judges!

THE WORD "CHRISTIAN" IN ACTS 11

What is a Christian? We will define the word from the Bible. We
look first in Acts 11:

> And the hand of the Lord was with them: and a great number believed, and
> turned unto the Lord (Acts 11:21).

A Christian is someone who believes in Jesus and turns away from
heathenism and paganism to the Lord. The Antiochians had been
worshiping Bacchus, the god of wine, in Bacchanalian festivals. They
had been worshiping Saturn in their Saturnalian festivals. Unspeaka-
bly vile, they had turned away from this idolatry and had accepted as
Savior the Lord Jesus.

We read further in the eleventh chapter "that with purpose of heart
they would cleave unto the Lord" (v. 23b). There they are committed

and consecrated to the Lord Jesus. Verse 26 states that "they assembled themselves with the church." Any time a man says, "I can be a Christian and not go to church," he is speaking foolishness. A man who is a Christian feels in his heart, "I want to be in the church with the people of the Lord." There you can gather together and listen to the expounding of the Word of God. Such is a Christian.

THE WORD "CHRISTIAN" IN ACTS 26

The second time the word "Christian" is used is in Acts 26:28, "Then Agrippa said unto Paul, almost thou persuadest me to be a Christian." The actual Greek word translated "almost," is *en oligo*, "to sum up," "in a little." Agrippa actually said, "In summary, you want me to be a Christian." Agrippa certainly knew what Paul was talking about. What is a Christian? A Christian is, and this was Paul's presentation to King Herod Agrippa II, "a man who has turned to accept the Lord Jesus." To the king, Paul had described his conversion and mandate from heaven. Paul had avowed that God sent him to the Gentiles "to open their eyes, and to turn them from darkness to light, and from the power of Satan unto God, that they may receive forgiveness of sins, and inheritance among them which are sanctified by faith that is in me . . . [so I preach] that they should repent and turn to God, and do works meet for repentance" (Acts 26:18, 20b). That is a Christian; someone who has turned away from the evil and iniquity of this world and has turned in faith to the Lord Jesus.

THE WORD "CHRISTIAN" IN 1 PETER

The third place where the word "Christian" is found is in 1 Peter 4:16: "Yet if any man suffer as a Christian, let him not be ashamed; but let him glorify God on this behalf." This is in a beautiful context. We read in chapter 4:

> But rejoice, inasmuch as ye are partakers of Christ's sufferings; that, when his glory shall be revealed, ye may be glad also with exceeding joy.
> If ye be reproached for the name of Christ, happy are ye; for the spirit of glory and of God resteth upon you: on their part he is evil spoken of, but on your part he is glorified.
> Yet if any man suffer as a Christian, let him not be ashamed; but let him glorify God on this behalf (vv. 13-14, 16).

A Christian is someone who has turned from the world, and has found forgiveness of sin and hope of eternal life in Christ Jesus. A Christian is one who assembles with God's people in prayer and in

Bible reading and study. A Christian is one who bears a reproach in the name of Christ and does it triumphantly and victoriously.

Alexander the Great's empire covered the civilized world. He was a great conqueror. In his army was a soldier who was the namesake of Alexander, but he was a notorious coward. Alexander the Great, who conquered the world when he was just twenty-three, called the soldier before him and said, "Is your name Alexander and are you named for me?" The trembling coward said: "Yes, sir. My name is Alexander and I was named for you." The great general said, "Then either be a brave soldier, or change your name!"

I feel that way about the Christian faith and about us. Let us live it, act it, and commit our lives to it, or let us change our name. Lord God, that I might be among those who are enrolled as being a Christian—not a heathen, not a pagan, not a worldly man, but a Christian!

13

The Christians of Antioch

And when he had found him, he brought him unto Antioch. And it came to pass, that a whole year they assembled themselves with the church, and taught much people. And the disciples were called Christians first in Antioch. (Acts 11:26)

When we think of a church such as Antioch, we sometimes think that it existed only in the days of the Bible. We read of the church at Antioch on the pages of the New Testament, but after the Bible closes, we suppose that it has little history thereafter. In this chapter we are going to follow the church at Antioch through the centuries beyond the Bible until the church and the city itself were destroyed in a vast earthquake in A.D. 526.

Antioch became the center of the worldwide missionary enterprise of the Church. In Acts 11, the propagation and world evangelization of the Christian faith is changed from Jerusalem to Antioch. From Antioch the Word of God spreads to the entire civilized world and ultimately around the globe. What of its history and what became of the mighty church?

THE STORY OF THE CHURCH AT ANTIOCH
CONTINUES IN GLORY AND POWER

Truly one of the most interesting and dynamic stories that one could ever read in history is the story of the progress and growth of the vast congregation in Antioch. One time when I was speaking at an

100

evangelistic conference I mentioned that the church in Antioch had at least 50,000 members.

One of the ministers came up to me after the service and said, "Where did you get the figure of 50,000 members in the church at Antioch?" I replied, "In reading I came across those statistics." He said, "Well, I do not believe it."

His response rather shocked me, so I went to my library and reread my books. What I read was this: John Chrysostom said that there were 100,000 members in the church in Antioch! I had actually understated the total membership.

IGNATIUS

After the Book of Acts closes in about A.D. 64 and before the apocalypse of John was written, the church at Antioch had a tremendous pastor named Ignatius. Ignatius was a dynamic, Spirit-filled, and godly preacher. He proclaimed the gospel in that Greek, heathen city. In about A.D. 70 and in the years thereafter Ignatius was turning the whole populace to the Lord.

Trajan, the Roman Caesar, came to visit Antioch to see what was happening concerning emperor worship, idolatry, and heathenism. He listened to Ignatius and saw the throngs who were turning to the Lord. Enraged, Trajan commanded that Ignatius be brought before him and he sentenced Ignatius to be exposed to the wild beasts in Rome.

The Roman colosseum was built about five years after the martyrdom of Paul, so that would mean that it was built in approximately A.D. 72. The historians say that the first Christian martyr to be exposed to the lions in the Colosseum was this pastor of the church in Antioch, Ignatius. In the long journey from Antioch to Rome and the Colosseum, he wrote beautifully inspired letters which are the treasures of Christendom to this day.

Finally arriving in Rome, Ignatius was placed in the middle of that great amphitheater with tiers of thousands of onlookers on either side. The cages were opened and the lions were let loose. When the leading lion ran toward God's preacher, Ignatius held out his hand to it. Above the crunching sound of bone and tendon, Ignatius was heard to say, "Now I begin to be a Christian!" What faith, what consecration, what triumph, what victory! No wonder the historian says, "The blood of the martyr is the seed of the church." After Ignatius died in the Roman colosseum, his friends gathered up what few bones were left, and buried them with great lamentation and gratitude for his life in Antioch.

SIMEON STYLITES

As time went by, an unusual man by the name of Simeon the Elder was born in Antioch. This man sought to withdraw himself from the world, so he entered a cage and locked himself up behind walls. He bacame known as a very holy man, so people began to come and see him. Finally, to separate himself from the world even more, he built himself a little pole which was about six feet high. He sat and lived on the pole. As the days and the years passed, people began to come from the ends of the earth to see this Simeon Stylites, pole-sitter, anchorite.

In order to separate himself still further from the world, he extended his pole ten feet high, then twelve feet high, then fifteen, then thirty, then forty, then sixty, and finally so high that one of the historians records that he extended the pole 120 feet in the air. From the ends of the earth people would come to see Simeon the pole-sitter. He became the most famous Christian who lived in that day, sitting on a pole all day and all night for thirty-seven years.

When Simeon Stylites died after thirty-seven years on that pole, they brought him down and the whole empire was officially represented in the procession that buried him in Antioch. Seven thousand Roman legionnaries followed that train.

For a thousand years thereafter, all over Christendom the order of Stylites or pole-sitters could be seen everywhere. That was an unusual development in Christendom.

There is a characterization of religion that is unusual, for there are more fanatical frenzies connected with religion than with any one thing in the earth. I do not know what it is, but if one is religious, then he somehow feels that he must behave in a different and noticeable manner.

Such behavior is so different from the men of God in the Bible. The Lord Jesus was someone who dressed like everyone else. Peter, Paul, and all of the disciples dressed like other people. They talked like other people, they lived a life like other people, and their holiness and piety came not in their eating or in their dressing, but came in the godliness of their lives and the beauty of their souls.

Two Bible Schools

In the empire two tremendous Bible schools developed. They represented schools of thought and interpretation. One was the school in Alexandria and the other was the school in Antioch, and they were as different as night and day.

The school in Alexandria was a spiritualizing school; that is, men would take the Word of God and spiritualize it, making it mean anything they pleased. Philo who lived in Alexandria, was a contemporary of the Lord Jesus, and he was also a spiritualizer. A tremendous intellect and a great Jewish philosopher, Philo would take the Old Testament, and in order to make it conform to Greek philosophy, he would spiritualize the Scriptures.

For example, this would be typical of Philo. If Philo was expounding the story of Adam and Eve in the Garden of Eden, he could say: "There were no such people as Adam and Eve. They never lived, but they represent you and me, the human race. There was no such thing as the Garden of Eden, but it represents your mind, your brain. The trees in the Garden of Eden represent your mental processes and thoughts—good thoughts from the good trees, and bad thoughts from the tree of the knowledge of good and evil. The four rivers that watered the Garden of Eden represent the four cardinal virtues of Greek philosophy." That is spiritualization.

Origen, who was a tremendous intellectual exponent of the Christian faith, lived in Alexandria and followed that way of interpretation. In my humble opinion, the poorest interpretation of the Word of God is spiritualization; that is, instead of letting the Bible say what it says and mean what it means, we take the Bible and spiritualize it. We make it mean anything we want it to mean, whatever comes to our mind. That school of theology developed in Alexandria.

Contrariwise, in Antioch was found an outstanding Bible school and a tremendous way of interpretation. The school in Antioch followed what one would call a historical-grammatical interpretation of the Bible. Men took the Bible in Antioch and they studied its language. They studied what God meant; they studied the textual grammar, its historical background, its setting, and where it originated. They expounded the Word of God according to what God says and what God means by what He says. To me, that is the correct way for a school to teach, and it is the one way I think a preacher ought to preach. He ought to take the Bible to see what God has to say, and then he ought to expound the meaning of what God says to our lives. That was the great school in interpretation in Antioch.

Their most brilliant and incomparable preacher was named John. So fluent and oratorical was John that they called him John Chrysostom, "John the Golden-mouthed." He was born into a noble family in Antioch and was pursuing an outline of study that would make him a great orator, rhetorician, and lawyer.

But John Chrysostom had a godly Christian mother named Anthusa. Libanius, who headed the oratorical school to which John was sent, wrote, "This is the young man whom we are preparing to take my place. [He was to be the great orator, rhetorician, lawyer, and philosopher of Antioch and the entire eastern world.] But his mother has prayed him into a life of piety."

John left the school, embraced the Christian faith, was baptized, and went into the desert to expose his soul before the Lord. When he returned, he was a flame of fire, a man of great intellectual and theological perception. When you read the outstanding biblical commentaries today such as Matthew Henry, Ellicott, Westcott, Jamieson-Fausset-Brown, Lightfoot, and Alford, you will find that their interpretations actually began with John Chrysostom. What a mighty preacher and interpreter of the Word of God he was!

John Chrysostom's Flaming Beginning as a Preacher

A riot took place in Antioch in the days when John Chrysostom was a young preacher. Theodosius, the emperor, had laid a heavy levy upon the city to support his Roman army and legionnaires. The city rebelled against that tax and a riot and uproar followed. The people destroyed the images of the emperor, an act that was not only sacrilege but treason as well. When the people of the city came to their senses and realized what they had done, they cowered and trembled for fear of a visit from the Roman Caesar with his army.

So the people of Antioch sent a committee to Theodosius in Rome to beg forgiveness and to apologize in order that their city might be spared and not be burned to the ground. While the emissaries were in Rome pleading with the Roman Caesar to forgive them their sacrilege and treason, John, the mighty preacher of God, seized the opportunity and every day and night preached the gospel of the Son of God with tremendous power. When the Roman Caesar came to the city, he saw that they were in the midst of a Spirit-leading, soul-saving revival. People were turning to the Lord and emperor Theodosius forgave them. Out of the vast outpouring of the Spirit of God and the tremendous revival in Antioch was crowned the magnificent church in Antioch which John Chrysostom stated was comprised of more than 100,000 members.

THE CHURCH STRUCTURE IN ANTIOCH

In Antioch, Constantine began the building and his son, Constantius, completed the construction of a vast edifice which had an enormous dome, even more marvelous than the church of St. Sophia in Istanbul. Now the church of St. Sophia is a miracle. Today huge buildings are built with steel, and large open places are structurally achieved because of the steel beams, but there was no steel in the days of the church at Antioch. Those buildings had to be built out of masonry. The St. Sophia Church in Istanbul is constructed with arches on top of other arches with the largest dome arch being larger than a baseball diamond, all made out of stone. So vast are those open spaces that one has the feeling of being outside. The church in Antioch which Constantine and Constantius built and in which John Chrysostom preached was even greater than the church of St. Sophia.

One might wonder how all 100,000 people could crowd into the church. It is a modern development that we have pews or chairs in a church. When the people came to church at Antioch, they all stood. In a vast area when people stood side by side crowding right up to the pulpit, thousands of people could crowd into a huge church such as the church at Antioch.

THE PREACHER

John Chrysostom's life ended in tragedy. He was called to be pastor of the church in Constantinople in the days of the Roman empress by the name of Eudoxia. Across the street in front of John Chrysostom's church, the empress had built a silver statue of herself, a shrine which was a place of godless orgy, immorality, and pagan worship. John Chrysostom stood in his pulpit and denounced Eudoxia, calling her "Jezebel." When Eudoxia replied that she was going to burn John Chrysostom at the stake, he stood in his pulpit and said: "Again, Herodias is raging; again, Herodias is dancing; again, Herodias is reaching out her hand for the head of John." She carried out her threat. She suborned men who cast John out of the pulpit, out of the church, out of the city, and tried to assassinate him. Instead, John Chrysostom, that great man of God, died of exposure and starvation.

Any true man of God, no matter in what generation, is a man who preaches the gospel fearlessly, honestly, and spiritually, according to the Word of the Lord. For example, in Oxford you will find a shrine where Hugh Lattimer and John Ridley, great preachers and mighty men of God, were burned at the stake. Lattimer had preached a sermon in the presence of Henry VIII which had greatly displeased his majesty. Thereupon, the king commanded Lattimer to return to the same place in the same church in the same pulpit and apologize for what he had preached in his presence. The following Sunday in the same pulpit, at the same time, Lattimer stood up to preach and spoke the following words:

> Hugh Lattimer, dost thou not know before whom thou art this day to speak, to the high and mighty monarch, the king's most excellent majesty who can take away thy life if thou offendest? Therefore, take heed that thou speakest not a word that may displease. But then consider well, Hugh, dost thou not know from whence thou comest—upon whose message thou art sent? Even by thy great and mighty God, who is all-present, and who beholdeth all thy ways, and who is able to cast thy soul into hell. Therefore, take care that thou deliverest thy message faithfully.

The history book continues: "He then proceeded with the same sermon he had preached the preceding Sunday, but with considerable more energy." I like that! God bless the preacher of God who was sent from heaven with a message from the Lord.

You may remember that when Bloody Mary ascended to the throne, the first thing she did was to burn Cranmer, and then burned Lattimer and Ridley together.

TWO CONCLUSIONS

We conclude with two facts. First, we stand in a noble line, in a great tradition. Think of it—John the Baptist, the Lord Jesus, Simon Peter, Saul [Paul] of Tarsus, Ignatius, John Chrysostom, Hugh Lattimer, John Huss, John Wycliffe, the martyrs of the Reformation, the martyrs of our mission fields, and the men of God, who, at this moment represent the Lord at the cost of their lives behind iron curtains in oppressive and communist lands. Yes, we stand in a great tradition!

Second, God has assigned us a great work. The purpose of this chapter is not just to recount facts of history, but also to remind us that as the men of old had a mandate from heaven in their day, we likewise have a mandate from the Lord in our day. We carry that torch under God's hands until He says, "It is enough," and calls us home. We are to be as true to our commitment in our day as they were in theirs, following through as fellow pilgrims with our faces toward God, doing God's word in the earth.

Lord, grant that we might be as true and as faithful in our generation as these were in theirs!

14

The Touch of an Angel's Hand

Now about that time Herod the king stretched forth his hands to vex certain of the church.

And he killed James the brother of John with the sword.

And because he saw it pleased the Jews, he proceeded further to take Peter also. (Then were the days of unleavened bread.)

And when he had apprehended him, he put him in prison, and delivered him to four quaternions of soldiers to keep him; intending after Easter to bring him forth to the people.

Peter therefore was kept in prison: but prayer was made without ceasing of the church unto God for him.

And when Herod would have brought him forth, the same night Peter was sleeping between two soldiers, bound with two chains: and the keepers before the door kept the prison.

And, behold, the angel of the Lord came upon him, and a light shined in the prison: and he smote Peter on the side, and raised him up, saying, Arise up quickly. And his chains fell off from his hands.

And the angel said unto him, Gird thyself, and bind on thy sandals. And so he did. And he saith unto him, Cast thy garment about thee, and follow me.

And he went out, and followed him; and wist not that it was true which was done by the angel; but thought he saw a vision.

When they were past the first and the second ward, they came unto the iron gate that leadeth unto the city; which opened to them of his own accord: and they went out, and passed on through one street; and forthwith the angel departed from him.

And when Peter was come to himself he said, Now I know of a surety, that the Lord hath sent his angel, and hath delivered me out of the hand of Herod, and from all the expectation of the people of the Jews. (Acts 12:1-11)

When we read the name "Herod" in the Bible, we can be sure that there will be trouble. Wherever a member of that family appears in the

Scriptures, there is conflict. The Herod in our text is Herod Agrippa I, the son of Aristobulus, who was the son of Herod the Great and Mariamne, the Herod of Jesus' birth.

Herod Agrippa I stretched forth his hand to "vex" the leaders of the church. The Greek word *kakos* means "bad," "wicked." The verbal form of the word is *kakoo*, which means "to treat terribly," "to oppress." "Herod the Great stretched forth his hand to crush, to vex, to oppress, to treat terribly certain of the church."

Notice that the verse begins with the phrase, "Now about that time." We know what time that is. Acts 11 closes with a great drought, a vast, world-wide famine. "About that time" refers to this time of trouble. But that is not all there is about "that time." Herod was stretching forth his hand to crush the infant church. One dies slowly by famine, but Herod had learned a faster way to bring oppression and death, so he seized James, the son of Zebedee, the brother of the sainted John, who wrote the Apocalypse, and beheaded him with the sword. Had James lived, I wonder what he would have become. Whenever in the Bible the two men, James and John, are named, James is always mentioned first. The reason one never hears particularly of James is because he forfeited his life under the cruel and murderous hand of Herod Agrippa I. When Herod saw that the murder of James pleased the people, he seized Peter also and placed him in prison awaiting the passing of the days of unleavened bread, the Passover season, in order to murder also our Lord's chief apostle.

Is not that the way of all iniquity? It does not like solitude. It is never found alone. Violence and crime always repeat in a succession or in a chain. Somehow those who perpetuate iniquity learn the skill of it, and when the first deed is done, the acts didn't seem so ghastly, so it is immediately followed by other crimes that are just as black. So it was with Herod when he killed James. Seeing that he prospered in murder, Herod seized Peter also that he might be murdered.

THE MURDER OF JAMES PLEASED THE JEWS

Our text reveals that Herod saw that his murder of James pleased the Jews. What an astonishing observation to be made about such a violent crime! Earlier the Jews had literally bathed their hands in the blood of Jesus, the Son of God, and in the blood of Stephen, and now in the blood of James. Further, they are preparing to bathe their hands in the blood of Peter.

Let me point out as I look at the text that this persecution is the tragic side of our faith in the Lord. Think of the Inquisition. On the pages of history, year after year, century after century, men and women were burned at the stake, drowned in rivers, and cast out of human society to die of exposure and starvation. Such a way of life is unthinkable to us, but it has characterized Christianity from its first day to this present hour.

If you enter Oxford University in England, you will find the monument to Lattimer and to Ridley who were burned at the stake.

The first time I visited Zurich, I asked the host to take me to the head of the Limont River which pours out of Zurich Lake, and I stood there in the place where they drowned the great Anabaptist leader, Felix Mantz.

The first time I was in Vienna, I asked to be taken to the place where men had burned Balthasar Hübmeier at the stake, then I asked to be taken to the place on the Danube River where three days later they bound and drowned his wife, who refused to repudiate the faith of her husband.

To make the story more sorrowful, look how faithfully and meticulously the Jews observed the proprieties and the amenities of the faith. They would not dare slay Peter during the days of the Passover, they said that after Easter, after the Passover, they would bring him forth to murder him.

I remember reading one day of two men who had robbed a bank, killed the bank president, and fled. The robbers finally came to a little cafe and stopped to eat. While they were eating the meal, one of them said, "Wait! This is Friday," and he pushed their plates away. They were comfortable in robbing a bank and killing the bank president, but ah, to eat meat on Friday! They were meticulous in observing the rituals and the ceremonies, while at the same time they were violating its foundational truths.

That is what we read in the Bible. May the Lord deliver us from ever observing all of the outwardness of the faith, but denying its inward reality.

THE FAITHFUL BAND PRAYED

So Peter was arrested and placed in prison to await his execution. Yet our text tells us, "But prayer was made without ceasing of the church unto God for him." Did you know that prayer is the real battlefield of the world? The whole universe looks down upon that little group interceding for the life of their chief apostle. God looks down upon it. The angels look down upon it. The hosts of heaven look down upon it. The powers that be, the ages look down upon it. The real battlefield where the decisive events of time and history are decided are in the faithful group of followers of the Lord who are down on their knees, praying without ceasing to God.

In Revelation 12 we read of the red dragon waiting to devour the child that was born. Likewise, Herod is stretching forth his hand to destroy the church. What does one do? How can he match his feebleness against the might and strength of Satan and of his stool pigeon, Herod Agrippa I?

So you call a prayer meeting. You bow before the Lord in intercession. "Prayer was made without ceasing of the church unto God for him."

Men often wonder at the permissive will of God. Why does God not intervene? Our text says that Herod stretched forth his hands to vex the church. Why did God not tear off that hand? He intervened in 2 Kings in the story of King Jeroboam. When the king stretched forth his hand to seize the prophet who came to denounce his idolatry in Bethel, the Bible says that his hand was paralyzed, and he could not draw it back. Why did God not do that with Herod?

What is the permissive will of God in allowing Jesus to die? What is the permissive will of God in allowing James to be slain of the sword? What is this permissive will of God that allows blood, terror, and oppression to the people of the Lord?

I have just one answer. As high as the heaven is above the earth, so are God's reasons and God's thoughts above our thoughts. I cannot explain the mystery of the permissive will of God. I cannot even explain His will in the trouble that we have in our lives, the sorrows that we know. Why does God allow them? Why does God allow the baby to die? Why does God allow the sorrows that sometimes overwhelm us like a flood? I cannot explain except for one thing I read in the text. It is this: When trouble and sorrow came, the people fell on their knees in real, agonizing prayer. I can see that in the lives of God's people. So often our prayers are peripheral. They are lifeless. They are cold. They are indifferent. They are repetitive. They have no blood in them, no tears in them, no agony in them. But when trouble comes and sorrow threatens, our prayers are no longer just syllables, sentences, and words. They are heartbeats, they are blood drops, they are agonies. So it is in this text. Bowed to their knees by an awesomeness of the slaughter of the infant church, the church goes to God in agonizing prayer.

CONFIDENCE AND ASSURANCE

Now notice the assurance and confidence of Peter. We read in the text, "And when Herod would have brought him forth, the same night Peter was sleeping between two soldiers, bound with two chains: and the keepers before the door kept the prison" (v. 6). The next day Peter was to be slaughtered, to be executed! He is like an animal in a cage awaiting the will and the time suited to the king to be slain. And we find him sound asleep. How beautiful is the tranquility that comes to the child of God who rests in the Lord. Think of Daniel in the lion's den, perfectly quiet, not afraid! You see, Peter belonged to God, for he was blood-bought, redeemed. Peter rested in the Lord, and it was in God's choice whether he lived or died. When Peter was free, he preached and served the blessed Jesus. When Peter was bound and in prison, he rested and slept. He was in the hands of God.

When John Wesley was returning to England from the failure of his missionary enterprise in Georgia, the little ship upon which he was sailing was caught in a furious storm. Wesley was scared to death. On board was a little band of Moravians, who, in the height of fury of the storm, were perfectly quiet, singing their hymns of praise, praying to the Lord God. John Wesley concluded: "I have not been saved. I am afraid; but these Moravians are quiet in the midst of the storm."

And so we see Peter, sleeping soundly on the day before his intended execution.

"And when he [Herod] had apprehended him, he put him in prison, and delivered him to four quaternions of soldiers to keep him" (v. 4). The guards took turns guarding Peter, changing every six hours, which means that a total of sixteen soldiers guarded him. What a preposterous arrangement! Peter is behind three gates, and is bound by two chains. As though that were not enough, Herod assigned sixteen soldiers to watch him!

Have you ever thought of the unconscious tribute that Satan pays to God's people? Look at the Lord Jesus on the cross. He surely must be dead because the soldiers thrust an iron spear into His heart and tore it apart. So He is placed in a sepulcher which has been carved out of solid rock and which was sealed by an enormous stone bearing a Roman seal. And the disciples had forsaken Him and fled. Here, Satan pays an unconscious tribute to God's people, for he placed a Roman guard to watch that dead man. Evidently Satan is afraid of a power that we do not see. So it is in our text. Herod had placed sixteen soldiers to guard a man in an iron cage, bound by two chains.

Those sixteen soldiers were either too many or too few. If Peter is behind walls and is chained inside an iron cage, then sixteen soldiers are too many. They are not needed.

But turn the situation around. If perchance those sixteen soldiers are fighting against God, against heaven, against the hosts of glory that the Lord can send to deliver Peter, then sixteen soldiers are too few.

We can read in Isaiah 38 that one angel was sent by the Lord over the vast army of the Assyrian Sennacherib, and the next morning, 185,000 dead corpses were counted.

DELIVERANCE

"And, behold, the angel of the Lord came upon him, and a light shined in the prison: and he smote Peter on the side, and raised him up" (v. 7). Do you know what problem we have here? We take in too small a field, too little a circumference. We follow the line, then it is broken off, and we are overwhelmed by the vice, the violence, the atheism, the iniquity, and all the sin of the world. We lose faith, and we are discouraged. Do you know why? We are judging the whole purposes of God by our little day, our little understanding, and our little time.

Wait, my friend. The universe is a great circle and it takes in the kingdoms of the whole creation. We can see just so small a part of it. There is an angel of the Lord awaiting in his day and his time to bring deliverance. Wait upon the Lord. He is not done. The last chapter has not been written.

The days of the Antedeluvians, the days of Noah, how tragic, how dark, they were. Wait; God is not done.

The days of Abraham, how the whole world was in idolatry. Wait; God is not done.

The days of the fiery furnace were days into which the Hebrew children were cast in Egypt. Wait; God is not done.

The days of the great apostasy in the time of Elijah were sad days. Wait; God is not done.

The days of the carrying away of the children of Israel into Babylon were grievous. Wait; God is not done.

The days of the awesome crucifixion were dark days. Wait; God is not done.

The days of the persecution of God's children and the church are still not finished. Wait; God is not done.

At the end of Revelation 19 we read that the Lord will come down with all His saints and the hosts of angels. He will establish His kingdom in His own might and power. Satan and his demons will be cast into the lake of fire. Then will follow the new heaven and the new earth, and we will have our assignment in a heavenly home, in a new Jerusalem, to live with God forever and ever. God is not done. Wait! Trust! Believe! Sleep at night in the assurance of the Lord. Some day God will send His angels and wake us up if we have fallen into a sleep in the dust of the ground, in the open grave. God will send His angel at the sound of the trumpet and wake us up. It is the Lord's good pleasure to let His children inherit the kingdom and all His creation. Happy day! Blessed day! Triumphant day! Glorious day when I received Jesus into my heart!

15

The Smiting of God's Angel

And, behold, the angel of the Lord came upon him, and a light shined in the
prison: and he smote Peter on the side, and raised him up, saying, Arise up
quickly. And his chains fell off from his hands. (Acts 12:7).

And immediately the angel of the Lord smote him, because he gave not God
the glory: and he was eaten of worms, and gave up the ghost. (Acts 12:23)

Our discussion in this chapter is based upon the unusual story of the
descent of the angel of the Lord twice in the twelfth chapter of Acts. In
each instance the angel is doing the same thing. Twice God's angel
smites, but how differently!

Peter we already know. He is the chief apostle, the preacher at
Pentecost. To him was given the keys of the kingdom to open the door
of salvation to the Jew first, to the half-Jew at Samaria, to the proselyte
at Caesarea, and then to the Gentile world.

THE NAME OF "HEROD" ALWAYS SPELLS TROUBLE

The Herod of Acts 12 we need to meet. Any time you find a Herod
in the Scriptures, it is a dark and troubled day. Herod the Great was the
king who destroyed the babes in Bethlehem. The next Herod we meet
is Herod Antipas, the son of Herod the Great. His niece had married
her uncle, Herod Philip, but she, finding Philip dull and uninteresting, left him and married her other uncle, Herod Antipas. When John
the Baptist denounced the adulterous union, it was Herod Antipas who
had John beheaded at the request of Salome, the dancing daughter of
Herodias by Philip.

Now we meet this Herod in Acts 12. He is the grandson of Herod the Great, the son of Aristobulus, who was executed along with his brother Alexander, and their mother, Mariamne, by Herod the Great. This Herod Agrippa I of Acts 12 was the father of Herod Agrippa II and of the two daughters, Drusilla and Bernice. It was before these Herodians that Paul appears in Acts 24 and 25. Bernice was the daughter whom Herod Agrippa II had enticed from her husband and with whom he was living in incest when they appear in the Bible. The other daughter is Drusilla, who was married to Felix, the Roman procurator.

The Herod in Acts 12, Herod Agrippa I, was as shrewd, cunning, and dangerously malicious as was his grandfather, Herod the Great. Sent to Rome to be educated, he was dissolute, extravagant, and finally left the imperial city penniless and in debt. He made appeal to his sister Herodias, who was married to Herod Antipas, that she help him. So Herod Antipas gave him a menial job in his new capital that he had built by the Sea of Galilee named Tiberias. But at a public occasion, Herod Antipas taunted and insulted this Herod Agrippa because of his enforced poverty. In bitterness and in anger, Herod Agrippa went back to Rome, and in a strange providence of life made a close and fast friendship with Gaius Caligula, heir to the throne of the Caesars. When Tiberias, the Caesar, heard Herod Agrippa say disparaging words concerning him and his stupidity, and that Caligula ought to be the Roman Caesar, he put Herod in prison. He weighted him down with an iron chain. When six months later Tiberias died and Caligula came to the Roman throne, Caligula liberated Herod and gave him a golden chain of the same weight as the iron chain by which he had been bound while in prison. Herod Agrippa, seeing his opportunity to destroy his uncle, Herod Antipas, accused Herod Antipas and persuaded Caligula to dismiss him in disgrace. Caligula, now the Roman Caesar, gave to this Herod Agrippa all the territories of his uncle, the deposed and exiled Herod Antipas. When Caligula was poisoned, Herod Agrippa made close friends with Claudius, the succeeding emperor. Cladius added to the kingdom of Herod Agrippa Samaria, Judaea, and Idumaea. Thus he reigned over the same extensive territories which Herod the Great, his grandfather, had reigned over.

When Herod Agrippa saw that it pleased the Jews to persecute the church, he seized James and executed him. Then when he saw that he gained further popularity in the execution of James, he seized Peter and placed him in prison and would have slain him. But because of the Passover, he delayed his execution until the feast days, the Feast of Unleavened Bread, should be passed. Peter is now in prison, awaiting execution the next day.

THE ANGEL OF THE LORD SMITES PETER

Even though on the following morning Peter is to be slain, he now is fast asleep. In calm self-assurance the apostle, pressed between those two Roman soldiers, bound with a heavy chain, behind three iron doors, rests in the confidence and assurance of the goodness of God. If he dies, he is to be with the Lord. If he lives, he is to serve the Lord. Then, in the middle of the night, an angel of the Lord suddenly descended and smote Peter with a gentle violence. Peter awoke; he was freed of his iron chain, and was able to go out into the liberty of God's great and abounding goodness.

THE ANGEL OF THE LORD WILL ALSO SMITE THOSE WHO ARE ASLEEP IN JESUS

This story is but a parable and a symbol of the smiting of God's angel in the days of consummation when the trumpet shall sound, the voice of the angel shall be heard, and those of us who have fallen asleep in Jesus will be raised to a new life in Christ. The chains of our sin will be loosed. The imprisonment of our carnality and the drag of our physical frame will be gone. We shall be liberated into the glorious likeness of the life, ministry, and service of our Lord, at the voice, at the smiting of the angel. Ah, what a day!

Paul wrote of that day saying, "O death, where is thy sting? O grave, where is thy victory?" (1 Cor. 15:55). Paul also wrote, "For me to live is Christ, and to die is gain" (Phil. 1:21). And again Paul said, "Henceforth there is laid up for me a crown of righteousness, which the Lord, the righteous judge, shall give me at that day: and not to me only, but unto all them also that love his appearing" (2 Tim. 4:8). The smiting of the angel of God will awaken those who have fallen asleep in Jesus.

The great Christian poets Browning and Tennyson wrote of that glorious day. On his deathbed, Robert Browning wrote a poem that always closes the publication of a collection of his poems; a poem which he read in his last illness to his daughter-in-law and his sister. Here is one of the stanzas:

One who never turned his back but marched breast forward,
Never doubted clouds would break,
Never dreamed, though right were worsted, wrong would triumph,
Held we fall to rise, are baffled to fight better,
    Sleep to wake.

The Victorian poet laureate of England, Alfred Lord Tennyson, wrote:

Sunset and evening star,
    And one clear call for me!
And may there be no moaning of the bar,
    When I put out to sea,

But such a tide as moving seems asleep,
    Too full for sound and foam,
When that which drew from out the boundless deep
    Turns again home.

Twilight and evening bell,
    And after that the dark!
And may there be no sadness of farewell,
    When I embark;

For tho' from out our bourne of Time and Place
    The flood may bear me far,
I hope to see my Pilot face to face
When I have crossed the bar.

Oh, the smiting of the angel of God, the gentle violence of the sound of His voice when He raises us up into the liberty of the Son of God!

The Same Angel of the Lord Smote Herod

That same angel of the Lord came and smote Herod. Our text says, "And [Herod] went down from Judaea unto Caesarea" (v. 19). Herod went down to Caesarea where the life was more frivolous. The rules and rituals of the Jewish life in Jerusalem were too dull for him, so he went down to the Roman city of Caesarea where the viands were better, the wine was redder, and the tempo was faster.

One great festival day, Herod appeared in the theater at Caesarea, the ruins of which are still standing in Israel today. Many have visited those ruins. Herod appeared in that theater dressed in a beautiful robe of wrought, woven silver. When he moved in the sun, his robe of solid silver shone in a brilliant, dazzling manner so as to almost blind one's eyes. Luke writes that when Herod appeared upon his throne and spoke that oration, the people gave a shout, saying, "It is a voice of a god and not of a man." It is an interesting study to read Josephus's account of the same incident. When Herod appeared the people shouted that he was a god, and they cried to him, saying, "Be thou merciful to us; for we are but mortal, but thou art immortal." According to Josephus, when Herod was immediately struck, he looked upon his friends and said, "I, whom you call a god, am commanded presently to depart this life; while Providence thus reproves the lying words you just now said to me; and I, who was by you called immortal, am immediately hurried away by death."

What an unusual experience! This Herod Agrippa I, appearing in the theater wearing his beautiful, solid silver woven robe, and the people crying out that he is a god. Then immediately he is struck by the angel of the Lord, he is eaten up of worms, and he gives up the ghost.

What an awesome imagery, eaten up of worms! The worms and the wicked are mentioned three times in Mark 9. Our Lord there speaks of the place where the wicked go, where the worm dieth not. Think of it! But how sadly and tragically true!

Lord Byron was the darling of the whole world. He was a peer in the House of Lords in England. He was not only reverenced and loved by the English-speaking world, but he was adored by the entire earth. Do you remember the last poem he wrote?

> My days are in the yellow leaf;
> The flower and fruits of love are gone;
> The worm, the canker, and the grief
> Are mine alone!

The title of that poem is "Upon My Thirty-sixth Birthday." Byron was as compromised and immoral as any figure in literature who ever crossed the horizon of human story. What a way to end a life, in despair!

COMPARING THE TWO SMITINGS

The two smitings of the Lord's angel represent all mankind in the presence of the Lord. The smiting of Peter, the gentle tenderness that awakened him to God; and the awful judgment, the smiting of the angel of the Lord to those who give their lives to worldliness and to wickedness. The same angel, the same smiting, but oh, how different!

All the providences of life, the same experiences, are so different and so opposite. The cloud to the Israelites was light and life, but that same cloud to the Egyptians was darkness. The ark that maimed the god Dagon and decimated the Philistines, blessed the house of Obededom. In 2 Corinthians we read:

> For we are unto God a sweet savour of Christ, in them that are saved, and in them that perish:
> To the one we are the savour of death unto death; and to the other the savour of life unto life. And who is sufficient for these things? (2:15-16).

All the providences of life are like that. They are dual in nature. Death to the child of God is a coronation. It is our entrance into glory. Heaven is opened and the pearly gates are filled with angels to welcome God's saints who have gone home. But what an ominous visage is that pale horseman of death to the wicked! Yet death comes to both the saved and the lost.

DUALITY IN EVERYDAY LIFE

Not only in the consummation of the age do we find that duality, but we find it through every experience of this life. To a child of God, it is precious to read the Scriptures. To a saved man, it is dear to receive a Bible, maybe written in Korean, in Hottentot, in Chinese, or in Auca. But how dull, how phlegmatic, and uninteresting are the Scriptures to those who despise them! What the world wants is pornography, salacious stories filled with all the evil, carnal suggestiveness of a vile and deprived imagination. the same type, the same alphabet, and the same language are used, but oh, how differently they are put together in the Word of the Lord from the way they are arranged in a suggestive, carnal story!

Prayer to the Christian is precious.

> What a friend we have in Jesus,
> All our sins and griefs to bear.
> What a privilege to carry
> Everything to God in prayer!

To the Christian, how much strength, comfort, and assurance there is in prayer! To a child of the world, one could not find an exercise more distasteful. If he had a thousand hours in every day, no minute of it would he give to intercession, to talking to God, to baring his soul open before the Lord. How different, the smiting of the angel of the Lord!

The Christian says, "I was glad when they said unto me, Let us go into the house of the Lord." The child of God loves attending the services of the church, calling upon His name, and listening to the expounding of the holy Word. To a worldly man, one who is not saved, what a dull waste of time! He thinks that he could be out doing a thousand things more interesting.

Think of the songs that we sing! There are no songs comparable to Christian songs, songs of praise and hallelujah. But a worldly man likes songs that are suggestive and sexual.

WE NEED A GREAT TURNING

What we need in life, in home, in heart, in every experience is a great turning to the Lord. Even though it is in some ways sad, the Lord spoke no truer parable than when He told the story of the prodigal son. The Scriptures say that the boy took his inheritance, the substance of his father, and he wasted it with harlots and in riotous living. When he hit town, everyone knew he was there. The fun and the frolic, the wine, the women, and the song! He lived it up. That is the way of the world.

But the day inevitably came when his money was gone, when his health was gone, when his youth was gone, when the good times were gone, and he was eating with hogs. He was eating the husks. Thank the Lord that this boy, the Bible says (as he sat on the top of a corral and watched the hogs eat), "came to himself." What a statement! He came into his right mind, into his right judgment. It is reasonable for a man to be a Christian, to love God. It is unreasonable, an aberration of the mind, for a man to leave God out of his life. The prodigal boy said: "Here I am in the hog pen. I will go back to my father's home." That is where he belonged, not in the hog pen, not in the world, not eating husks.

We belong in the house of the Father in all of the blessing and glory of the gracious hand of God our Lord! We need to get out of the world into the life of Christ, out of the poverty of the cheap repercussions and rewards of the world, into the riches of the abounding ableness, providence, and largess of God. How could a man choose to die, when he could live!

16

The Work Whereunto God Has Called Us

As they ministered to the Lord, and fasted, the Holy Ghost said, Separate me Barnabas and Saul for the work whereunto I have called them. (Acts 13:2)

Acts 13 is a great continental divide in the Word of God, for there is a new and significant departure in this chapter. This is the beginning of the vast missionary enterprise, the ultimate outreach of the purpose and plan of God. Heretofore, in the Book of Acts, the center of the church was Jerusalem. Now it is in pagan, gentile, Antioch. Heretofore, the story concerned mostly Peter. Now it concerns Saul or Paul. Heretofore, the message had been built around the Jew. Now it is a message concerning the gentiles. Heretofore, the involvement had been largely with one people. Now it is with all peoples. Heretofore, the outreach was with one nation. Now it is with all nations. Heretofore, the gospel had been bound up with Jewish legalism. Now it is the message of justification by faith alone. So when we come to this chapter we are in a new, a different world.

THE FOREIGN MISSION ENTERPRISE OF PAUL

As Barnabas and Saul left on their journey led by the Holy Spirit, they journeyed from Antioch to Seleucia. The beautiful Orontes River, situated between the Lebanon and Anti-Lebanon ranges, flows due north, then before it reaches the Taurus Mountains, turns immediately west and pours into the Mediterranean Sea. At the turn of the river was located the ancient, beautiful Greek city of Antioch, the third city of the Roman empire, where Barnabas and Paul stopped.

Then, having gone the sixteen miles on land from Antioch down to Seleucia, they sailed to Cyprus, 125 miles to Salamis, where they preached the Word of God. Then they walked through the island of Cyprus from Salamis to Paphos, which is the capital of the island, where they preached the gospel. Paphos is apparently where Saul changed his name to Paul after the conversion of the Roman proconsul of Cyprus, named Sergius Paulus. From Cyprus they crossed the Mediterranean Sea and traveled 175 miles north to Perga, in the Roman province of Pamphylia. From Perga they walked ninety miles to Antioch in the Roman province of Pisidia and preached the gospel there. Then from Pisidian Antioch they journeyed to Iconium, to Lystra, and to Derbe, the churches of Galatia. Paul continued beyond that in his second and third missionary journeys, and finally carried the message to Rome itself.

A WORK OF THE HOLY SPIRIT

The work of the Holy Spirit is a great and marvelous work, and it was a work that was in the mind of God from the beginning. Our text says, "Separate me Barnabas and Saul for the work whereunto I have called them." The word in Greek is *proskeklemai* and is in the perfect tense. It is taken from the word *proskaleo*, which means "to call for." Here in the Greek perfect tense it expresses something that is in the mind of God, something that is perfected, complete in the ages past, and now finds its implementation in all the centuries that follow after. In other words, this call of God, expressed in the church in Antioch, is not an adventitious thought nor is it due to a present inspiration, but it was an expression of a divine, elective purpose from the beginning of time.

One can easily see that divine purpose in the revelation of the elective calling of God in human history, as it is revealed to us in the Holy Scriptures. The Lord God said to Abraham when He called him: "And in thee shall all the families of the earth be blessed" (Gen. 12:3). There is a divine purpose in the mind of God. In Exodus 20 are found the oracles of the Lord, the Ten Commandments, which were given to the people of Israel. But chapter 19 comes before chapter 20. In chapter 20 God gave to Israel the Ten Commandments, but in chapter 19 He said to Israel, "[Thou] shalt be unto me a kingdom of priests, and an holy nation" (v. 6). What does He mean by a kingdom of priests? A priest is someone who represents a man to God and God to man. That is, before God gave His oracles into the hands of Israel, He first said to them: "You are to be the teachers, the ambassadors, the missionaries, and the evangelists of the Word of God to all the earth. You are to receive these oracles from My hand and you are to teach them to all the nations of the world."

We find what God intended from the beginning in the revelation of the coming Savior of the world in the prophets. For example, a typical passage is Isaiah 49:6 where God is speaking of the coming Messiah and Savior of the world. He says, "I will also give thee for a light to the Gentiles [the nations], that thou mayest be my salvation unto the end of the earth." The divine purpose of God from the beginning finally found expression in the incarnate Son of heaven. The story in Matthew, Mark, Luke, and John always consummates in the Great Commission. "Go ye therefore, and teach all nations, baptizing them in the name of the Father, and of the Son, and of the Holy Ghost" (Matt. 28:19). "Ye shall be witnesses unto me both in Jerusalem, and in all Judaea, and in Samaria, and unto the uttermost part of the earth" (Acts 1:8). This is the divine mind of God.

The story of Saul's conversion is recounted three times in the Book of Acts (the ninth, the twenty-second, and the twenty-sixth chapters), and each time it is told the same thought is there. The Lord says to the new convert, Paul, "I have called you and appeared to you for this reason, that you may preach My name and this gospel to all peoples of the earth." Paul is to be the missionary to the gentiles. When Paul speaks of that conversion in Galatians 1, he avows the same idea; that from his mother's womb God had set him apart to be the emissary of heaven to all the people of the earth. What we read here is an expression of the divine mind of God from before the foundation of the world. "Separate me Saul and Barnabas for the work whereunto [*proskeklemai*] I purposed for them before the world was made."

GOD REVEALS HIS PURPOSE THROUGH HIS APPOINTED INSTRUMENT

Notice again the instrument through which God reveals His purpose. Barnabas and Saul were in the church at Antioch and as they sacrificed and ministered, the Lord said to that serving church, "Separate me Barnabas and Saul for the work whereunto I have purposed for them." Is that not a divine revelation? God's purposes of grace are expressed through and implemented by His church. The church is unlike any other organization or organism in the world. It is unique, it is separate, and it has an assignment that no other body or organization in the world has. The church is set in the world to be God's emissary and evangelist for the conversion of all the nations on the face of the globe. The church is different from a fraternal organization. It is different from any political entity. It is even different from philanthropical and civic organizations. It is different from the legislature, from the judiciary, from the executive. It is different from the great banking and merchandising establishments. The church is set apart in the world for one great, divine purpose, namely, the conversion of the world to Jesus Christ. Its task and assignment is to preach the gospel of Christ, to call men to repentance and to faith in Him. This is our high calling and the divine purpose of God for us in Christ Jesus. When the church is sensitive to the call of God, its people can be found engaged in outreach ministries to the ends of the world.

> If I have strength, I owe the service of the strong;
> If melody I have, I owe the world a song;
> If I can stand when all around me the weak are falling,
> And if my torch can light the dark of any night,
> Then I must pay the debts I owe with living light.
>
> If heavn's grace has dowered me with some rare gift;
> If I can lift some load no other's strength can lift;
> If I can heal some wound no other's hand can heal;
> If some great truth the speaking skies to me reveal,
> Then I must go to each broken and wounded thing,
> And to a broken world my gifts of healing bring.
>
> For any God-given gift I am taught to say:
> Gifts are most mine when I most give them away.
> God's gifts are like His flowers
>   which show their right to stay,
> By giving all their bloom and fragrance away.
> Riches are not gold or land, estates or marts;
> The only wealth transported to heaven
>   is found in human hearts.

A church that is sensitive to the mind and will of God is a church that offers itself in God's grace to the world, to be used of God that men might be saved.

THE WORK TO WHICH THE SPIRIT CALLS

Do you notice what the mandate of heaven turned out to be when Barnabas and Saul obeyed it? The divine purpose of the calling of Barnabas and Saul was to be realized in the church and God purposed for that church to present the ministering grace of the Lord to the world. So, being sent by the Holy Ghost, they preached the gospel in Seleucia, in Salamis, in Paphos, in Perga, in Attalia, in Pisidian Antioch, in Iconium, in Lystra, in Derbe, in Ephesus, in Philippi, in Thessalonica, in Berea, in Athens, in Corinth, and in Rome. Through the converts of those apostles, the gospel was spread to the whole world, and it was finally brought to my father and mother and to me. This is what God purposed when He said, "Separate me Barnabas and Saul for the work whereunto I have called them," namely, the ministry of the Word of God to all people everywhere.

You may see many accouterments in your church to help in the divine worship of our living Lord, but God never said anything about them. The only thing the Lord said was, "Remember My lambs, and feed My sheep." The church does not deal with inanimate objects. It is not concerned with freight, boxes, and containers. The church is concerned with people.

Some years ago a famous radio entertainer delivered his version of Lincoln's Gettysburg Address. His presentation was so different that he was deluged with mail after he delivered the address. You see, the entertainer did some research and found that when Lincoln delivered that address, he put an emphasis upon one word in that dedication. We always say: "That government *of* the people, *by* the people, and *for* the people should not perish from the earth." But the entertainer found out that when Lincoln delivered his speech he said, "that government of the *people*, by the *people*, and for the *people* should not perish from the earth." Lincoln emphasized not a preposition, but the *people*. He was moved by the people. That is the emphasis that ought to be in our work and in our assignments. Our work concerns people. It concerns human souls.

When we look at the continents of the world, we see people. When we hear the cries of the urban and rural communities of the earth, we hear the cries of people. When we consider the needs of the nations of the earth, we consider the needs of people. When one reads the revelation of the love of God in Christ Jesus who died on the cross, we find God's infinite love for the people. Thus our heavenly mandate is to reach people for the Lord.

I began my pastoral work in Oklahoma in the days of the depression, when people were hungry, when they lost their homes and farms because they could not pay the mortgage, when cotton sold for five cents a pound, when people labored all year long and yet could not pay the debt of the grocery bill at the store. A friend of mine was talking to me one day and told me what happened when they had conducted their every-member canvas in his church. In the church was a hungry family, which consisted of a man and his wife, and seven ragged, half-starved children. A deacon was to call on them but he said to his pastor, "Pastor, I will not do it. I will not go to that man and ask anything of him. He is too poor, too hungry, and too ragged, and he does not have a job. I will not go." The pastor said to him, "But, brother, it is an every-member canvas, and that does not mean every member except him." The deacon said, "Pastor, I do not care what you say; I am not going to do it." The pastor said, "Deacon, if I go with you, will you go?" He said, "No, I will not." Then the pastor said: "Then I will do it myself. Will you come with me?" The deacon replied: "Yes, I will go with you with the understanding that I am not going to say a word. You are to do all the talking." So they went to this home, and were invited into the poverty-stricken hovel. The pastor sat down with the family and explained to them the work of the church, the preaching of the gospel, its teaching of the Word of life, and its great outreach ministries including the foreign mission enterprise. In the midst of this, the man broke down and cried. The pastor said to me: "I thought I would die. I never felt such a wanting to hide myself as I did then. I thought that I had hurt the heart of that man. He could not give, and here I was asking him to help." The pastor added, "The deacon was seated in the room listening to me and hearing the sobs of that man, and I thought that I had come to the end of the way." The preacher said, "You know, when the man was able to control his emotions, he lifted up his face, dried the tears away, and said, 'Pastor, this is the first time anyone has ever come asking us to help.'" The man continued: "This is the first time we have ever been treated like other folks. They have always passed us by. We are too wretched, too poor. We have been outside of their interest, their calls, their visits, and their asking to help. Pastor, give me nine of those cards." That poor fellow took nine of those cards and passed them out. Then he said, "Each one of us will fill it out for five cents a Sunday." Then he gathered them up and put them in the hands of the pastor, saying, "I do not know where the money is coming from, but we will trust Jesus for it." The pastor said, "In the days immediately following the man found a fine job and he entered a new day. At every service nine members of that family filled up a pew. And I have now baptized all seven of those children."

When we read of the delivery of the message of the gospel of Christ to the Roman empire, we saw that there were some who rejected the message. In fact some even created trouble in rejection. When we bear the message of salvation in Christ, not everyone will respond. They will not all turn and believe; they will not even be grateful that we took the time to invite them to the Lord. But the Word of the Lord tells us that even though we may not win all of them, we will always win some. There will always be some who will respond.

O Lord, keep on blessing. What kind of a barrier, what kind of standard do we raise against the vast floodtides of communism and atheism, except the preaching of the gospel of the Son of God. How do we battle the vast inroads of evil, iniquity, violence, and blood except in the preaching of the gospel of the Son of God. What hope do we have for our own beloved nation of America except the pouring out of the Spirit and blessing of the Lord upon us. What hope do we have for the peace of the children of our generation except that God shall empower us to carry out the Great Commission of the Son of God. That is the communion and the faith that we pledge our lives to share with the world.

17

Facing the Pagan World

So they, being sent forth by the Holy Ghost, departed unto Seleucia; and from thence they sailed to Cyprus.

And when they were at Salamis, they preached the word of God in the synagogues of the Jews: and they had also John to their minister.

And when they had gone through the isle unto Paphos, they found a certain sorcerer, a false prophet, a Jew, whose name was Bar-jesus:

Which was with the deputy of the country, Sergius Paulus, a prudent man; who called for Barnabas and Saul, and desired to hear the word of God.

But Elymas the sorcerer (for so is his name by interpretation) withstood them, seeking to turn away the deputy from the faith.

Then Saul, (who also is called Paul,) filled with the Holy Ghost, set his eyes on him,

And said, O full of all subtilty and all mischief, thou child of the devil, thou enemy of all righteousness, wilt thou not cease to pervert the right ways of the Lord?

And now, behold, the hand of the Lord is upon thee, and thou shalt be blind, not seeing the sun for a season. And immediately there fell on him a mist and a darkness; and he went about seeking some to lead him by the hand.

Then the deputy, when he saw what was done, believed, being astonished at the doctrine of the Lord.

Now when Paul and his company loosed from Paphos, they came to Perga in Pamphylia: and John departing from them returned to Jerusalem. (Acts 13:4-13)

The story in our text took place on the first missionary journey of Paul which began in about A.D. 45. Paul and Barnabas went down to Selucia, the port city of Antioch, about fifteen miles away. Then they set sail for Cyprus and began their ministry there.

129

THE CREDIBILITY OF LUKE

In reading this passage in Acts, we have an opportunity to examine the credibility of Luke, of the Bible, the Word of God. When Saul and Barnabas came to Cyprus they found the province governed by a man named Sergius Paulus who three times is called a "proconsul," an *anthupatos*, translated in the King James Version as a "deputy." In verses 7, 8, and 12 Sergius Paulus is referred to as the "deputy." It is not just an adventitious reference. It is by stated purpose that Luke called him *anthupatos*, because he was an appointee of the Roman senate and was not appointed by the imperial Caesar.

For years critics of the Bible have attempted to find errors, and they point to this reference in Acts with great glee. They say that here is an error in the Word of God for the province of Cyprus was imperial, not senatorial. A senatorial province was one that was at peace, such as Cyprus or Asia. It needed the army to keep its peace and was under the Roman Caesar. The governor of an imperial province was called a "procurator," in Greek, a *hegemon*. Judaea, for example, was an imperial province under the Roman army, and therefore was ruled by a Roman procurator like Pilate, Felix, or Festus. The people were volatile and restive; for example, in A.D. 66 the Jewish people rebelled in an awesome conflict.

Critics refer to Strabo, who plainly says in his history that Caesar Augustus divided the empire into two kinds of provinces, senatorial and imperial. Augustus kept Cyprus for himself and ruled it by the army with a procurator. Luke, however, says that Cyprus is a senatorial province, not imperial, and is ruled by an *anthupatos*, not a *hegemon*; it is ruled by a proconsul, not by a procurator.

Then in recent years an obscure passage of Dio Cassius, a Greek historian whose works are almost all lost, was discovered which said that five years after Augustus Caesar divided the provinces and kept Cyprus for himself, he made an exchange with the senate and relinquished Cyprus to the senate for another province that he wanted for himself. So after five years, and at the time in our text, Cyprus was a senatorial province ruled by a proconsul. Later, in digging among the ruins of Paphos and other places in the island (and I have been there and looked at them), archaeologists have found coins to substantiate this proconsular rule. Finally, men have discovered two inscriptions which list the names of the proconsuls of Cyprus, and the name of this very man, Sergius Paulus, is listed as one of them.

This gives me an opportunity to say that for hundreds of years archaeologists have been digging in the tells, the mounds, and the ruins of the ancient Levant, and every spade of dirt turned up confirms the Word of God! In a thousand instances the critics have hammered at the Book, saying, "Here is an error, there is a misconception, and here is a mistake." But the archaeologist confirms the divine record. The Bible is inerrant, infallible, and inspired by the Holy Spirit of omniscience. Praise God for the Book that reveals to us the mind of our Lord!

THE PEOPLE INVOLVED

Now we will look at the figures, the personalities whom Saul and Barnabas meet in their first missionary journey and upon their first preaching of the gospel. First, is a proconsul, translated here, a "deputy," named Sergius Paulus. He is described by one of the best adjectives in the Greek language. The word used to describe him is *sunetos*, translated here "prudent," a magnificent description of Sergius Paulus. The verbal form of the word is *suniemi*, which literally means "to put together." The adjectival form, *sunetos*, refers to a man whose mind would be able to put things together. Thus the word actually means "intelligence," "making for understanding." This Sergius Paulus, an aristocrat of the Roman senate, was *sunetos*, a man who was learned, intelligent, a man of understanding. Sergius Paulus sent for Barnabas and Saul and heard from them the Word of the Lord. He was willing to learn, and to hear what the Lord had to say to him. He was the first aristocrat to be converted to the Christian faith.

There is a reason for the parentheses in Acts 13:9, "Then Saul, (who also is called Paul,)." Heretofore, Paul had been called "Saul of Tarsus," but from this moment on he is called Paul, the preacher of Christ, Paul, the missionary. Why should Luke have placed the parentheses here? There is a possibility, of course, that Paul had both names from the beginning. Saul, a Hebrew name, Paul, a Roman name, since he was a Roman citizen. Could it be that he took the name Paul from his first aristocratic, illustrious convert? Or could it be that, being sent to the Roman empire, he takes a Roman name, Paul, meaning "small," "little," referring to the humility with which he does his work before the Lord? He is now a preacher to the Roman citizens, to the Roman empire, to the Roman provinces, thus he is hereafter called Paul. In any event, to me it is significant that at the conversion of Sergius Paulus, Saul's name becomes Paul.

Now look at another character we meet on the first missionary journey. In the capital city of Paphos, where Sergius Paulus had his seat of government, there was a Jew, a sorcerer, named Elymas. The word translated here "sorcerer" in Greek is *magos*, and our word "magician" comes from it. The word actually means "astrologer." So this Jew was an astrologer. In Aramaic, or in Arabian, he is called Elymas, that is, "the wise one." But Luke calls him a "false prophet." This man controls the mind and life of Sergius Paulus. How could such a thing be, for Sergius Paulus has been described by one of the finest Greek adjectives, *sunetos*, a man of tremendous intelligence and a man of great understanding and learning? Yet he is under the complete domination of this astrologer. We can never understand such a development unless we are acquainted with Roman history. You see, in Paul's day, the East for the first time was open to the West, and the western world was totally captivated by all the mysticism that poured out of the East. The eastern culture was astonishing to the western world and to the Roman mind. Consequently, these astrologers simply took over the mind of the Roman empire. For example, all the great military Roman leaders such as Marius, Pompey, Crassus, and Caesar consulted their astrologers before they entered into any great military campaign. Juvenal, the famous Roman satirist-poet, described Emporer Tiberius Caesar as "sitting on his rock Capri surrounded by his flock of Chaldeans" [astrologers].

We may remark that these dupes lived two thousand years ago. But the same is true today. There is not an influential newspaper in the country that would dare go to press without a column on astrology. And if you would ask the editor why he puts those blantant superstitions in his newspaper he would tell you he couldn't sell the paper without them. There are millions of people today who follow those astrological prognostications. It is unthinkable.

I once had a friend who was a successful businessmen who, to my amazement, in all of his business decisions first conversed with a medium, a necromancer.

The people who do not love God and do not serve the Lord are subject to the most unbelievable demonic influences. I am not referring to ghetto, underprivileged, and submarginal people. I am talking about the aristocrats of the land. We are all alike. If a man turns aside from God, it is amazing to what he turns. That is what happened to the brilliant, learned, and intelligent Sergius Paulus. The men of God, Paul and Barnabas, stood before him, and Paul, under the power of the Holy Spirit, confronted that necromancing, demon-possessed astrologer, named Elymas. The Bible is against all sorcery, witchcraft, astrological prognostications, and all the divinations that mediums and spiritists are supposed to deliver to us. The Bible, from the beginning to end, hammers against sorcery.

THE CONFRONTATION

Let me make a comment about how Satan works. He is a remarkable being. He is brilliant beyond anything we could imagine. Who would ever think that Satan is of all things religious! He is for religion, but perverts, uses, and misuses it just as he is doing here with the false prophet, Elymas. For example, when Paul and Barnabas finally came to Ephesus, they created a riot in the city. Over what? Religion! The whole city was in an uproar crying, "Great is Diana of the Ephesians." Religion is Satan's best tool.

In Acts 17, we see that Paul walked through the greatest intellectual center the world has ever known. I do not think there will ever be another city like the city of Athens. There will never be architects, philosophers, or poets who will exceed those in that great Athenian culture. When Paul stood up to speak, he said, "Ye men of Athens, I perceive that in all things ye are," and the King James Version translates it, "most superstitious." That would have been an insult. What he said was, "Ye men of Athens, I perceive that in everything you are *deisidaimonesteroi*, which means, "deeply religious." In everything you are "deeply religious," you are "most reverent." "For as I passed by I saw an altar with the inscription, *Agnosto Theo*, To the Unknown God," lest they should have left out one! Can you believe that? Athens was the most intellectual center in the world, and at the same time it was the most reverent, the most devout. But Satan perverts religion.

There is a book entitled *This Believing World*. In it we read that there are more than 300,000,000 people who worship Hindu gods. Other millions are following Mohammed the prophet. In modern Japan many people are following the doctrines of Shinto. Recently, I read that many Japanese are trying to reinstate their emperor as the god and son of heaven. In America practically the entire nation worships at the shrine of hedonism, materialism, or humanism. The Christian faith faces the ancient and the modern pagan world. How does it do it?

Look at how Paul spoke under the power of the Holy Spirit. He said to the false prophet, "O full of all subtilty and all mischief, thou child of the devil, thou enemy of all righteousness, wilt thou not cease to pervert the right ways of the Lord?" (Acts 13:10). What language Paul used! Why do preachers not speak like that today. So often the preacher preaches a half-Christ, a half-truth. Always it is Jesus-love, Jesus-grace, Jesus-pity, Jesus-mercy. All these things about Jesus are true, but just half true. There is another side to this gospel and it is one of judgment, denunciation, and condemnation. For example, Revelation 6 says that the condemned cry to the mountains and rocks to fall on them to hide them from the face of Him who sits on the throne, and from the wrath of the Lamb (v. 16). Think of the words, "the wrath of the Lamb." A lamb is so gentle, cuddly, and pure, but the Scripture speaks of *the wrath* of the Lamb. Think of the passages in Hebrews 10 and 12: "It is a fearful thing to fall into the hands of the living God" (10:31). "For our God is a consuming fire" (12:29). Oh, the truth of the whole message of God makes one tremble and fills one with fear before the Lord.

Saul stood before Elymas, the astrologer, with powerful and godly condemnation. Such circumstances are repeated through the years. I think of Elijah standing before Ahab, or Amos standing before Amaziah. I think of John the Baptist standing before Herodias, or John Chrysostom standing before Empress Eudoxia. I think of Savonarola standing before Cesare and Lucrezia Borgia. I think of John Knox standing before Bloody Mary, Queen of England. I think of Martin Niemöller standing before Adolph Hitler. A true man of God will always bring the Word of the Lord: "Except we repent, we face judgment, condemnation, and damnation." That is God's message, and that is the word delivered here.

This powerful testimony is delivered only in the power of the Holy Spirit. Were it not for the power of the Holy Spirit of God, Christianity long ago would have been swallowed up by the darkness of the world. It is in the power of the Holy Spirit that Jesus lives, moves, converts, and saves.

One time a man described for me a great throng gathered in a city auditorium. The meeting was advertised as a public confrontation between the Christian religion and other religions of the world. That night the Buddhist priest, suave, learned, and gifted, presented the religion of Buddhism, a faith of contemplation, of meditation. The people listened, enthralled by this priest's words. When the Christian preacher stood up to deliver his speech for Christianity, he was plainly confused. His arguments that God was to become a man and be incarnate, his arguments that God could die upon a cross for our sins—everything he said became limp and lacked power. When the Christian finished, both men were allowed a rebuttal. The Buddhist priest stood up, and in a calculated, clever way, decimated the idea of the Christian faith and of Jesus, the Son of God. When he sat down, someone in the top of the highest balcony stood up and began to sing,

> All hail the power of Jesus' name!
> Let angels prostrate fall;
> Bring forth the royal diadem,
> And crown Him Lord of all.

As he started the second stanza, other people began to pick it up:

> Ye chosen seed of Israel's race,
> Ye ransomed from the fall,
> Hail Him who saves you by His grace,
> And crown Him Lord of all.

When they got to the third stanza, the great throng stood up and joined in the paean of praise:

> Let every kindred, every tribe
> On this terrestrial ball,
> To Him all majesty ascribe,
> And crown Him Lord of all.

The man told me that the Buddhist priest in humiliation silently walked away while the people rejoiced in the power and the presence of the Lord. "It is not by might, nor by power, but by my Spirit, saith the Lord." It is not by learning, it is not by argument, but it is by the convicting presence of the power of God that there is revealed to us who have found refuge in Him, the truth of the revelation of God in Christ Jesus.

Bless His name that God opens our hearts to the message of the faith of the Lamb of God!

18

The Forgiveness of Sin

Be it known unto you therefore, men and brethren, that through this man is preached unto you the forgiveness of sins. (Acts 13:38)

Acts 13 concludes with the message that the apostle Paul delivered to the people who lived in Pisidian Antioch. Beginning at verse 13 we read:

Now when Paul and his company loosed from Paphos, they came to Perga in Pamphylia: and John departing from them returned to Jerusalem.

But when they departed from Perga, they came to Antioch in Pisidia, and went into the synagogue on the sabbath day, and sat down.

And after the reading of the law and the prophets the rulers of the synagogue sent unto them, saying, Ye men and brethren, if ye have any word of exhortation for the people, say on.

Then Paul stood up, and beckoning with his hand said, Men of Israel, and ye that fear God, give audience (vv. 13-16).

Then follows the message that Paul preached:

Be it known unto you therefore, men and brethren, that through this man is preached unto you the forgiveness of sins:

And by him all that believe are justified from all things, from which ye could not be justified by the law of Moses.

Beware therefore, lest that come upon you, which is spoken of in the prophets;

Behold, ye despisers, and wonder, and perish: for I work a work in your days, a work which ye shall in no wise believe, though a man declare it unto you (vv. 38-41).

PAUL'S SERMON IN PISIDIAN ANTIOCH

This message of Paul at Pisidian Antioch sounds strangely familiar,

136

as though we've heard it before. It is a message which recounts the dealings of God with Israel up to the coming of Christ in whom are fulfilled all the promises of the Lord in the Old Covenant. As I think of the construction of Paul's message and how it ends, I remember where I heard the sermon before. It was the message of God's first martyr, Stephen. It was the sermon that Stephen preached in the Cilician synagogue before the Sanhedrin of the Jewish nation. Paul's sermon and Stephen's sermon follow the same course. Remember that the young rabbi, Saul from Tarsus, listened as he heard Stephen deliver his message in the synagogue. And he must have listened intently. We can know what the Lord meant when He said to Saul on his way to Damascus, "It is hard for thee to kick against the pricks." Saul had violently persecuted the church and had guarded the garments of those who stoned Stephen to death. The message that Stephen delivered moved in Paul's heart, and his violent reaction to it could not drown its message or its truth. Now this persecuting Saul has picked up the torch, picked up the same message, and is delivering it to the Gentile world in Pisidian Antioch.

The heart of the message is this: "Men and brethren, children of the stock of Abraham, and whosoever among you feareth God, to you is the word of this salvation sent" (Acts 13:26). Look at the Greek word for "word," *logos*. We are familiar with the word *logos*, for we read in John 1, "In the beginning was the [*Logos*] Word, and the [*Logos*] Word was with God, and the [*Logos*] Word was God" (John 1:1). "The Word" applies to God, to the Holy Scriptures, to the revelation of God's grace in the blessed Jesus—"to you is this *logos* of salvation (*soteria*) sent." What does *soteria* mean? *Soter* is the word for "savior," a word that is applied to God and the Lord Jesus who is our *Soter*, our Savior. *Soteria* is what He saves us from. Our salvation is from eternal death. The word of this salvation is "sent," *apostale*, the passive voice of *apostello*, "to send as a messenger." An *apostolos*, is "one who is sent," "an apostle." God has sent his saving, incomparable word of deliverance and salvation to us. What a marvelous gospel and an incomparably precious announcement!

WHAT IS THIS GOSPEL OF SALVATION?

What is this gospel of salvation that God has sent to us? Paul describes it in the message he delivers in our text. In verse 23 Paul says, "God according to his promise raised unto Israel a Savior, Jesus!" In verse 33 he says, "God hath fulfilled the same unto us their children, in that he hath raised up Jesus again." That is also what Paul writes in Romans 1:4, "And declared to be the Son of God with power, according to the spirit of holiness, by the resurrection from the dead." Then we are given the glorious consummation of the Good News:

> Be it known unto you therefore, men and brethren, that through this man is preached unto you the forgiveness of sins:
> And by him all that believe are justified from all things, from which ye could not be justified by the law of Moses (Acts 13:38-39).

That is the glorious Good News of the gospel of the Son of God.

TO WHOM THE SAVING MESSAGE IS SENT

To whom is this message sent? It is sent to the whole world. Verse 47 declares, "For so hath the Lord commanded us, saying, [then Paul quotes Isaiah 49:6] I have set thee to be a light of the Gentiles, that thou shouldest be for salvation unto the ends of the earth." The message of salvation is for all men everywhere. Each gospel concludes with the Great Commission.

Picture in your mind Peter coming up to the Lord, when He had delivered the words of the Great Commission (that this message of salvation, forgiveness, and justification is to be delivered to all men everywhere), saying, "Lord Jesus, do you mean that we are to declare the message of forgiveness even to the men who slew You, who crucified You, who nailed You to the cross?" The Lord replies, "Yes." Peter continues, "Do you mean that the message of forgiveness and salvation is to be delivered to the man who planted the crown of thorns and pressed it upon Your brow?" "Yes." "Is the message of forgiveness, salvation, and justification to be delivered to the men who drove those nails into Your hands and feet?" "Yes." "Do you mean that the word of salvation and forgiveness is to be delivered to the Roman soldier who thrust the iron spear into Your heart?" "Yes, to all men everywhere." Every tribe, nation, tongue, and family under the sun, all are included in the great message of forgiveness, grace, and love of God in Christ Jesus.

HOW THE MESSAGE IS SENT

How is this message of salvation to be sent? The answer is found in the beginning of Acts 13: "Separate me Barnabas and Saul for the work whereunto I have called them" (v. 2b). The Lord sent them out. The preached message of the grace of God is delivered by the apostles, by missionaries, by evangelists, and by preachers who crossed the seas and continents of the world. And we still preach and write about the gospel to countless millions today. Paul concludes:

> Beware therefore, lest that come upon you, which is spoken of in the prophets;
> Behold, ye despisers, and wonder, and perish: for I work a work in your days, a work which ye shall in no wise believe, though a man declare it unto you (Acts 13:40-41).

The author of Hebrews asks the question: "How shall we escape, if we neglect so great salvation . . ." (Heb. 2:3). The weight, the burden, and the responsibility of preaching and listening to the gospel of Christ is as though heaven and earth depended upon our doing it and our answering it.

THE CLIMAX OF PAUL'S SERMON

The climax of Paul's sermon begins in verse 38:

> Be it known unto you therefore, men and brethren, that through this man is preached unto you the forgiveness of sins:
> And by him all that believe are justified . . . (vv. 38-39a).

That is the great conclusion of the sermon that Paul delivers to the people at Pisidian Antioch.

Paul's message has to do with the forgiveness of sins and our justification before God. His message concerns a universal experience of every human heart, the experience of sin, wrong, and guilt. Job cries: "I have sinned; what shall I do?" (Job. 7:20).

We do wrong in two ways. First, we do wrong against others. I once read of a Kentucky mountain preacher who could not read or write but who could preach the gospel in a way that could move any soul. In one of his stories he talked about the wrong that we do others. He spoke of a mountaineer who had an obsession with money. He raised grain for the hogs and would sell the hogs to make more money, to buy more land, to raise more grain, to feed more hogs, to make more money, to buy more land, to raise more corn, to feed more hogs, to make more money. He said that the man's wife, who toiled by his side, came to her husband one day and asked for a new dress. The mountaineer refused, for he had to buy more land, to raise more grain, to feed more hogs, to make more money, to buy more land. His wife would ask him for a new hat, but he had to make more money, to buy more land.

Whatever his dear wife asked for, the mountaineer refused her because he had to have more money, to buy. After years of toil, his wife died. The sorrow upon her death broke the mountaineer's heart and mind. One day, those who knew him found him in the cemetery with bolts of silk and satin wrapping them around her tombstone. We do wrong to others.

Second, we do wrong against God. Crime is a wrong against a person. Vice is a wrong against society. But sin is a wrong against God. David cried in Psalm 51: "Against thee, thee only, have I sinned, and done this evil in thy sight" (v. 4a). Sin is against God.

OUR HELPLESSNESS BEFORE SIN

We are helpless before sin, both in commission and in remission. How can a man keep from sinning? Solomon prayed his prayer of dedication for the beautiful temple he built. He spoke of its being a place where the people could pray and where God could hear and forgive, because, Solomon said, "there is no man that sinneth not" (1 Kings 8:46).

In Romans 7 the apostle Paul writes: "For the good that I would I do not: but the evil which I would not, that I do" (v. 19). The experience of sin is universal. A man is not perfect, nor can he be perfect. Neither is a man able to remit his sins. What does he do, having sinned?

One of the most poignant experiences one could ever imagine in human literature occurs in Shakespeare's *Macbeth*. Macbeth had as his guest Duncan, King of Scots. Because of a fiendish hope for the securing of the crown for himself, Macbeth took a dagger and plunged it into the heart of his guest, the king. But the blood flowed out like a fountain and covered Macbeth's hands. When he came back into the chamber, Lady Macbeth looked at Macbeth's hands and said:

> Go, get some water,
> And wash this filthy witness from your hand.
> A little water clears us of this deed;
> How easy is it, then!

Macbeth walked over to the fountain to wash the blood from his hands, and as he walked, this is what he said:

> Will all great Neptune's ocean wash this blood
> Clean from my hand? No, this my hand will rather
> The multitudinous seas incarnadine,
> Making the green one red.

All the waters in all the oceans of all the world cannot suffice to wash the stain of sin out of our souls. We are helpless before the awesome judgment of our sins.

GOD'S PROVISION FOR MAN

The gospel of the good news of the grace of the Son of God is that God has made provision for our cleansing and for our forgiveness. He is the Lamb slain from before the foundation of the world. It was in His mind, purpose, and heart from the beginning that we should have salvation in Christ Jesus. This was the message of the apostle Paul and of Stephen, and that is the message that comes to us today. Through the providences of God, Jesus came into the world to die for our sins according to the Scriptures and to be raised from the dead to declare our justification. Every sacrifice in the Old Testament points to Him. Every lamb that was slain points to Him. The great Day of Atonement was a day that prefigured the Lord. Paul had a marvelous message in the Good News; namely, that to anyone, anywhere, any time, if they would accept the atoning sacrifice of Jesus Christ, God would do for them two things. One is positional and the other is experiential.

Positionally, the Lord will justify a man who will accept the atoning death of Christ. Our text says, "And by him all that believe are justified from all things" (Acts 13:39). That is a marvelous thing. The Greek word *dikaios* means "just," "righteous." The verbal form is *dikaioo*, which means "to make righteous," "to make innocent," "to declare to be pure," "to cleanse and free from all guilt and accusation." God does for us a positional thing; not that we are righteous, not that we are perfect, not that we are sinless, but God declares us so. He justifies us; that is, He declares that we are pure, innocent, and righteous. The Scriptures search out the most amazing images to declare what God does for us when we accept Jesus as our Savior. For example, in Psalm 103 the Lord says: "As far as the east is from the west, so far hath he removed our transgressions from us" (v. 12). How far is that? As far as east goes east and west goes west, just so far does God take our transgressions from us. In Isaiah 38, he says, ". . . for thou hast cast all my sins behind thy back" (v. 17b). Our sins are never seen, they are never recalled. They are forgotten; they are put behind the Lord. In Isaiah 44 God says, "I have blotted out, as a thick cloud, thy transgressions, and, as a cloud, thy sins . . ." (v. 22a). In Micah 7 the Lord says: ". . . and thou wilt cast all their sins into the depths of the sea" (v. 19b). God declares us righteous. He justifies us. It is as though we had never sinned. God looks upon us as He looks upon His own Son. The righteousness of Jesus is given to us and we stand in His presence sinless and pure. That is the first thing God does for those of us who accept Jesus as Savior. For His sake, God justifies and declares us righteous.

The second thing God does is experiential. He gives to us forgiveness of sins. If we were given an opportunity to stand up and to say how we were saved, every one of us would have a different story describing the time and the place in our life when we met the Lord Jesus. But however our lives were introduced to the Savior, one thing we would all have in common, namely, that in Him we have an incomparable assurance and rejoicing that God, for Christ's sake, has forgiven our sins. Because of the experiential part of our salvation, God puts a song in our heart and He puts praise and gladness in our souls. For example, Acts 13:48a says: "And when the Gentiles heard this, they were glad, and glorified the word of the Lord." The chapter ends with, "And the disciples were filled with joy, and with the Holy Ghost" (v. 52). That is why Christians sing, giving experiential response to what God has done for us.

Did you know that out of all the religions of the world, the only religion that exaltingly sings is Christianity? Christians are people who have found salvation in Jesus Christ. Could you imagine Handel's *Messiah* and the beautiful "Hallelujah Chorus" being sung in a Muslim mosque? They do not sing in Muslim mosques. In a Buddhist pagoda? They do not sing in them. In a Shintoist shrine? They do not sing in them. In a Hindu temple? They do not sing in them. But wherever you find God's people gathered together in the name of the Lord, there you will find those people singing. Singing is a marvelous outpouring of our hearts and spirits in gratitude and thanksgiving to God for forgiving us and justifying us.

I once read about an international assembly of God's saints who wanted to do something in which all of them could share. The people decided to sing a song, each one singing in his own language. The song they chose was:

> Rock of ages, cleft for me,
> Let me hide myself in Thee;
> Let the water and the blood,
> From Thy wounded side which flowed,
> Be of sin the double cure,

Save from wrath and make me pure.

Could my tears forever flow,
Could my zeal no languor know,
These for sin could not atone;
Thou must save, and Thou alone:
In my hand no price I bring,
Simply to Thy cross I cling.

A song of praise and thanksgiving to God for the cleansing of our souls is what all of the redeemed of the Lord love to sing.

Before I ever baptized in a baptistry inside a building, I would baptize in creeks, in rivers, and in ponds. Every time I baptized out in those country streams and led the candidates into the water, God's redeemed saints would stand on the shore and sing:

Happy day, happy day,
When Jesus washed my sins away!
He taught me how to watch and pray,
And live rejoicing every day;
Happy day, happy day,
When Jesus washed my sins away!

That is the Christian faith, a faith of singing, rejoicing, and gladness, for Jesus has washed our sins away!

19

The Word of the Lord

And when the Jews were gone out of the synagogue, the Gentiles besought that these words might be preached to them the next sabbath.

Now when the congregation was broken up, many of the Jews and religious proselytes followed Paul and Barnabas: who, speaking to them, persuaded them to continue in the grace of God.

And the next sabbath day came almost the whole city together to hear the word of God.

But when the Jews saw the multitudes, they were filled with envy, and spake against those things which were spoken by Paul, contradicting and blaspheming.

Then Paul and Barnabas waxed bold, and said, It was necessary that the word of God should first have been spoken to you: but seeing ye put it from you, and judge yourselves unworthy of everlasting life, lo, we turn to the Gentiles.

For so hath the Lord commanded us, saying, I have set thee to be a light of the Gentiles, that thou shouldest be for salvation unto the ends of the earth.

And when the Gentiles heard this they were glad, and glorified the word of the Lord: and as many as were ordained to eternal life believed. (Acts 13:42-48)

When we look at Acts 13, we find that the chapter refers to the Word of the Lord seven different times. It is mentioned in verse 5: "And when they were at Salamis, they preached the word of God. . . ." It is mentioned again in verse 26: ". . . to you is the word of this salvation sent." We see God's Word referred to again in verse 42: ". . . the Gentiles besought that these words might be preached to them. . . ." It is mentioned also in verse 44: ". . . the whole city (came) together to hear the word of God." It is mentioned again in verse 46: ". . . It was necessary that the word of God should first have been spoken to you [to the Jew first, and also to the Greek]." In verse 48 we read: "And when the Gentiles heard this, they were glad, and glorified the word of the Lord." And finally in verse 49 we read: "And the word of the Lord was published throughout all the region." That is a tremendous emphasis upon the Word of the Lord. But if we think that Acts 13 has so many references, we will be interested to learn that in the concordance there are 1,153 instances in the Bible where the Word is used. Such emphasis reflects the entire spirit and attitude of the revelation of God that we hold in our hands.

THE ALMIGHTINESS OF GOD'S WORD

There is an almightiness about the weight and burden of the meaning and significance of the Word of God. In Psalm 119 is written: "For ever, O LORD, thy word is [*natsav*] settled in heaven" (v. 89). The Hebrew word, *natsav*, translated in the King James Version, "settled," literally means "fixed" or "established." For ever, O Lord, Thy word was fixed in heaven before it was ever written down in the Bible. What does the psalmist mean by "thy word is fixed in heaven"? Is the Word on a great tablet? Is it engraved in angelic marble? Is it written on the sides of the golden city?

Another typical passage which proclaims the almightiness of God's Word can be found in Psalm 89: "My covenant will I not break, nor alter the thing that is gone out of my lips" (v. 34). We can depend upon the Word of God. Heaven and earth may change, it may pass away, but the Word of God will never pass away.

It was the Word of God that Jesus used in Matthew 4 to defeat Satan in every temptation. Jesus answered the tempter with a word from the Book of God. It is no less amazing that in Revelation 12 the inspired writer says that as the people faced Satan, "they overcame him by the blood of the Lamb, and by the word of their testimony" (v. 11a).

Someone described the Christian faith as being "The Great Confession." It is precisely that. The apostle Paul wrote to us in Colossians 3: "Let the word of Christ dwell in you richly in all wisdom" (v. 16a). The wisest man who ever lived wrote:

> My son, attend to my words; incline thine ear unto my sayings.
> Let them not depart from thine eyes; keep them in the midst of thine heart.
> For they are life unto those that find them, and health to all their flesh (Prov. 4:20-22).

What a remarkable thing! The words of God are life and health.

A WONDERFUL CALLING TO DECLARE GOD'S WORD

How wondrous that God should call us to be instruments to be used of Him. Acts 13 begins: ". . . the Holy Ghost said, Separate me Barnabas and Saul for the work whereunto I have called them" (v. 2b). What work? When Barnabas and Saul go out to do the work God has called them to do, this is what the work is. Seven times in the story that follows they are teaching and preaching the Word of God. What a heavenly mandate! Psalm 119 says: "My soul cleaveth unto the dust: quicken thou me according to thy word" (v. 25). Imagine what it is to be used of God not only to raise people out of the pit, out of the mire and clay, and out of the dust of the ground, but to raise them up to the Word of God, to the angelic, beatific vision of the Lord Himself, reading God's Word, thinking God's thoughts, storing them in our souls.

THE GREAT ASSIGNMENT AND DEDICATION OF THE CHURCH

One may deduct from God's Word this first avowal: the tremendous mandate of the church is to teach the Word of the Lord. That is why God has called us, commissioned us, and sent us out. We are to preach and to teach the Word of the Lord. Paul wrote to his son in the ministry in 2 Timothy 2: "And the things that thou hast heard of me among many witnesses, the same commit thou to faithful men, who shall be able to teach others also" (v. 2). That is our heavenly assignment, teaching those, who, in their generation, shall teach others also.

In keeping with that, the school has always been in the church, teaching the Word of the Lord. The Greek word *katekeo* means "to instruct." New converts into the faith were called "catechumens" who were instructed, *katekeo*, with a "catechism." I think that the four Gospels, Matthew, Mark, Luke, and John, were little tracts that were used to teach the catechumens the words of the Lord. From the beginning, the school was in the church. All of the old great universities were church schools. The ancient schools in Rome, in Germany, in France, in England, and in America, without exception, were church schools.

The public school system also was in the church. In 1780 Robert Raikes, the editor of the *Gloucester Journal* in England, seeing all of the children out in the streets, gathered them together in a Sunday school. As the days passed and the Sunday school movement grew, it was decided that on Sunday the Bible, the Word of God, would be taught. Then on the week days they would teach reading, writing, and arithmetic. So the church school was divided.

Education, teaching, has always been in the church, and it ought to stay there. To teach without God is to deliver to the world Frankensteins, evolutionists, atheists, materialists, and secularists. Teaching is an assignment for the church, the people of God.

In the session of the Southern Baptist Convention in Augusta, Georgia, in 1863, Dr. Basil Manly, Jr. (professor and later president of Southern Seminary), offered the following resolution:

> "Resolved, that a committee of seven be appointed to inquire whether it is expedient for this convention to attempt anything for the promotion of Sunday Schools."

> Ablest men were chosen and Dr. Manly served as chairman of the committee. The committee later made the following report:

> "All of us have felt that the Sunday School is the nursery of the church, the camp of the instruction of her young soldiers, the great missionary to the future. It goes to meet and bless the generation that is coming, to win them from ignorance and sin, to train future laborers when our places shall know us no more."

The report of the committee recommended the appointment of a Sunday school board. The Southern Baptist Convention adopted the report and recommendations unanimously. The new board was located in Greenville, South Carolina, home of the seminary. Dr. Manly was the president of the board, Dr. John A. Broadus was secretary, and Dr. James P. Boyd was vice-president.

At that time the convention met biennially. Because of the tragic war between the states, the convention failed to meet in 1865. In 1866 at Russellville, Kentucky, the new Board made its first report, which was written by possibly the greatest scholar the Southern Baptist denomination has ever produced, Dr. John A. Broadus. This is what he said:

> In conclusion, the Board affectionately urges upon the convention of the churches the incalculable importance of the Sunday School work. Besides its powerful direct influence upon the welfare of society, and its vast and blessed result in the salvation of souls, the Sunday School is a helper to every other benevolent agency. The preacher and pastor finds in it the aid of many subordinate preachers and pastors, each laboring for the benefit of a little flock, and all finding their gifts and graces developed and exercised, as his own are, by efforts for the religious good of others. Everything Christians care for would greatly

suffer if its influence were lost; everything will gain in proportion as its influence is extended.

Great! But the war's destruction was too much for the town. The seminary leaders were struggling to keep the institution alive, and they finally moved it to Louisville, Kentucky. It was not until 1891 that they were able to continue the work, this time in Nashville, Tennessee, where the Baptist Sunday School Board is still located. Just think of the dedication and the wisdom of those men and the wisdom of God in the church through the years, giving itself to a tremendous teaching program!

THE CONSTRAINING MOTIVE OF TEACHING THE WORD IS GOD HIMSELF

Let me point out that not only is teaching a dedication of the church, a commitment from God, but the constraining motive that lies back of teaching God's Word is from the Lord Himself. When we are teaching the Word of the Lord, we are doing God's work in the earth. Look in the Great Commission at the word "teach." We are to "go into all nations, teaching them in the name of the triune God, *teaching* them all the things that I have commanded thee." When one is doing God's work, he is teaching the Word of the Lord. A teacher is seated before the class with a Book in his hand. In front of the teacher sit a boy and a girl. The boy also has a Book in his hand. The assignment of the teacher is to implant the message of the Bible into the hearts of the boy and the girl. That is why we need the Holy Spirit to help us. The youngster may understand the syntax of a sentence that describes the grace of God, but does he know the grace of God? He may be able to learn all of the historical and geographical background of the Bible, but does he know the God of the land and the Lord of the people? With the Spirit of the heavenly Father helping us, this is our great work—to get the Word of God into the hearts of those who sit before us, who study with us, and to lead all of us into the kingdom.

THE PRICE OF EXCELLENCE

The price of excellence in the teaching of the Word of God is twofold. First, it is the paying of attention to detail. What an inconsequential reason! Instead of talking about the Word of God, about lifting souls out of the dust, and elevating people into the kingdom of God's dear Son, it sounds like I'm going to talk about inconsequentials, about paying attention to detail. That may not be as far from the mind of God as one might think. Exodus 31 tells us that the Holy Spirit filled Bezaleel and Aholiab. One might assume that they were going out to conquer the whole earth since the Holy Spirit filled them! But what did Bazaleel and Aholiab do? Filled with the Holy Spirit of God, they made pots, pans, snuffers, stobs, curtains, and tashes for the tabernacle. That is how God works.

We can find the same workmanship of God in nature. One time a scientist came to me and said, "Look through the microscope." He had a slide of an object that had been painted. When I looked at the slide with the naked eye, the object looked to be just painted red, but when I looked at it through the high-powered microscope, I never saw such blobs in my life. There was a blob from one side to the other. Then the scientist changed the slide and asked me to look again. He had taken a butterfly wing and had mounted it. When I looked through the microscope at the butterfly wing, I saw that from one side of the wing to the other, it was as smooth as silk and satin. There was not a blob in it. The Lord God who fashioned that little butterfly wing went down into the atomic and molecular structure of the wing and made it perfect. It looked like something that only God's hand could do.

Think of a snowflake. A snowflake is a beautiful crystal under a microscope, yet there have never been two snowflakes alike out of the trillions of snowflakes created. That is God!

Think of a flower. The poet Alfred Lord Tennyson wrote this poem about a flower:

> Flower in the crannied wall,
> I pluck you out of the crannies.
>
> I hold you here, root and all, in my hand,
> Little flower—but if I could understand
> What you are, root and all, and all in all,
> I should know what God and man is.

The poet saw the very breadth and presence of God in the arrangement of a little flower growing out of a crack in a stone wall. That is God, paying attention to detail.

In the Parthenon in Athens, above the porch of the columns, is a great pediment. Phidias, the incomparable sculptor, made beautiful marble carvings for the pediment. But when Lord Elgin conquered Greece, he took all of those beautiful marble pieces down and gave them to the British Museum in London where they are now on exhibition. When I was in London, I went to the London Museum to look at the Elgin Marbles because I wanted to look on the back side of the statues. There is a story about Phidias when he was working on those sculptured pieces. They were to be placed high above the porch in the pediment. Phidias was carefully working on the back side just as he had labored over the front side. A man came by and asked, "Phidias, why are you carefully working on the back side trying to make it just as beautiful as the front side? Do not you know that the figures are going to be placed so high that no one will ever see the back side."

Phidias replied, "I know, but God can see it."

Even though he was shaping those sculpures to be placed where no human eye could even see from so great a distance, he wanted the back side of the marble to be just as beautifully and carefully carved and shaped as the front side. That is art!

When I was in Florence, Italy, I went to the Academy of Fine Arts to look at Michelangelo's *David*. Here again is a world-famous story of heroic proportion. Michelangelo carved the statue of David out of a hugh block of marble. When he had finished the statue, a friend came by and said: "That is magnificent. You have done it."

Michelangelo replied, "Yes, almost."

That same friend came by several months later and saw Michelangelo still working on that statue of David. He was making ever so slight adjustments in the shape of a curve or in the expression on the face. The friend said, "I thought you had finished the statue months and months ago; what are you doing?"

Michelangelo replied, "I am just trying to change a little contour of the muscle here and soften the expression there."

His friend said: "Listen, Michelangelo. Those are trifles!"

Then the famous reply was uttered by Michelangelo, "Trifles make perfection, but perfection is no trifle." That is excellence! There are multitudes of little details that go together to make for excellence.

The same is true of an effective teaching ministry in the church. Is there a place to park at the church? Is the room comfortable for the class? Is the temperature adjusted for the seasons of the year? Is the teacher prepared? Is the work organized well? Put it all together and you have ingredients for excellence in reaching the lost for the Lord.

The pastor also must prepare. You can be sure that I have spent hours and hours in preparing messages, even though the messages may sound extemporaneously delivered.

Every one of us in the Sunday school is to be like that, paying attention to little details, acquiring patience in doing what makes for a powerful teaching ministry.

Do you remember Isaiah 28:10? Isaiah's enemies were mocking, ridiculing, and scorning him. They said: "This is Isaiah, line upon line, precept upon precept, here a little, there a little. We are so tired of that we do not know what to think. Isaiah is going over the same thing, over and over again." But that is the message of the prophet, just staying with it, delivering the message of the Lord, line upon line, precept upon precept, here a little, there a little.

ADULTS LEAD THE WAY

The ministry of teaching the Word of God is always to be led by the adults. The Lord tells us, "Study to shew thyself approved unto God, a workman that needeth not to be ashamed . . ." (2 Tim. 2:15a). We are to study, to read God's Word, and to open our hearts to the truth of the Lord. Then we are to train our young people. We are commanded to "train up a child in the way he should go . . ." (Prov. 22:6a).

One time I read an unusual article about "The Inaccessible Boy." A fellow was seated by a boy with his arm around him. The boy was prodigal and wayward, a boy of the street. The man was trying to get the boy to come to his Sunday school class. He said: "We have candy and cookies. Will you be there?"

The boy said, "No."

The man said: "We have games and a gymnasium. Will you come?"

The boy said, "No."

The man said: "We have books and we have materials to place in your hands for you to study. Will you come?"

The boy said, "No."

The man said: "We sing songs and you can be in the choir. We have the best time in the world. Will not you come?"

The boy said, "No."

The fellow was discouraged and walked away dejected.

The boy said, "Say, will *you* be there?"

The man answered, "Yes, I will."

The boy replied, "Then I will be there, too."

The boy did not know anything and cared less. But he was touched by the warm embrace of the teacher. His heart was moved by the friendship of someone who took a little interest in him. The boy would have followed the man either to the saloon or to the church. We have an awesome responsibility to reach our young people for Jesus!

FAITHFUL IN WORKING

A survey was made of the Sunday school and it was found that one-half of all of the pupils in the Sunday school are lost because of the indifference of the teacher. The tie between the teacher and the pupil is so frail and is broken so easily.

One time I was talking to a man in North Carolina in a large knitting factory. As I talked to the man, he worked on the loom, keeping his eyes on the loom, carefully looking at the threads. We must thus watch over our pupils.

On another occasion I was visiting with a rancher in west Texas. All the years of his life his eyes were fixed on the herd and the calves. Our students are worth more.

One time I heard a man say: "You know, I am sorry that I joined that church. Before I was converted, they came to see me, they talked to me, and they paid attention to me. But now that I am saved and belong to the church, no one says anything to me and no one pays any attention to me." That is tragic! We must love our children, care for them, teach them the Word of the Lord, and grow in grace together with them. This is God's finest and best assignment.

God will not let our effort fall to the ground. When we carry out God's Word, He never lets it fail.

One time a Sunday school teacher decided to quit teaching her class. She said: "Pastor, I am a failure. I am so discouraged."

Meanwhile a soldier who was killed in a battle had talked to a friend and said, "Go see my Sunday school teacher and tell her that I thank her for winning me to Jesus, for teaching me the way to die and that I will meet her in heaven."

The soldier came back and told the Sunday school teacher what the dying boy had said. The teacher said, "O God, to think that I have been discouraged and wanted to quit!"

No word that we deliver in God's name ever falls to the ground. This is God's assignment and work for us in the earth.

May the Holy Spirit help us as we strive to carry out His precious mandate!

20

The Doctrine of Election

And when the Gentiles heard this, they were glad, and glorified the word of
the Lord: and as many as were ordained to eternal life believed. (Acts 13:48)

The doctrine of election is introduced in Acts 13:48, in which the
author, Dr. Luke, writes a concluding clause: "And as many as were
ordained to eternal life believed." Whether we like it, believe in it, or
accept it, the Bible says "And as many as were ordained to eternal life
believed." This is a work of God like the wonder of the creation above
us, around us, and beneath us. Just as the creation is a work of the
hand of almighty God, His purpose of redemptive grace in human
history is as much a sovereign work of His.

It is unusual the way Luke has chosen to say, "And as many as were
ordained to eternal life believed." The translation "ordained" is a
following of Jerome's Latin Vulgate. The word is a periphrastic past
perfect participle, passive voice, indicative mood, *hesan tetagmenoi*.
The basic form of the verb is *tasso*, which is a military verb referring to
"an orderly arrangement." If we were to translate it precisely as Luke
wrote it, we would translate it "appoint," "arrange," "set," "assign," or
"allot." Let us take the word "appoint." Luke writes, "And as many as
were appointed to eternal life believed." He does not say who did the
appointing. Could it be, as some say, that the Gentiles were so disposed to listen and to respond that they believed, they accepted the
Lord? Was it their disposition that thus opened for them the gates of
heaven? Or did God dispose their hearts to believe, and in that belief,
appointed them to eternal life, as John Calvin and his followers would

153

avow? Certainly it is said here that they believed, they trusted, they opened their hearts. In my humble opinion, as I study the text as best I can, I think it is both. I think that the elective, ordained, predestined purpose of God was that they would believe, accept the Lord, and thus be appointed to eternal life. I am persuaded also that their response arose out of them. "And when the Gentiles heard this, they were glad, and glorified the Lord, and as many as were ordained, as many as were appointed to eternal life, believed." You see, the response of the Gentiles is in contrast to the Jews who rejected that message. "Then Paul and Barnabas . . . said, It was necessary that the word of God should first have been spoken to you: but seeing ye put it from you, and judge yourselves unworthy of everlasting life, lo, we turn to the Gentiles" (Acts 13:46). When Paul turned to the Gentiles, they were disposed to believe and were appointed to eternal life.

Two Scriptural Facts of God's Election

There are two great facts that Scripture fully reveals. One of the facts is the sovereign, eternal, elective purpose of God, which is as much in evidence as a work of the Almighty as the creation that we see around us. He made the universe, the galaxies, the sidereal spheres, the stars, and all of the firmament. God also purposed a divine election of the redeemed from the foundation of the world. The Bible plainly uses those words describing the elective purposes of God. Just listen to these words as we read them out of the Book of Ephesians:

> . . . he hath chosen us in him before the foundation of the world (1:4).

> Having predestinated us unto the adoption of children by Jesus Christ to himself . . . (1:5).

> Having made known unto us the mystery of his will, according to his good pleasure which he hath purposed in himself (1:9).

> In whom also we have obtained an inheritance, being predistinated according to the purpose of him who worketh all things after the counsel of his own will (1:11).

That is the great Almighty who intervenes in human history. Listen again:

> For whom he did foreknow, he also did predestinate to be conformed to the image of his son, . . .
> Moreover whom he did predestinate, them he also called: and whom he called, them he also justified: and whom he justified, them he also glorified.

Who shall lay any thing to the charge of God's elect? It is God that justifieth (Rom. 8:29, 30, 33).

It is a fact in the Holy Scriptures that God chooses. He always has and He still does. God chose Abraham out of idolatry. He chose Moses and sent him down into the land of Egypt. He chose Aaron, and He chose the Levites for the ministries in the tabernacle. He chose David and anointed him above his brethren. He chose the twelve apostles. He intervened in the life of the archpersecutor, Saul of Tarsus. God chose him and made him the apostle Paul. And the Lord chooses to this day.

I have a brother. We had the same mother. We had the same father. We grew up in the same home. Every outward circumstance, culture, life, education, church, pastor, and influence around me was around him. He never felt any call to the ministry. I did, from as far back as I can remember, I have felt that God has called me to be a pastor. He did not call me to be an evangelist, a professor, or a teacher, but a pastor. Why did God not call my brother? That is in the mystery of His sovereign will. Why did God not call the boy who lived next door to me in that little town in which I lived? I do not know. God called me. The elective purpose and choice of the Lord almighty is a regnant will that is as much in vogue, in sight, and in purpose today as it was in the beginning.

The other fact plainly revealed to us on the sacred page is no less dynamically pertinent and true. This also is a fact in life and in the Holy Scriptures both. It is that God made us free. We are human agents able to choose for ourselves. We are free, but we are morally responsible. We can choose for ourselves, and we do. The apostle Paul tells us in 1 Timothy 2, that Adam was not deceived. Eve was deceived. The subtle serpent led her astray, but not Adam. Adam chose to eat the forbidden fruit. He chose to die with his wife rather than to live without her. He had the power of choice. He made the decision that has followed through all the generations since and comes down to us. Choice is a fact of human experience and human life.

Moses stood in the midst of the camp as the Israelites danced naked around the golden calf and called, saying, "Who is on the LORD'S side? let him come unto me" (Exod. 32:26).

The grand hero of the faith, the captain of the host of Israel, Joshua, closes his book with an address in which he concludes, "Choose you this day whom ye will serve . . . but as for me and my house, we will serve the LORD" (Josh. 24:15). In 1 Kings 18, Elijah is on top of Mt. Carmel saying to the people of Israel, "If the LORD be God, follow him: but if Baal, then follow him" (v. 21). The power of choice is given to us.

How many beautiful, precious, and tender appeals we can find in the word, in the heart, and in the language of the Lord Jesus! He says, "Come unto me, all ye that labour and are heavy laden, and I will give you rest" (Matt. 11:28). He gives us the freedom of choice.

In his second Corinthian letter Paul says, "Now then we are ambassadors for Christ, as though God did beseech you by us: we pray you in Christ's stead, be ye reconciled to God" (5:20).

The last invitation closes the apocalypse, "And the Spirit and the bride say, Come. And let him that heareth say, Come. And let him that is athirst come. And whosoever will, let him take the water of life freely" (Rev. 22:17). The elect, the whosoever wills; the non-elect, the whosoever will nots—the power of choice is as much written on the sacred page as the elective sovereignty of God.

This truth revealed in the Scriptures is always in God's perview and in God's revelation. Sometimes we have difficulty seeing all of the things of God in all of the things of us, but we will never view it clearly until we are able to see both the ability and the sovereignty of the Almighty and the free human choice we have in our lives. There is a language that describes the Lord in heaven, and there is another language that describes us here in the earth, we who are mortals. There is a language, a vocabulary that is used only for God in glory. That language and vocabulary will use words like this: "almightiness," that is God; "sovereignty," that is God; "foreknowledge," that is God; "election," that is God; and "predestination," that is God. That is the language of heaven.

There is another vocabulary that describes us down here in the earth. The words we will use to describe mortal men are "free moral accountability," "free agency," "free will," the "power of choice." Our problem arises when we misapply and mix up those words. We cannot take the words that apply to the Almighty and make them apply to us. It becomes ridiculous and inane. The words do not fit.

The monarch who reigned the longest in Europe, and probably in the world, was Louis XIV of France. He was a despot of the first order. He said, "I am the State." When Louis XIV died, the priest who presided at the memorial service looked down at the casket a long time.

Then he raised his head and looked up toward heaven. Finally, he said, "Only God is great."

"Foreknowledge" is a word that applies only to God. It does not apply to us. God knows the future for the aeons and the ages yet to come. He prophesies in His Book things that are coming years hence. The eternity is just present before him. But we? If you have foreknowledge two minutes, I will tell you how to be a billionaire. Just buy a stock on the New York Stock Exchange before it goes up and then sell it just before it goes down. You will be a billionaire in no time. Words that apply to the great mightiness of God do not apply to mortal man. When we talk about God, we talk about sovereignty, purpose, God's will through the ages, foreknowledge, election, and predestination. But when we talk about man, we know nothing of those things. There is no almightiness in us, no foreknowledge. That is God. When we talk about ourselves, we talk about free moral agents, spiritual responsibility, and freedom of choice.

When we think about those two facts, to us they are diametrically contradictory. How can a man be free, and at the same time God be sovereign? How can God carry through His elective purpose, and at the same time I be perfectly able to make any choice that I like?

OUR INABILITY TO UNDERSTAND

Our problem lies in our astigmatism, our spiritual and moral near-sightedness. We can see one thing at a time, but apparently we are incapable of seeing two. We can see the sovereignty and almightiness of God, and we can see the free moral agency of a man, but because of our astigmatism, we cannot see both at the same time. To us they are contradictory. When we try to understand what God has done, we immediately come into the unfathomable. There is an inexplicable side about doctrine in the Bible, and no less is there an unfathomable facet about every work of the creative hand of God. For example, in astronomy there is a force called centripetal force, which is a force that pulls a thing to the center. There is also a centrifugal force, a force which flings things to the outside. To us they are opposites, but in the mightiness of God that is what keeps planets in their orbits. There is a force that would pull the earth into the sun called gravity. There is also a centrifugal force that would fling it out into space, as these planets swing in their orbits. The force of the one that pulls it back, and the force of the other that flings it afar, keeps the planet in its orbit without a second of variation through all the ages. To us they are two forces diametrically opposed to each other, but if we had the mind of God, we would see them as one.

The same thing is illustrated time and again in physics. There are laws that are seemingly so contradictory in physics. One is the law of expansion and contraction in cold and heat. The law of physics says that if an object gets colder and colder it will contract. The same law states that if an object gets hotter and hotter it will expand. We can see the law of physics that an object contracts when it gets colder. But then, in the mystery of God in His universe, water gets colder and colder and contracts in volume, and then suddenly, for no reason at all, another law of God intervenes. When water becomes 32° and freezes, it expands, which is the opposite of the law of contraction. To us, those are opposites, but if we had the mind of God, they would be just one. That is why the apostle Paul closes his marvelous discussion of election in Romans 9-11 with an exclamation, "O the depth of the riches both of the wisdom and knowledge of God! how unsearchable are his judgments, and his ways past finding out!" (11:33).

The Purpose of God's Election

I cannot understand. We do not understand. All we do is observe. We do not explain anything nor does anyone else explain anything. We just look. The mysteries of this world are voluminous and infinite. Finite man cannot encompass the infinitude of God. We cannot contain Him in our mental processes. We are not big enough to hold God in our hearts and minds. But in the revelation of the Lord, there are things that show us why the sovereignty, why the election, and why the foreknowledge and predestinary decrees of God. They are twofold. One concerns us and the other concerns our blessed Lord Jesus. First, why the election of God? It is for our sakes. It is an election, a decree of grace, of pity, of mercy, of redemption, of salvation. Election, or predestination, is the working out of the purposes of grace and redemption in the human race. God has chosen that in a world of sin, damnation, and judgment, there will be also salvation through grace, mercy, and His love. The human race by nature is perverse and finds aversion to the will of God. Every newspaper we read blatantly headlines that fact in every issue on every page. The human race is lamentably sinful and it is heading toward its own self-destruction. The human race has in it the seeds of perdition and finally death. Nor is there any hope for the future, for there are no generations that will ever be born that will be any different from the sinful generations that are in the past and to which we also belong. We live in a lost, condemned, and dying world. But God intervenes in grace, in mercy, in love, and in salvation. All the decrees of God are for our redemption. He never decrees damnation and judgment. It is the will of God that all come to repentance and to salvation, as the Lord said in Ezekiel:

As I live, saith the Lord GOD, I have no pleasure in the death of the wicked; but that the wicked turn from his way and live: turn ye, turn ye from your evil ways; for why will ye die, O house of Israel? (33:11).

God is always intervening in His divine sovereignty, in grace, in mercy, in love, in redemption, and in salvation. There is only one place in the human story where election is without pity, without mercy, and without human kindness, and that is the position taken by the pseudoscientists of the world. They take the word "election" and put an "s" in front of it, calling it "selection"; that is, the doctrine of the survival of the fittest, the doctrine of evolution. That is the horrible doctrine of the fang, the tooth, and the claw that has no part of love and mercy. That is election as the pseudoscientist and evolutionist teaches and believes it. When the child of God looks at human history and the revelation of the purposes of God, he sees in that doctrine the merciful, tender, loving presence of the Lord God, and His choices always are that we might be saved. God chose Israel and they are His chosen people. But God chose Israel that they might be missionaries, witnesses, and teachers of the whole world. Isaiah 43 says, "Israel is my witness" (v. 10). In Exodus 19 the Lord God said:

Ye shall be unto me a kingdom of priests, and an holy nation (v. 6).

A kingdom of priests means that Christians are to represent man to God and God to man. They are to be the teachers, the preachers, and the missionaries witnessing to the whole world. It is no less in His church. In 1 Peter we read:

Ye are a chosen generation, a royal priesthood, an holy nation, a peculiar people; that ye should shew forth the praises of him who hath called you out of darkness into his marvelous light (2:9).

The whole world ought to see the beauty of the Lord in us that they might be drawn to the Savior. All individual election is like that. The Lord said about Saul of Tarsus:

Go thy way: for he is a chosen vessel unto me, to bear my name before the Gentiles, and kings, and the children of Israel:

For I will shew him how great things he must suffer for my name's sake (Acts 9:15-16).

All the elections of God are for the healing of the nation, for the salvation of the lost, that we might find eternal life in Jesus.

God's sovereign election is not only for us, it is also for Jesus. The Lord in heaven said to the blessed Savior, "You suffer and You die for the sins of the race, and I promise You that You will have a people who will love You, believe in You, and give their hearts, lives, and souls in trust to You." That is election and the purpose of the sovereign redemptive grace of God.

In John 6 the Lord said:

All that the Father giveth me shall come to me; and him that cometh to me I will in no wise cast out (v. 37).

God promised Jesus a people. Those whom God has promised to the blessed Jesus will come to Him. The Lord with open arms stands ready to love, to bless, and to receive them.

O God, how could I thank You enough, that in Your providence, Your grace, and Your purpose, I heard the gospel message. I listened to it when I was young. I responded to it with my heart and soul. How shall I thank You, God in heaven, that my name should be included in that Book of Life, that I should have been an object of the tender love and mercy of the Lord Jesus. How shall I thank You enough, that my heart was disposed to receive You, believe in You, accept You, trust You, and love You? O the depths and the heights of the love of God in Christ Jesus that reached down even to me!

It is God's love, grace, election, and purpose that Jesus should have a people. That means all of us. His divine purposes of grace are being realized in us this day. "And as many as were ordained to eternal life believed."

21

Apostolic Christianity

And it came to pass in Iconium, that they went both together into the synagogue of the Jews, and so spake, that a great multitude both of the Jews and also of the Greeks believed.

But the unbelieving Jews stirred up the Gentiles, and made their minds evil affected against the brethren.

Long time therefore abode they speaking boldly in the Lord, which gave testimony unto the word of his grace, and granted signs and wonders to be done by their hands.

But the multitude of the city was divided: and part held with the Jews, and part with the apostles.

And when there was an assault made both of the Gentiles, and also of the Jews with their rulers, to use them despitefully, and to stone them,

They were ware of it, and fled into Lystra and Derbe, cities of Lycaonia, and unto the region that lieth round about:

And there they preached the gospel.

And there sat a certain man at Lystra, impotent in his feet, being a cripple from his mother's womb, who never had walked:

The same heard Paul speak: who stedfastly beholding him, and perceiving that he had faith to be healed,

Said with a loud voice, Stand upright on thy feet. And he leaped and walked.

And when the people saw what Paul had done, they lifted up their voices, saying in the speech of Lycaonia, The gods are come down to us in the likeness of men.

And they called Barnabas, Jupiter; and Paul, Mercurius, because he was the chief speaker.

Then the priest of Jupiter, which was before their city, brought oxen and garlands unto the gates, and would have done sacrifice with the people.

Which when the apostles, Barnabas and Paul, heard of, they rent their clothes, and ran in among the people, crying out,

And saying, Sirs, why do ye these things? We also are men of like passions with you, and preach unto you that ye should turn from these vanities unto the living God, which made heaven, and earth, and the sea, and all things that are therein:

Who in times past suffered all nations to walk in their own ways.

Nevertheless he left not himself without witness, in that he did good, and gave us rain from heaven, and fruitful seasons, filling our hearts with food and gladness.

And with these sayings scarce restrained they the people, that they had not done sacrifice unto them.

And there came thither certain Jews from Antioch and Iconium, who persuaded the people, and, having stoned Paul, drew him out of the city, supposing he had been dead.

Howbeit, as the disciples stood round about him, he rose up, and came into the city: and the next day he departed with Barnabas to Derbe.

And when they had preached the gospel to that city, and had taught many, they returned again to Lystra, and to Iconium, and Antioch,

Confirming the souls of the disciples, and exhorting them to continue in the faith, and that we must through much tribulation enter into the kingdom of God.

And when they had ordained them elders in every church, and had prayed with fasting, they commended them to the Lord, on whom they believed.

And after they had passed throughout Pisidia, they came to Pamphylia.

And when they had preached the word in Perga, they went down into Attalia:

And thence sailed to Antioch, from whence they had been recommended to the grace of God for the work which they fulfilled.

And when they were come, and had gathered the church together, they rehearsed all that God had done with them, and how he had opened the door of faith unto the Gentiles. (Acts 14:1-27)

In our study of the Book of Acts, we continue with chapter 14, and as a background for the exposition of the whole chapter, let us look at verse 27:

And when they were come, and had gathered the church together, they rehearsed all that God had done with them, and how he had opened the door of faith unto the Gentiles.

As we expound the Word of the Lord, we must remember that we are not talking about modern Christianity, European Christianity, or American Christianity. The subject concerns apostolic Christianity, the kind that was delivered to the world under the hands of the apostles. What was apostolic Christianity, how did it begin, and how did it progress?

APOSTOLIC CHRISTIANITY WAS A FLAME AND A SWORD

My first observation is that apostolic Christianity was a flame and a fire. It was a sword and a tumult. It was a challenge and a confrontation. Look at the Word of the Lord. God called Saul and Barnabas for a stated assignment, "for the work whereunto I have sent thee." This is God's work which is mandated from heaven. So these men, emissaries from heaven, with the Word of the living God in their souls, went forth, sent by the Holy Spirit of the Lord. The record of that missionary journey begins in Acts 13. How did it end?

The missionary endeavor ended in a tumult, in a persecution, in an expelling out of the city and from the whole country. We read in Acts 13:

> But the Jews stirred up the devout and honourable women, and the chief men of the city, and raised persecution against Paul and Barnabas, and expelled them out of their coasts (v. 50).

That is how their mission ended in Pisidian Antioch.

So Paul and Barnabas went to Iconium to preach the gospel of the Lord God. How did their efforts end in Iconium? We read in Acts 14:

> But the multitude of the city was divided: and part held with the Jews, and part with the apostles.
> And when there was an assault made both of the Gentiles, and also of the Jews with their rulers, to use them despitefully, and to stone them (vv. 4-5).

Then Paul and Barnabas fled to Lystra. How did their missionary endeavor end in Lystra? We read again in Acts 14:14:

> And there came thither certain Jews from Antioch and Iconium, who persuaded the people, and, having stoned Paul, drew him out of the city, supposing he had been dead (v. 19).

Remember that we are talking about apostolic Christianity and not bland, innocuous, modern Christianity. Are you not surprised that the Word of God and the precious preaching of the love of Jesus should ensue in division, tumult, stormy persecutions, stonings, blood and death? One would think that surely the sweet message from heaven would bring peace on the earth. It is just the opposite. There is no peace, there is no rest, and there is no quiet. There is division in the town and in the city. There is tumult, there is persecution, there is stoning, there is blood, and there is death. How could such a thing be? Remember, we are talking about apostolic Christianity, the Christianity of the Bible.

APOSTOLIC CHRISTIANITY CONFRONTS EVIL WITH FLAMING TRUTH

The answer is obvious as I read the Bible. First of all, apostolic Christianity was a challenge to evil, wickedness, heathenism, and wrong wherever it was found. It was fierce and courageous. That has always been the way of God. It is not peculiar in Acts 13 and 14. That has been the way of God through the centuries.

For example, in the Old Testament Ahab said to Naboth, "I would love to have your little garden next to the palace in which to raise roses, petunias, and all kinds of pretty plants." According to the Word of God, Naboth replied, "I cannot sell the inheritance of my fathers. God has allotted that to my family forever. It cannot do it." So Ahab sulked, went to bed, would not eat, and turned his face to the wall.

Jezebel asked him: "Why do you not eat? Why do you lie in bed? Why do you turn your face to the wall?"

Ahab answered: "I want the vineyard of Naboth next to our palace. He will not give it to me."

So Jezebel said: "I will get it for you."

So they hired witnesses and accused Naboth of blaspheming God and of being a traitor to the king. Then they took Naboth out and stoned him to death.

Jezebel came and said to Ahab: "Arise, possess. Naboth is dead. Take the vineyard."

So in gladness, Ahab rose up and went into the vineyard of Naboth.

Then the Scripture says, "But God." That is always the concluding paragraph and sentence. The Lord said to Elijah; "Arise up and meet Ahab. He is in the vineyard of Naboth."

When Ahab rose to enter and possess the vineyard of Naboth, there stood the prophet of God, Elijah. When Ahab saw him he said, "Hast thou found me, O mine enemy?"

Elijah said, "In the place that the dogs licked up the blood of Naboth, shall dogs lick up your blood." That is God.

It is no different in the New Testament. John the Baptist stood before Herod Antipas who had enticed and wooed away his brother's wife, Herodias. John the Baptist confronted the king and said, "It is not right for you to have your brother's wife." That is God.

It was the Lord Himself who said:

> But whosoever shall deny me before men, him will I also deny before my Father which is in heaven.

Think not that I am come to send peace on earth: I come not to send peace,
but a sword (Matt. 10:33-34).

That is apostolic Christianity, and it faces evil, paganism, and atheism
courageously and fearlessly.

There is a young student in our church who is dedicated to the
Lord. In a university his professor mouthed words of blasphemy and
the student stood up and challenged the professor, "What you say is
not true." The professor flunked him. That is all right. That is the faith
of apostolic Christianity.

APOSTOLIC CHRISTIANITY REFUSES TO COMPROMISE

How does apostolic Christianity create confrontation and tumult? It
is a noncompromising faith. It is all-inclusive and authoritarian.
Apostolic Christianity never says, "I will give a little and I will take a
little." There is no room for any other god or any other faith. It is truth
itself.

Have you ever considered why Rome persecuted the Christian faith?
The Roman empire was the most lenient and sympathetic of any
empire. We sometimes have a wrong concept of the Roman Empire. It
was a conquering force under the iron hand of the Caesars, but when it
conquered a province, it was most gracious in the administration of the
government. Whatever the people wanted to do, whatever god they
chose to worship, the Roman Empire was most lenient and understanding. Then why did the Roman empire persecute Christians?

The answer is obvious. Agrippa, the friend of Julius Caesar, had
built in Rome the Pantheon where all gods were worshiped. They
would conquer Athens, and Athens worshiped Athena. So in the
Pantheon there is a beautiful niche for Athena, the goddess of the
Athenians. They would conquer Egypt, and Egypt worshiped Isis and
Osiris. They placed in the Pantheon a beautiful niche for Isis and
Osiris. For every province they conquered, they placed the god of that
province in the Pantheon. When the gospel of Christ was preached,
the Romans offered to place right beside the niche of Jupiter a niche
for Jesus Christ. But the Christian apostles said that Jesus could not be
placed alongside any other Gods. "He is Lord alone."

That was why the Roman empire persecuted the Christians. You do
not stitch the Christian faith to some old dirty rag of paganism or
heathenism or atheism. Christianity is a seamless robe. You do not add

to it, you do not take away from it, and you do not rend it. It is woven one throughout.

The Christian faith is noncompromising. It faces evil fearlessly. Did the Lord not say:

> Is not my word like as a fire? . . . and like a hammer that breaketh the rock in pieces? (Jer. 23:29).

Daniel said:

> Thou sawest till that a stone was cut out without hands, which smote the image upon his feet that were of iron and clay, and brake them to pieces.
> Then was the iron, the clay, the brass, the silver, and the gold, broken to pieces together, and became like the chaff of the summer threshingfloors; and the wind carried them away, that no place was found for them: and the stone that smote the image became a great mountain, and filled the whole earth (Dan. 2:34-35).

That is Christianity from horizon to horizon, filling all space and all time because the faith is all true.

APOSTOLIC CHRISTIANITY ALWAYS SAVES OR SLAYS

Why the persecution and why the storm? What is it about apostolic Christianity that leads to persecution? Because it is a mandate of God, is a revealed truth of the Word, and is in opposition to the sin and evil of the world, it always results in one of two things. Apostolic Christianity always results in salvation or damnation. It results in someone being saved or someone being lost. Paul describes it like this:

> For we are unto God a sweet savour of Christ, in them that are saved, and in them that perish:
> To the one we are the savour of death unto death; and to the other the savour of life unto life. And who is sufficient for these things? (2 Cor. 2:15-16).

The Christian faith is always one of two things. It builds up a soul gloriously and fills it with the life and presence of God, or else it digs a hell and casts into it all wickedness, disobedience, rejection, and unbelief. The Christian faith always has been one or the other, and it is that today if it is apostolic.

APOSTOLIC CHRISTIANITY IS A SUPREME COMMITMENT TO GOD

What kind of a faith is apostolic Christianity? Let us look again at our text:

And when they were come, and had gathered the church together, they re-hearsed all that God had done with them, and how he had opened the door of faith unto the Gentiles (Acts 14:27).

Not only is the apostolic faith a storm and a furor, not only is it a flame and a fire, not only does it confront and challenge the heathenism and the paganism of the world, but it also is a supreme commitment to the Lord. It is a costly and exhausting devotion. Look again at the Scripture: "And they rehearsed all that God had done with them" (Acts 14:27). But didn't we just read about persecution?

But the multitude of the city was divided (Acts 14:4a).

We read about assault, contempt, and despicable treatment, and about stoning and dragging out to death. But it also says in the Bible, "And when they were come, and had gathered the church together, they rehearsed all that God had done with them." I must revise my ideas of the faith. The apostle is saying that the providences that overwhelm us and the confrontations that we face are from God. These early Christians did not say, "Oh, the things we have suffered, the heart-aches we have endured, the troubles that plague us!" They never referred to them. "They rehearsed all the things God had done with them." How many times do we speak of all the troubles that we have, of the disadvantages under which we labor, and of our discouragements and trials? We must remember that in apostolic Christianity the whole outcome ultimately is of God. The Lord is teaching us, He is trying us, and He is placing us in the fire that He might melt out of us the dross of our souls to make us pure in the sight of God. We are not to complain or to find fault. God is in everything. We accept from God's hands every handicap, every problem, every stoning, every storming, every confrontation, every disadvantage, and every distress. Hardships and difficulties just make us more devoted to the Lord.

Paul did not stand before the church to give the report of his first missionary journey and say, "The way is most difficult." Instead, Paul stood before the church and said, "The way is open." God opened the door to the Gentiles. Paul did not say, "If you go to the Gentiles, they will stone you, they will persecute you, they will treat you contemptuously, and they will expel you." He made the report and said:

For a great door and effectual is opened unto me, and there are many adversaries. (1 Cor. 16:9).

It was that kind of a shocking, sacred enthusiasm that turned the world upside down. Christianity without the persuasion that God is in it, that the Lord is going to work with us, that He is going to give us victories, and that the door is opened by the mighty, omnipotent hand of God Himself is like a Vesuvius without fire, like a Niagara Falls without water, like a firmament without the sun. The faith becomes a speculation and not the truth. God is in everything, and the opposition itself is but an open door to confront the world with the gospel of the Son of God.

Apostolic Christianity Cannot Be Destroyed

Apostolic Christianity is unbeatable and undefeatable. Even if it is stoned and dragged out for dead, it rises and goes back into the city. Is not that what the Bible says?

> . . . and, having stoned Paul, drew him out of the city, supposing he had been dead (Acts 14:19b).

Does the Scripture say, "When he came to, he escaped for his life, he fled"? No, the Scripture says:

> Howbeit, as the disciples stood round about him, he rose up, and came into the city: and the next day he departed with Barnabas to Derbe.
> Confirming the souls of the disciples, and exhorting them to continue in the faith, and that we must through much tribulation enter into the kingdom of God (Acts 14:20, 22).

What are you going to do with a man like that? What are you going to do with a faith like that? Beaten, stoned, dragged out of the city and left for dead, yet the man rises up and announces that it is through heartache, persecution, trouble, trials, and tribulation that we enter the kingdom of God. There is the Christian faith again. Try to kill it, bury it, cast rocks, stones, and dirt upon it, but out of the dust of the ground, out of the depths of the grave, and out of the heart of the earth, like a little plant in the spring time, there it is bursting from the very grave in which it has been buried.

I quote a Rumanian:

> With about thirty other Christians I was in a prison cell in Rumania. One day the door was opened and a new prisoner was pushed in. It took us a little time to recognize him in the darkness of the cell. When we did recognize him we were amazed to see not a fellow Christian but a well-known Captain of the Secret Police who had arrested and tortured us. We asked him how he had come to be a fellow prisoner.

He told us that one day a soldier on duty reported that a twelve-year-old boy, carrying a bouquet of flowers, was asking to see him. The Captain was curious and allowed the boy to enter. When the boy entered he was very shy. "Comrade Captain," he said, "You are the one who arrested my father and mother, and today is my mother's birthday. It has always been my habit to buy her a bouquet of flowers on her birthday—but now, because of you, I have no mother to make happy.

"My mother was a Christian and she taught me that we must love our enemies and reward evil with good. As I no longer have a mother, I thought these flowers might make the mother of your children happy. Could you please give them to your wife?"

The Communist torturer is also a man. There is a chord in his heart that still vibrates at the word of truth and burning love. The Captain took the boy's flowers and embraced him with many tears. A process of remorse and conversion began. In his heart he could no longer bear to arrest innocent men. He could no longer inflict torture. In the end he had arrived with us in prison because he had become a defender of the faith he once destroyed.

How do you kill Christianity? One may think he has slain it and put it in the grave. But it rises again, even in the form of a twelve-year-old boy whose father and mother had been slain. That is the faith!

22

Tribulation and Triumph

Confirming the souls of the disciples, and exhorting them to continue in the faith, and that we must through much tribulation enter into the kingdom of God. (Acts 14:22)

In our study of the Book of Acts we are in chapter 14. The text is found in verse 22: ". . . that we with much tribulation enter into the kingdom of God." The context would begin at verse 19 when Paul preached at Lystra:

And there came thither certain Jews from Antioch and Iconium, who persuaded the people, and, having stoned Paul, drew him out of the city, supposing he had been dead.

Howbeit, as the disciples stood round about him, he rose up, and came into the city: and the next day he departed with Barnabas to Derbe.

And when they had preached the gospel to that city, and had taught many, they returned again to Lystra, and to Iconium, and Antioch,

Confirming the souls of the disciples, and exhorting them to continue in the faith, and that we must through much tribulation enter into the kingdom of God (Acts 14:19-22).

The Greek word which is used is *thlipsis*, which means "tribulation," "affliction." The translation in English comes through the Latin Vulgate, "tribulation." *Tribulum* was the Latin word for the flail that the farmer used to thrash wheat. From the use of the word *tribulum* came our English word "tribulation." "Through much *tribulation* we must enter into the kingdom of God."

170

TRIBULATION IS COMMON TO MAN

There is a sorrow of the world, a common tribulation, that is known to all mankind. It is something we all have in common. There are tears of childhood which are just as real as the tears of manhood. There are tears of teenagers, disappointments and frustrations that young people know. There are many struggles that manhood and womanhood endure. And of course, there is the inevitable and inexorable approach to old age and finally death. All mankind are one in that *tribulum*.

Job said that a man's days are few and full of trouble (Job 14:1).

Notice how the Lord closed His Sermon on the Mount. He spoke of a man who built his house on the rock, and the rains descended, the floods rose, and the winds blew and beat on the house. Then He spoke of a man who built his house on the sand, and the rains descended, the floods rose, and the winds blew and beat on that house. A logical question would arise. "Why did both men build their houses in a riverbed where the floods would rise and beat against the house?" The answer is obvious. There is no other place to build our house but in the path of the storm and flood, and in the path of sorrow, disappointment, heartache, age, and death. There is a sorrow that is common, a tribulation that is shared by all mankind.

TRIBULATION IS COMMON TO WORLDLINGS

There is also a sorrow and a tribulation that is known to the world, to the unrighteous, to those who have every hope and every dream centered in this life. A typical example of that kind of a worldly sorrow would be a beautiful girl in Hollywood whose entire life centers around her youth and beauty. Every dream she has and every prospect for every golden tomorrow lies in her being a sex symbol, a movie star, or some glamorous creature that is exploited by the movie world. Then one day she looks in the mirror and begins to find evidences of the fading beauty and the loss of her youth. We often read that many of these Hollywood starlets, having no alternative, commit suicide. That is a sorrow of the world.

CHRISTIANS MUST ENDURE TRIBULATION ALSO

But there is also a tribulation that is unique to the child of God, just the opposite of what one might think. We can easily understand how God links unrighteousness and iniquity with judgment and tribulation.

But how is it that the child of God also falls into the same category of trouble, trial, and sorrow? Yet the Bible plainly presents it, and not only in this text. This is the teaching of the Holy Spirit all through the Scriptures. For example, in Paul's first letter to the church at Thessalonica, he says:

> And sent Timotheus, our brother, and minister of God, and our fellow-labourer in the gospel of Christ, to establish you, and to comfort you concerning your faith:
>
> That no man should be moved by these afflictions: for yourselves know that we are appointed thereunto.
>
> For verily, when we were with you, we told you before that we should suffer tribulation; even as it came to pass, and ye know (1 Thess. 3:2-4).

These were God's people, fellow Christians in the church at Thessalonica, so Paul sent Timothy to comfort them that they should not be moved by their afflictions.

Then look at what Paul wrote in his last letter:

> Yea, and all that will live godly in Christ Jesus shall suffer persecution (2 Tim. 3:12).

One would think that we who are Christians, who have found refuge in Christ, would have no trouble, no sorrow, no tears, and no suffering. We are Christians now and we have given our lives to God; therefore, we are delivered from these trials and troubles. It is just the opposite, which is an amazing revelation in the Word of God and in our own experience. Because I am a Christian does not mean that I do not weep during trial and that I do not feel the afflictions and oppressions of the world; that I do not fall into sorrow, frustration, and disappointment.

I was once visiting in the home of a godly deacon and his wife who had one child, a girl of about sixteen years of age. While I was there the girl went through the living room beautifully dressed. A car of young people was out in front and she had a date. She went out the door happy, got into the car, and drove away with the young people on the date. I was still at the home later when the girl returned home. She walked through the living room, looking neither to the right nor to the left, and she did not speak. She went down the hallway and opened the door of her bedroom. I was seated in the living room near her bedroom, and soon I could hear her crying pitifully. The mother stood up, excused herself for a moment, and went to her daughter's room. After awhile she came back into the living room and said: "My daughter tells me that when she was out with the group of young people, she refused to become involved in promiscuity, so they shoved her out of the car and made her walk home. That is why she is crying."

Every honest businessman knows what it is to pay a price for integrity and honesty. Every Christian knows what it is to face trial and compromise. In the world the Christian will suffer tribulation.

The Lost Man Meets Tribulation in Despair

How does the worldling, the sinner, the one who rejects Christ, face trial, trouble, and inevitable tribulation? He does it in despair. He has no other alternative. He does it in absolute darkness and frustration.

Disraeli, who fashioned the British Empire under Queen Victoria, said: "Youth is a blunder; manhood is a struggle; and old age is a regret." The turn of modern philosophy is existentialism, the philosophy that all we know is our bare existence, the consciousness of our being alive. It says that we do not know where we came from, we do not know where we are going, and there is no meaning or tomorrow in life. It is a philosophy of indescribable and infinite despair. That is the philosophy of the modern world.

Tolstoy, the incomparable Russian novelist and philosopher, in his *My Confessions and My Religion* summarized four attitudes men take toward life's problems. He classified all men into the following four categories:

1. There are those who view life as all bad and get drunk to forget it.
2. There are those who view life as all bad and struggle against it.
3. There are those who view life as all bad and by suicide remove themselves from it.
4. (Tolstoy included himself in this one) There are those who view life as all bad but we live on, irrationally accepting it as it comes.

This comes from one of the finest minds regarding the definition of the purpose and meaning of life. Man is either to get drunk and forget it, he is to struggle against life hopelessly, he is to commit suicide and get out of it, or he is to accept life irrationally as it is, as it comes, with no meaning or purpose, just enduring it until the grave swallows him up.

But There Is Also God

According to the Word of God, there is also a fifth alternative that Tolstoy did not name. It could be there is a divine reason and a divine purpose in life. There could be in life a God who had infinite reason, infinite plan, and infinite, sovereign grace for us who have found refuge in Him.

Alfred Lord Tennyson and Thomas Carlyle were looking at two busts. One was of the German poet, Goethe, and the other was of the Italian poet, Dante. Tennyson said to Carlyle, "What is it in the face of Dante that one misses in the face of Goethe?"

Immediately Carlyle responded, "God."

God makes the difference as we face life in all of its vicissitudes, fortunes, trials, and tribulations. God in the revealed Word says that in our trial and in our trouble we glorify Him.

In John 21, the Lord told Peter that he would die by crucifixion, by the outstretched hand. Then the next verse avows:

> This spake he, signifying by what death he should glorify God (v. 19).

The glory of God is found in the fire, the flame, and the trial of His people, singing songs in the night, praising Him in the midst of indescribable sorrow and heartache. There is a reason for the trials that we know in life. Maybe God is teaching us, maturing us, and preparing us for a glory that is yet to come. In Romans 5 the apostle Paul writes:

> . . . we glory in tribulations also: knowing that tribulation worketh patience;
> And patience, experience; and experience, hope:
> And hope maketh not ashamed; because the love of God is shed abroad in our hearts by the Holy Ghost which is given unto us (vv. 3b-5).

Trouble and tribulation lift a man's soul upward to God.

LEARNING THE TRUE VALUES OF LIFE

In the days of the desperate depression in which I began my ministry as a pastor, in the days when men committed suicide because they lost all they possessed, there was a rich merchant who went into bankruptcy, who lost everything he had in the world. He was lamenting: "I have lost everything. Everything is gone. I have lost everything." His pastor came to visit and to comfort him. The rich merchant, who had descended from affluence to poverty, from riches to rags, lamented his loss to the pastor.

The pastor said: "How sad, how tragic! You have lost everything. You have lost your good name and you have lost your reputation."

"Oh, no," said the man. "No, pastor, my name is unsullied and my reputation is above reproach. I have not lost my name or my reputation."

"Oh," said the pastor. "Now I understand. You have lost everything. Your wife has turned her back upon you and she treats you with disdain and contempt."

"No," said the man. "My wife is an angel standing by my side, a trooper and warrior with me. No, my wife is so faithful. I have not lost my wife."

The pastor said: "I understand. You have lost everything. You have lost your children. They have turned their backs on you and they treat you in sordid disgust."

"Oh, no," said the man. "Not my children. I never really did know my children until this disaster came. I have not lost my children."

Then said the pastor. "I see now. You have lost everything. God has turned his back on you; you have lost Jesus, you have lost your faith, and you face nothing but damnation and hell. I see now."

"No," said the man to his pastor. "I have not lost God. I have been praying to Jesus and He has never been so dear and so precious to me. I have not lost God and I have not lost heaven."

Then the pastor said: "You have lost everything? What have you lost?"

The man confessed, "Pastor, I have just lost some money."

The Book of Hebrews says:

> Whose voice then shook the earth: but now he hath promised, saying, Yet once more I shake not the earth only, but also heaven.
> And this word, Yet once more, signifieth the removing of those things that are shaken, as of things that are made, that those things which cannot be shaken may remain (12:26-27).

It may be that the trials and the losses that we experience in life exist so that we might come into the true riches to know God's eternal values, the goals that do not perish, that moth and rust cannot corrupt. There is a godly purpose in every trial and trouble that the Christian endures. God is training and preparing us for the upward life and the upward look, one of faith and glory.

The Lord says in John 16:

> In the world ye shall have tribulation; but be of good cheer; I have overcome the world (v. 33).

In Luke 12 the Lord says to His disciples:

> Fear not, little flock; for it is your Father's good pleasure to give you the kingdom (v. 32).

We shall inherit the kingdom. God hath purposed it in sovereign, elective grace for us.

There is an effective painting of blind John Milton seated in an armed, high-backed chair with the light from the window spreading over him. He is dressed in a black velvet suit, long, dark hose, and a large, white Puritan collar around his neck. To the side is a table. Beyond sits one of his daughters sewing. In the corner stands a second girl looking at her father. At the end of the table is the third daughter with a quill in her hand, writing the dictated word of her father. He had lost his eyesight contending for the cause of religious liberty for the Puritan Commonwealth under Oliver Cromwell.

But now everything was lost. Oliver Cromwell was dead. Roger Williams, who taught him the Dutch language, was in exile. His fellow Baptist, John Bunyan, was in prison in Bedford. Every institution that he despised was now restored. He fought against the tyranny of kings. Now the king had been restored. He fought against the empty shallowness of an authoritarian state church, and now the church was more authorized, more established than ever before. All of his peers had been executed, and why he was not sent to the scaffold in the four years that he was a refugee, no one can understand. All England had failed, it had fallen into sordid distress, but he had not failed.

John Milton sits there in his blindness dictating. What is he dictating? Could it be the sonnet, "On His Blindness," that closes with the last verse: "They also serve who only stand and wait"? Could it be the opening lines of the greatest epic in human literature, *Paradise Lost*?

> Of man's first disobedience, and the fruit
> Of that forbidden tree whose moral taste
> Brought death into the world, and all our woe,
> With loss of Eden, till one greater man
> Restore us, and regain the blissful seat,
> Sing, Heavenly muse . . .
> . . .
> —What in me is dark
> Illumine; what is low raise and support:
> That, to the highest of this great argument,
> I may assert Eternal Providence,
> And justify the ways of God to man.

After *Paradise Lost* Milton wrote the equally great epics, *Paradise Regained* and *Samson Agonistes* out of his own blindness. Who is the monarch who supplanted him? Who is the king who placed John

Bunyan in prison? Who is the regency who placed his peers on the scaffold? Who had been restored to kingship in England? It was Charles II, a terrible king. He hired governmental employees to scour all England to bring him an endless succession of mistresses. He never had a legitimate child but did have many illegitimate children. He brought England down in sordid promiscuity to filth and dirt. So the poet sits at the table with every cause that he loved dashed to the ground. He is blind, outcast, living in disgrace and repudiation. But he writes. He is a great Protestant—Baptist, individualist, and an idealist. He writes about the authority of an infallible Bible, the inspired Word of God. He writes treatises on scriptural baptism and on the sacredness of the Lord's Day. He writes doctrinal studies about the deity of Christ and about the Holy Spirit. Facing the sunset of life in obscurity and in repudiation, he sits there dictating in his blindness.

You be the judge. How many times have you ever read in any history where men have searched through the pages of the story of our people seeking what Charles II said or did not say? How many people have you ever known who sought to emulate the life of the degraded Charles II?

But contrariwise, how many of us have looked in faith, in encouragement, and in blessing to the life, the example, and the epic poetry of that blind Puritan who wrote of God and believed in the faith and in the ultimate triumph of the sovereign grace of the Almighty? John Milton wrote:

> That, to the highest of this great argument,
> I may assert Eternal Providence,
> And justify the ways of God to men.

God lives, God reigns, and the sovereign destiny of the world is in His almighty hands.

For the moment it may appear that atheism, secularism, and sin flood the whole world. It looked that way in the days of John Milton, but in his blindness that Puritan poet and fellow warrior saw the glory of God, gave himself to the faith, and today we reap the rich inheritance and reward of his great, godly mind and his incomparable, spiritual commitment. My brethren, we will not lose. "Do not be afraid, little flock; for it is your Father's good pleasure to give you the kingdom." It shall be ours. God has purposed the best for us. He cannot fail, He cannot lie, and He is never discouraged. It is into a like faith and a like commitment that we invite you to pilgrimage with us!

23

The All-Sufficient Savior

And certain men who came down from Judaea taught the brethren, and said, Except ye be circumcised after the manner of Moses, ye cannot be saved.

When therefore Paul and Barnabas had no small dissension and disputation with them, they determined that Paul and Barnabas, and certain other of them, should go up to Jerusalem unto the apostles and elders about this question.

And, being brought on their way by the church, they passed through Phenice, and Samaria, declaring the conversion of the Gentiles: and they caused great joy unto all the brethren.

And, when they were come to Jerusalem, they were received of the church, and of the apostles and elders, and they declared all things that God had done with them.

But there rose up certain of the sect of the Pharisees who believed, saying that it was needful to circumcise them, and to command them to keep the law of Moses.

And the apostles and elders came together for to consider the matter. (Acts 15:1-6)

We now come to chapter 15 of the Book of Acts which is a recounting of the first Jerusalem Conference. What is written in this chapter is also written privately by the apostle Paul in Galatians 2. We have before us the historical record of the conference and in Galatians we can read Paul's private, inside confrontation. First, we shall consider the background of the conference in order that its discussion may be pertinent and understood by us today.

THE BACKGROUND OF THE CONFERENCE

On their first missionary jorney, Barnabas and Saul were sent out from the Gentile church in Antioch. They made their journey to Cyprus then across to Pamphylia and then to the region of Galatia where they established the Galatian churches. It was a marvelous thing that God had done in giving the missionaries the hearts of these pagan Greeks, for they came immediately, out of their paganism into the faith of Jesus Christ, with no intermediate step in between. The Scriptures tell us what happened when Barnabas and Paul came back from that journey.

> And when they were come, and had gathered the church together, they rehearsed all that God had done with them, and how he had opened the door of faith unto the Gentiles (Acts 14:27).

That was in Antioch. When they were challenged by what they had done on their journey, they did the same thing in Jerusalem. We read in Acts 15:

> And, when they were come to Jerusalem, they were received of the church and of the apostles and elders, and they declared all things that God had done with them (v. 4).

Wonderful! Marvelous! These heathen, idol-worshiping Greeks had turned from their licentious idolatry to receive Christ as Savior. But the passage also states that Paul and Barnabas abode a long time with the disciples in Antioch after their first missionary journey, and during that time certain men came down from Judaea who said, "Except ye be circumcised after the manner of Moses, ye cannot be saved" (Acts 15:1b). Then later in the Conference, the Pharisees said the same thing. When Paul and Barnabas described the marvelous outpouring of the Spirit upon the Gentiles, certain Pharisees, the legalists who believed, said that it was needful to circumcise converts and to command them to keep the law of Moses; otherwise, they could never be saved.

When I look at these legalists, I am in a quandary as to whether we are better off with them or without them. I do not know whether it is better to have them in or out of the church, but the Pharisees, the legalists, are very much in the Jerusalem church. Their doctrine is simple and plainly stated. In clear and understandable language, they avow, "Except ye be circumcised after the manner of Moses, ye cannot be saved." What they are saying is: "A man cannot be saved by trusting Jesus alone. In order to be saved, one must trust Jesus, *and* he must do something else." In this instance, they avow that one must be circumcised and obey all of the ceremonial, ritual, and traditional laws of the Mosaic legislation. So these legalists say to all of the new converts, "If you are circumcised and keep all of the laws of Moses, then we will be happy to welcome you into the church."

CIRCUMCISION WAS AN ANCIENT, SACRED RITE OF JUDAISM

Lest we look upon these men with scornful disdain, it might be profitable for us to recall that the ancient and sacred rite of circumcision had already been in vogue among the children of God for at least two thousand years. How could one express his filial love and loyalty to the revelation of God more than to circumcise his sons in obedience to the command of God? It was God Himself who commanded circumcision. In Genesis 17 we read that God gave the ceremonial rite to Abraham, and it was to be in perpetuity through all the generations that followed this father of the faithful. The rite of circumcision was instituted by no human authority. It was instituted by the authority of God; therefore, no human authority could abolish it. The rite of circumcision held, I suppose, first place among all the rituals of the Mosaic law. To perform the rite did not violate the holy Shabat, the Sabbath Day. Circumcision was performed on the Sabbath Day in keeping with the holiness of that sacred day. No one could eat the Passover who first had not been circumcised. It was a necessary observance for a man to come into the presence of God and the family of the Lord.

In Luke 1, it was upon the circumcision of John the Baptist that his relatives wanted to name him Zecharias, for his father. The angel Gabriel had spoken to Zecharias, and because of Zecharias's unbelief that he and his aged wife would have a child, the angel said, "You will not be able to speak until this comes to pass." At the time of the circumcision of the child, Zecharias shook his head when the people wanted to name the baby after him. They brought Zecharias a piece of paper and he wrote, "His name is John." It was then that God loosed his tongue and he praised the Lord.

In Luke 2 we read the story of the circumcision of Jesus. On the eighth day after His birth, at the time of His circumcision, His parents gave Him His name, "Savior," "Joshua," "Jesus."

The Pharisees had a strong case, and the thrust and march of those legalists was fierce indeed. In Galatians 2, after his Conference in Jerusalem, the apostle Paul writes:

But when Peter was come to Antioch, I withstood him to the face, because he was to be blamed.

For before that certain came from James, he did eat with the Gentiles: but when they were come, he withdrew and separated himself, fearing them which were of the circumcision.

And the other Jews dissembled likewise with him; insomuch that Barnabas also was carried away with their dissumulation (vv. 11-13).

Peter exhibited the flaw of timidity in his character. He quailed before a little maid who accused him of being one of the disciples of the Lord Jesus when the Lord was on trial before the Sanhedrin. He swore and cursed, saying: "I never saw Him. I do not know Him." Peter is doing the same thing here over the question of circumcision. When the Pharisees came from Judaea years after this Conference was over, Peter played the hypocrite, and pulled away from the Gentiles who had not been circumcised.

The lines are distinctly drawn. We read our text:

And certain men which came down from Judaea taught the brethren, and said, Except ye be circumcised after the manner of Moses, ye cannot be saved (Acts 15:1).

Listen to the apostle Paul as he writes in Galatians 5:

Behold, I Paul say unto you, that if ye be circumcised, Christ shall profit you nothing.

Christ is become of no effect unto you, whosoever of you are justified by the law; ye are fallen from grace.

For in Christ Jesus neither circumcision availeth any thing, nor uncircumcision; but faith which worketh by love (vv. 2, 4, 6).

That is plain enough. The Judaizers, the legalists, say, "Except a man be circumcised, he cannot be saved." The apostle Paul says, "Behold, I Paul say unto you, that if ye be circumcised, Christ shall profit you nothing."

So they came together to consider the matter, and that constituted the first Jerusalem Conference. More lies in the offing and in the balance than we realize; namely, how can a man by saved? How does one face God some day and live?

The Speakers at the Conference

Now we are gong to consider the speakers at this Jerusalem Conference, and they were God's greatest apostles. The question was how to answer the legalist. They were learned men; they knew Talmudic tradition from the days of their childhood. They were gifted in all manners of forensic discussion. They were brilliant. You just have to look at the Talmud to find that it is the most impressive group of books imaginable. Every syllable of it was written down one hundred years *after* Christ. All of that vast amount of academia was in the writers' minds by memory. So how would you answer these Pharisees, Talmudic scholars, who, all of their lives, had given themselves to the learning of the law?

They were answered by Paul. In Philippians 3 he calls himself "a Pharisee of the Pharisees." I am beginning to understand what God meant when He said to Ananias, "Go, put your hands upon him, for he is a chosen vessel unto me to bear my name." God always has His man. He who found water in the rock, He who found honey in the desert, knows how to find His man in a great confrontation.

Do you remember the story of the people of the Lord when they were oppressed in the land of Egypt? God's man, Moses, was on the back side of the desert, but God sent him to deliver his people.

In the days of Saul, king of Israel, Goliath, the uncircumcised, blaspheming Philistine, stood on the other side of the vale of Elah and cursed God's people and challenged them to combat. But God had His boy, a stripling, fresh from the sheepcoat, a little unshaven fellow whose name was David.

In the days of Jezebel, she took advantage of that weak and spineless king, Ahab, and brought apostasy into Israel with all of the priests of Baal. God had His man, Elijah, the sole champion of the Almighty.

When these Pharisees stood up, God placed before them Paul who was learned in all Talmudic scholarship and understanding. He did something that was most effective. In Galatians 2 we read:

> And I . . . communicated unto them that gospel which I preach among the Gentiles, but privately to them which were of reputation, lest by any means I should run, or had run, in vain.
> But neither Titus, who was with me, being a Greek, was compelled to be circumcised (vv. 2-3).

To me it was a stroke of genius when the apostle Paul, sent by God to go to Jerusalem, took Titus with him to the Conference. Titus appears many times in the scriptural record. He must have been a tremendous servant of the Lord and a preacher of the gospel. Timothy was timid. Titus was bold and fearless. Titus was the kind of a person who, no matter what the problem was, in no time at all had the problem solved. He was bold and courageous in the faith. When Paul went up to the Conference in Jerusalem, he took Titus with him to be Exhibit A. When Paul said that a man could be saved just by trusting Jesus, by simply coming out of his idolatry, heathenism, and paganism, he pointed to Titus and said: "There he stands, Exhibit A, of what God can do with a man who just trusts his heart and life to Jesus Christ. Look at him!" That is the power of the Christian message. It is not in words, in syllables, in sound, in furor; it is in the consecrated, regenerated lives of those who have been saved by the grace of the Son of God.

A minister was challenged by an infidel to a debate. The preacher said: "Fine, I will be happy to debate, but this shall be the procedure. I will bring one hundred men who have been marvelously regenerated and saved out of the lives of sin and depravity, saved by the grace of the Gospel of the Son of God. You bring one hundred men who have been saved by the gospel of infidelity. Then we will have our debate." The debate never took place. Where could anyone find one hundred men who had been saved by infidelity? In fact, where could anyone find in all of the literature of the music world one song extolling infidelity? Many years ago when I was a boy, I read that there were 400,000 hymns dedicated to Jesus. Since that time I suppose that men have written 400,000 more.

Paul went up to the Conference and brought with him Titus, a Greek who stood as a monument and trophy to the grace of God. Then the apostle delivered his message of salvation, salvation in Christ alone.

THE MIGHTY GOSPEL

Paul spoke to the conference saying that he knew a man was not justified by the works of the law, but by the faith of Jesus Christ. We follow the story in Galatians 3:

> Wherefore the law was our [*paidagogos*] schoolmaster to bring us unto Christ, that we might be justified by faith.
> But, after that faith is come, we are no longer under a schoolmaster.
> For ye are all the children of God by faith in Christ Jesus.
> For as many of you as have been baptized into Christ have put on Christ.
> There is neither Jew nor Greek, there is neither bond nor free, there is neither male nor female: for ye are all one in Christ Jesus.
> And if ye be Christ's, then are ye Abraham's seed, and heirs according to the promise (vv. 24-29).

We are children of God by faith in Christ. And in Him there is neither Jew nor Gentile, for we are all alike in His sight.

All of the rites, rituals, and ceremonies of the Old Testament were types prefiguring the great spiritual reality that we find in Christ Jesus. Even the rite and ceremony of circumcision was a type. It has a typical spiritual significance. When the realization comes of what the rite typified and symbolized, then the rite is automatically abolished. All rites and ceremonies are abolished when the spiritual reality that they typified comes to pass. It is not needed any longer.

For example, noon abolishes the dawn. Summertime abolishes spring. Manhood abolishes infancy. A growing oak abolishes the acorn. The Lord's return will abolish the Lord's Supper.

So it is with all the rites and ceremonies of legalism, of the Mosaic legislation. Now that we are in the presence of the Lord, we do not need the type any longer. We have the Lord Himself.

Then Peter spoke at the Conference and had a word that described the legalism of Pharisaism and Judaism. Peter said, "Why do you tempt God to place on them a yoke that neither we nor they could bear?" All of the rites were yokes which were burdensome to bear. They denied the fullness of the freedom that God intended for His children.

The next person to speak at the Conference was James, the Lord's brother, who was the pastor of the church in Jerusalem. He quoted Amos 9:10-12. He spoke of the Gentiles who came to the Lord, the heathen who were prophesied to come to Jehovah God. But the prophecy did not mention that they would come by circumcision or by the rites and ceremonies of legalistic legislation. They came by faith to the blessed God. Then James delivered the sentence that closed the conference, "So we shall not interfere or disturb what God has done. We shall but rejoice in heaven's favor upon those who have found refuge, strength, regeneration, and salvation in the Lord Jesus."

That is the way it is to this day, except that the legalists and the Pharisees are forever with us. They never seem to die out.

ONE MIGHT THINK THAT THIS IS OUT OF DATE

When we read of the Jerusalem Conference, our first reaction might be that this is something that happened almost 2,000 years ago and has no pertinency for us today. Actually, this is one of the most pertinent issues that we face in our generation. What must I do to be saved? The legalist stands up and says: "This you must do to be saved. You must trust in the Lord Jesus Christ, *and* do good works, or you cannot be saved. You must trust in the Lord Jesus Christ, *and* you must belong to the mother church, because mother church is the one that takes you to heaven." Modern legalism states that you must believe in the Lord Jesus Christ, *and* keep the Sabbath Day. If you do not keep the Sabbath Day, you will be damned and lost. It is the mark of the beast to not observe the Sabbath Day. Modern legalism states that we must believe in the Lord Jesus Christ, *and* be baptized. If we have already been baptized, modern legalism will say that we must be baptized again by them. Pharisaism today continues to try to add something to the gospel of the grace of the Lord Jesus Christ. It is as true today as it was in the day of the apostle Paul. We defeat and deny the power and efficacy of the cross any time we seek to add something to it by man's hand. If something must be added, then the death of Christ is in vain. The gospel of Paul is this: a man is saved by faith in the Lord Jesus Christ, receiving Him into his heart, into his soul, and into his life.

> Could my tears forever flow,
> Could my zeal no languor know.
> These for sin could not atone;
> Thou must save, and Thou alone.
> In my hand no price I bring,
> Simply to Thy cross I cling.

We are saved by trusting Jesus and Him alone. He washed my sins away. He sent the Holy Spirit of regeneration into my heart. He wrote my name in the Book of Life. He has promised to keep me forever and to present me some day in the presence of the Father. Thereafter, what I do is just out of love and praise to the blessed Lord who saved me. I do not go to church because I would be damned if I did not. I go to church because I love Jesus. I do not do good works in order to be saved. God says that my good works are as filthy rags in His sight. I am trying to do good, to magnify the wonderful name of the Savior. I want to obey Him in baptism, to partake of the breaking of bread and the sharing of the cup and to love the brethren. Then the whole life thereafter flows in one paeon of praise, in one glory of worship in gratitude to the blessed Jesus.

When we get to heaven we are going to sing a song that is presented in the Book of Revelation. The song says, "Worthy is the Lamb that was slain, to receive power, and riches, and wisdom, and strength, and honour, and glory, and blessing, for he hath redeemed us out of every tribe, family, nation, and race under the sun, and hath made us kings and priests unto God."

That is the gospel. There will be no praise to us in heaven. All of the praise is going to be to Jesus. He died for us. He poured out His blood for our sins, and He promised to keep us if we would trust Him. Then the rest of our life flows in praise and love to the blessed Redeemer!

24

James, The Lord's Brother

And after they had held their peace, James answered, saying, Men and brethren, hearken unto me:

Simeon hath declared how God at the first did visit the Gentiles, to take out of them a people for his name.

And to this agree the words of the prophets; as it is written,

After this I will return, and will build again the tabernacle of David, which is fallen down; and I will build again the ruins thereof, and I will set it up:

That the residue of men might seek after the Lord, and all the Gentiles upon whom my name is called, saith the Lord, who doeth all these things.

Known unto God are all his works from the beginning of the world.

Wherefore my sentence is, that we trouble not them, which from among the Gentiles are turned to God:

But that we write unto them, that they abstain from pollutions of idols, and from fornication, and from things strangled, and from blood.

For Moses of old time hath in every city them that preach him, being read in the synagogues every sabbath day. (Acts 15:13-21)

The Jerusalem Conference was called to consider the question of whether a man could be saved just by trusting Jesus, or whether, as all the Judaizers avowed, he could be saved only by trusting Jesus, *and* by keeping all the ceremonial, ritualistic legislation of Moses.

Today we are going to look at something which is most significant in the passage; if we were not careful, we might miss it. Beginning at Acts 15:12, the Scripture says:

Then all the multitude kept silence, and gave audience to Barnabas and Paul, declaring what miracles and wonders God had wrought among the Gentiles by them.

And after they had held their peace, James answered, saying, Men and brethren, hearken unto me (vv. 12-13).

Then James spoke of how God revealed His will to Peter concerning Cornelius and the Gentile household in Caesarea. He quoted from the prophet confirming the opening of the door to the Gentiles and said,

Wherefore my sentence is, that we trouble not them, which from among the Gentiles are turned to God (Acts 15:19).

When we read that passage, we sense something about this man. James waited until all the debate and forensic discussion is complete, and then he avowed, "Wherefore my sentence is." James stood as the preeminent figure in all the Christian world in the first century. It is not Paul, not Barnabas, not John, not Simon Peter, but James.

JAMES IS A COMMON NAME IN THE NEW TESTAMENT

The name "James" is one of the most common names in the Jewish household. The name in Hebrew is *Jacob*, and becomes "James" in English. There are three "Jameses" of note in the New Testament. One is James, the son of Zebedee, the brother of John, one of the apostles. He was beheaded by Herod Agrippa I and was the first apostle to lay down his life for the Lord. Because he was cut down at the beginning of his apostolic ministry we can't imagine what he might have been and done.

The second James we know only as the apostle called "James the Less" or "James the Little."

The third James in the New Testament is the one in our text. He is one of the most striking and impressive of all of the figures in the first Christian century.

THE VAST PROMINENCE OF JAMES

Taking our cue from Acts 15, we see that it is James who presides over the conference in Jerusalem and who gives a final judgment like a presiding Chief Justice of the Supreme Court of the United States. The apostle Paul describes the same conference discussed in Acts 15, in Galatians 2. Paul says that he went to Jerusalem in order to present for the discussion of the matter concerning how a man could be saved. He says:

And when James, Cephas [Simon Peter], and John, . . . perceived the grace that was given unto me, they gave to me and Barnabas the right hands of fellowship (Gal. 2:9).

Do you see something there? All my life I thought of Peter and John being named first among the disciples, but Paul names James first. You will find this James as the leader of the entire Christian world and especially as pastor of the mother church in Jerusalem.

For example, when Peter was delivered by an angel out of prison from the hand of Herod Agrippa I, he came to the little band praying for him, and said, "Go tell James and the brethren what God has done with me." In Galatians 1, when Paul came back from Arabia, he says he went up to Jerusalem and visited James. In Acts 33 when the disciples gathered the offering from the churches of Achaia, Macedonia, and Galatia, Paul went up to Jerusalem and presented the offering to James. He listened to James tell him how to allay the bitter antipathy of the Jewish people toward him. When Jude wrote his letter, he introduced himself as "the brother of James." James is the great, towering giant of the first Christian century.

James Is Important in Literature Outside the New Testament

You can find the importance of James in apocryphal literature; that is, all of the vast literature that is not inspired but is a part of Christian life and tradition. For example, there is an apocryphal book entitled *The Apocalypse of James*. In addition, there is a book called *The Ascents of James*; that is, what James spoke on each one of the steps as he entered into the temple.

Hegesippus is the first Christian historian. He was born about A.D. 100 before all the apostles had died. Hegesippus wrote a long passage about the martyrdom of James, pastor of the church in Jerusalem. He said that James was holy from his mother's womb. He was a Nazarite, who did not cut his hair or drink strong drink. He was a vegetarian; he did not eat meat. He gave his whole life to prayer and the worship of God. Hegesippus states that James' knees were dry and hard like camels' knees from bowing on the pavement in the temple of God, praying for the people. He also says that James was so holy and devout that he was called "The Just."

As the days passed, appeal was made to James that he stand on the gable of the temple and speak to the great throngs below at Passover season, against the vast numbers who were turning in faith to the Lord

Jesus. (I wish to point out that evidently the holiness and the ceremonial, Mosaic rectitude of this man so impressed the Jewish nation that they were inclined to forget that he was a pastor of a Christian church.) Instead, James glorified the Master, the Messiah, the Christ of God. When he did so, it infuriated the scribes, the elders, and the priests, and they cast him down. Not being slain by the fall, he was stoned, and then Hegesippus said a fuller; that is, a tailor who beats cloth with a club; clubbed James to death. He added, "And straightway Vespasian laid seige to them." As you know, Vespasian and his son Titus destroyed the nation, destroyed the city, and destroyed the holy temple. Hegesippus says that the reason for the judgment of God falling thus upon the nation until it was destroyed was because of their clubbing and stoning to death of James.

When we look at the continuing story in Christian literature beyond the New Testament, it follows the same astonishing pattern. Clement of Alexandria, one of the great scholars of all time, born in about A.D. 150, follows that same story concerning the asceticism, the Nazarite vow, the holiness, and the martyrdom of Jesus. Eusebius, the greatest Christian historian who ever lived, born in Caesarea in A.D. 275, the man who wrote the Nicene Creed, recounts all of this in his ecclesiastical history. To my surprise, at least when I was first introduced to it, the only Christian leaders about whom Josephus writes is James. His story is a little different. Josephus said that when Festus the Roman procurator died (the one before whom Paul made his final appeal), between the time of the death of that Roman procurator and the coming of the following governor, that Ananias the high priest called the Sanhedrin together and condemned James and stoned him to death, for which the Roman government deposed him in shame and ignominy.

All of this is to bring to our minds the fact that James, who was the pastor of the church of Jerusalem, was the towering personality over all the Christians of the first century.

THE FAMILY OF JAMES

James was the leader of the family of our Lord who lived in Nazareth, but he was not a believer. Lest we condemn James too harshly, I just wonder about myself, and how I would have responded had I been brought up with Jesus in the same household and family? I could understand how I could love the Lord, but worship Him? Believe Him to be the Son of God and the Messiah promised by the Old Testament prophets? I do not know. Mark 3 records:

> And when his friends heard of it, they went out to lay hold of him: for they said, He is beside himself (v. 21).

Notice that the translation of the King James version is, "He is beside himself," that is, he is mad. Who are these people who seek to lay hold on the Lord and who say that He is beside Himself and has lost His mind? In the same chapter a few verses down, we read:

> There came then his brethren and his mother, and, standing without, sent unto him, calling him.
> And the multitude sat about him, and they said unto him, Behold, thy mother and thy brethren, without seek for thee.
> And he answered them, saying, Who is my mother, or my brethren?
> And he looked round about on them which sat about him, and said, Behold my mother and my brethren!
> For whosoever shall do the will of God, the same is my brother, and my sister, and mother (vv. 31-35).

As though that were not enough, listen to the passage in Mark 6:

> And when the sabbath day was come, he began to teach in the synagogue: and many hearing him were astonished, saying, From whence hath this man these things? and what wisdom is this which is given unto him, that even such mighty works are wrought by his hands?
> Is not this the carpenter, the son of Mary, the brother of James, and Joses, and of Juda, and Simon? and are not his sisters here with us? And they were offended at him.
> But Jesus said unto them, A prophet is not without honour, but in his own country, and among his own kin, and in his own house (vv. 2-4).

It is evident that there was a deep repudiation of the Lord Jesus by James, and he led his family after him. A confirmation of that is found in John 7 where we find a dialogue between James, the brethren of the Lord, and the Lord Jesus concerning His appearance in Jerusalem at the Feast of the Tabernacles. We follow the passage:

> Now the Jews' feast of tabernacles was at hand.
> His brethren therefore said unto him, Depart hence, and go into Judaea, that thy disciples also may see the works that thou doest.
> For there is no man that doeth any thing in secret, and he himself seeketh to be known openly. If thou do these things, shew thyself to the world.
> For neither did his brethren believe in him (vv. 2-5).

James and his brothers did not believe in the Lord. One sees another confirmation of that when Jesus was dying on the cross. His mother was standing near the cross. Would you not have thought Jesus would have said to James, "James, take good care of her"? James was her son. James was the Lord's brother. Instead, the Lord turned to John and said, "John, look after your mother," and "Mother, look to your son." John adds, "From that day on, he took her to his own house."

The Conversion of James

If this were all, I doubt if I would have mentioned it. This was just one of the sorrowful events our Lord endured over which He wept and cried. But there are more.

There is a truth that God has revealed to us. After the Lord was raised from the dead, the apostle Paul names in 1 Corinthians 15 the three great leaders of the Christian faith to whom the Lord intimately and personally appeared. Paul tells us that first the Lord appeared to Peter. Second, He appeared to James, the Lord's brother. Third, He "was seen of me as one born out of due time." So the Lord, raised from the dead, appeared to those three men, and all three of them have something in common. Peter, denying and cursing, exclaimed, "I never saw Him; I do not know Him."

Jesus later appeared to Peter and asked him, "Lovest thou me?"

Peter replied, "Lord, Lord, You know I do."

The Lord replied, "Then shepherd my flock; feed my sheep."

The second person the Lord named was James, His own brother.

The third one was Paul, breathing out threatening and slaughter against the disciples of the Lord with letters to various cities to bring them bound to Jerusalem. All three of these men had repudiated the Lord. They had that one thing in common.

In that personal confrontation and revelation, the *apokalupsis*, the self-revelation of our Lord, He won James to the faith. James won his brethren to the faith. The Book of Acts begins with a prayer meeting, and Dr. Luke is careful to note that in the group is James and the brethren of the Lord, all of them in the kingdom, all of them in the church.

Let me point out the humility of James. Though he was the brother of Jesus, in his epistle he describes himself as *"Iakobos, Iesou Christou Deoulos,"* "James, a slave of the Lord Jesus Christ."

The Great Prophecy of Jewish Conversion

The conversion of James and of Paul is a great prophetic type. I know this is my interpretation, but it is one that I profoundly believe. The apostle Paul says that Jesus appeared to Cephas, then appeared to James, "then last of all, he appeared to me *ektroma*," translated, "as of one born out of due time." The meaning of the word *ektroma* is "abortion." That is, the child is born before the day it was supposed to be born. "He appeared to me in an abortion, before the day." What does he mean when he says "as of one born out of due time, before the time, in an abortion, before I should have been"?

This is what I think that means. In the great prophecy of Zechariah 12-14, the prophet says that the Lord Jesus will personally appear to His brethren, to His nation. He says that they will look on Him whom they pierced, and they shall say, "Whence these scars, these nail prints in your hands and in your feet?" The Lord will say, "These are the scars I received in My own house among My own people from My own brethren." Then the prophet says, "There shall be a great morning in Israel, like that at Hadadrimmon when they mourned over good king Josiah." In that day there will be a fountain opened for cleansing, and the nation will be cleansed, will be saved, and will accept their Lord who shall be King over the whole earth.

Before the time the Lord appears to His own people, before the time they are converted and saved by a personal appearance of the blessed, risen Lord, He appeared to Paul as in an abortion. This same ultimate experience and prophecy are seen in the conversion of James and the family of the Lord.

THE CONVERSION OF JAMES AND PROPHECY

Let me project the conversion of James in prophecy concerning the end time. I do not know of a race of people to whom we owe a greater debt than to Israel. Abraham, Isaac, Jacob, the patriarchs, the Bible, the Son of God are all gifts to us from the Jewish people. Why are we not white savages? Because of the preaching of the gospel of the grace of the Son of God brought to us by Christian missionaries. The hope we have for heaven lies in what Israel has done for us, having given us our Bible, having given us the great monotheistic revelation of God. Shall I rejoice in their damnation? Shall I be glad that at the consummation of the age they are shut out forever? No. As I am glad that before He returned to glory he appeared personally to James and won him to the faith, so I am glad knowing that when He comes again, He will appear to His brethren, and in a great confession and mourning, they will turn in faith to the Lord. In the millennium all Israel and the Gentiles will believe in Jesus and all of us in one voice will sing together, "Worthy is the Lamb that was slain, to receive power, and riches, and honor, and glory."

Oh, the infinite mercy, compassion, and grace of our blessed Jesus!

25

The Compassionate Sovereignty of God

And after they had held their peace, James answered, saying, Men and brethren, hearken unto me:

Simeon hath declared how God at first did visit the Gentiles, to take out of them a people for his name.

And to this agree the words of the prophets; as it is written,

After this I will return, and will build again the tabernacle of David, which is fallen down; and I will build again the ruins thereof, and I will set it up:

That the residue of men might seek after the Lord, and all the Gentiles upon whom my name is called, saith the Lord who doeth all these things.

Known unto God are all his works from the beginning of the world.

Wherefore my sentence is, that we trouble not them, which from among the Gentiles are turned to God. (Acts 15:13-19)

In our text, James is giving a final answer to the problem that was brought to the elders and leaders of the mother church in Jerusalem. Up until Acts 10, the message of the Lord had been directed toward a Jew or a Jewish proselyte. It had never occurred to any of the Jewish people who comprised the church in Jerusalem that the gospel message would ever be delivered to anyone who was not a Jew, either by birth or as a proselyte. In Acts 11 we read about Hellenists from Jerusalem who had been hounded out of the city in the persecution that arose around Stephen. They came to Antioch and preached the gospel of the grace of the Son of God to Greek idolaters, to heathen. To the amazement of the Christian community, those Greek idolaters turned to the Lord. They were wonderfully saved.

As though that were not enough, God's Holy Spirit called Barnabas and Saul to go on a missionary tour. They went to the central part of Asia Minor, what is called in the Book of Galatians, "the churches of Galatia," and there they preached the gospel again to heathen idolaters. They, likewise, accepted the Lord as their Savior and were wonderfully saved.

The problem that arose in Jerusalem was what to do with the former heathen who confessed their faith in the Lord Jesus and had been saved. The Judaizers said: "These men cannot be saved just by trusting the Lord. They must be circumcised and must be taught to keep all the Mosaic legislation. If they are not circumcised and if they are not taught to keep the law of Moses, then they cannot be saved."

Silas, Paul, Barnabas, and the Hellenists with them said: "Not so. A man is not saved by trusting Jesus *and* anything one can name. He is saved only by trusting the Lord. He is saved by faith." So the question as to how a man was to be saved was brought to the council in Jerusalem.

After much disputation, James, the pastor of the church in Jerusalem, and the towering personality of that first Christian century, gave a final verdict. This is what he said:

> James answered, saying, Men and brethren, hearken unto me: Simeon hath declared how God at the first [referring to the pouring out of the Spirit of the Lord at Caesarea] did visit the Gentiles, to take out of them a people for his name (Acts 15:13b-14).

Let us take a look at what James avowed. He said it was something that God had done. It was not by decision on the part of man. Look how the Lord did it.

In the English sentence the meaning is not clearly revealed, but the word for "gentiles" and the word for "a people" in Greek are *ethnon laon*. In the English sentence they are separated, "God did visit the *Gentiles* to take out of them *a people* for his name." But in the Greek sentence, James placed them side by side *ethnon laon*; he placed them in vivid and emphatic contrast, these idolatrous heathen and people of the Lord. This is because of the Judaizers who were saying that the idolaters could not be saved just by trusting the Lord Jesus. They had to be Jews before they could be saved. They had to be Jews first and then they could accept the Lord as Savior. The Judaizers avowed: "We are *the* people; we are God's people. We are the chosen people. We are the accepted of God."

Then the inevitable corollary is that everyone else is a heathen, is a Gentile. They belong to the nations.

But James avowed that God had taken out of the heathen *a* people and they are as much *a* people of God as Israel ever was. This marvelous grace and compassionate sovereignty of the Lord, this called-out people, is the *ekklesia*, the church of the living God.

THIS IS SOMETHING THAT GOD HAS DONE

James says this is something God has done. Notice when you read Acts 15 how many times it says that God has opened the door of salvation to the Gentiles.

In verse 8 we read, "And God, which knoweth the hearts, bare them witness, giving them the Holy Ghost, even as he did unto us."

Verse 9 tells us it is God who puts no difference between us and them, between the Jew and the Gentile.

Verse 14 says it is God who at the first visited the Gentiles, and it is God who had chosen to take out of them a people.

Verse 18 says, "Known unto God are all his works from the beginning of the world."

Then James bolsters that decision with an avowal of what Simeon had declared. Simeon declared to the conference that God made choice among them, and that he was chosen of the Lord to open the door to the Gentiles, to the heathen of the world. (This is recorded in Acts 10 at Caesarea.) The Holy Spirit of God fell upon Cornelius, the Roman centurion, and upon all his household, the soldiers and the servants in the praetorium. The Holy Spirit of God was poured out on them just as He was poured out on the Jew in Jerusalem at Pentecost. God in His mercy and compassionate sovereignty has included them. They also are a people chosen, delighted in, accepted, saved, and loved by the Lord.

James had one other avowal. He said, "To this agree all of the prophets." He used the word "prophets," plural, and he quoted just one, Amos 9:11-12. I think James could have quoted Scripture for the entire time of the conference. He could have quoted Isaiah 2:

And it shall come to pass in the last days, that the mountain of the LORD'S house shall be established in the top of the mountains, and shall be exalted above the hills; and all nations shall flow unto it.

And many people shall go and say, Come ye, and let us go up to the mountain of the LORD, to the house of the God of Jacob; and he will teach us of his ways, and we will walk in his paths: for out of Zion shall go forth the law, and the word of the LORD from Jerusalem (vv. 2-3).

He could have quoted from the glorious Isaiah 11:

They shall not hurt nor destroy in all my holy mountain: for the earth shall be full of the knowledge of the LORD, as the waters cover the sea.

And in that day there shall be a root of Jesse, which shall stand for an ensign of the people; to it shall the Gentiles seek: and his rest shall be glorious (vv. 9-10).

He also could have quoted from Isaiah 66:

And it shall come to pass, that from one new moon to another, and from one sabbath to another, shall all flesh come to worship before me, saith the LORD (v. 23).

It was never the intention that the grace and the mercy of God should be in that small area known only to the Jew, but it was the purpose of God that the whole earth know the Lord, be a people saved by His grace and mercy. This is the sovereign, compassionate goodness of the Lord God. That is what the Jerusalem conference was all about, and that is the benedictory decision that was finally made. The Book of Acts says in the fifteenth chapter that when the people heard it, they were glad and rejoiced in the goodness and grace of the Lord.

NOW THE CHURCHES REJOICE

We still rejoice today that the goodness and the sovereign, compassionate mercies of the Lord have come even unto us, for we are Gentiles. We do not belong to the family of Abraham. We are not of the seed of Isaac and Jacob. We are the *ethnon*; we are the Gentiles; we are the nations. To us the compassionate mercy of God has been extended by the Holy Spirit whom He sent abroad in our hearts and in this world.

Left to itself, the human race is abjectly, abysmally, and tragically lost. The tendency of the human heart is to lower itself, to go downward. I see that in every area of life. When people start telling jokes, it is not long before they descend into an off-colored story. In a movie it is not long until the picutres that are shown on the screen are promiscuous, immoral, and x-rated. There is a drive of damnation in sin that seizes every nation, every family, and every heart. God says, "The heart is desperately wicked; who can know it?" Even the imaginations of the soul are vile. When we consider the lostness of the nations and peoples of the world, there are two things about the sovereign, compassionate grace of God that we must remember.

GOD ALWAYS INTERVENES

First, God always intervenes. There is no time in the sordid and sinful story of humanity in which God does not intervene. In His compassionate mercy, looking upon the lost of the human race, God does something. His heart is moved. He is like us. When He sees us so pitifully undone in sin, He intervenes. He always does.

When our first parents fell, He covered their shame with a sacrifice, shed the blood of an innocent animal, and clothed their nakedness with the skins thereof. God did it.

In the days of the Antediluvians when the earth was filled with blood and violence, God intervened, saved Noah and his family, and taught him how to build the ark to the saving of his house.

In the day of universal idolatry, God called out Abraham.

In a time when the people of the Lord were to be crushed by the iron hand of Pharaoh, God intervened and raised up Moses to "deliver my people."

In the days of universal apostasy, God raised up Elijah.

It is the story through all of the centuries. God is moved by the lostness of the human race, our sadness in sin, and He always intervenes.

GOD IS ALWAYS INCLUSIVE

In that intervention, God is always inclusive in His love, in His attitude, and in His mercy. In the Bible we have the story of the coming of the Messiah through a family, the children of Israel. But we are sometimes persuaded that because the story of the Bible is confined to the Israelites, to the children of Abraham, God therein has excluded out of His mind, His love, and His grace all the other families of the earth. Nothing could be further from the truth. Let me illustrate.

Not only does God intervene in the lostness of the human family and the human race, but He also is all-inclusive in the outpouring of His love and grace.

The Bible calls Rahab a harlot. She was an innkeeper. Her name in Hebrew means "broad." Vulgar people will refer to a woman as "a broad." What about Rahab? She was one of the progenitors of our Lord Messiah. She was the great-great-grandmother of David, God's king. She was in the genealogy of our blessed Lord. In Matthew 1, the goodness, grace, and sovereign mercy of God are extended to Rahab. How amazing that out of the darkness of her life, she also is included in the family of God.

Ruth was a Moabitess; she was not of the seed of Israel. I challenge you in all human literature—Greek, Roman, English, French literature—to find a more beautiful, pastoral story than can be found in the story of Ruth. She was the grandmother of David and a progenitor of the Lord Jesus Christ even though she was a Moabitess and not a Jew.

As though that were not enough, the Assyrian was to the Jew a veritable ogre. Five times in the life of Isaiah alone, the bitter, ruthless, and merciless Assyrians invaded Judah. It was the Assyrians who destroyed the northern kingdom, destroyed Samaria, and took into captivity the northern ten tribes. The hatred and the bitterness of the Jew toward Assyria is impossible for us to describe.

One day the Lord God said to Jonah, "Arise, and preach the gospel of redemption to Assyria, to Nineveh."

Jonah replied, "I will not do it." He bought a ticket on a ship and fled in the other direction.

I can understand Jonah. Preach the gospel of grace to that ruthless and merciless Assyria? Never. So God prepared a big fish and put Jonah in it. When finally Jonah got right with the Lord, he came to Nineveh and preached: "Yet forty days and God is going to damn Nineveh in hell, and He is going to destroy this city." Jonah liked that. If he was to preach to the Ninevites, then he was going to preach hell and damnation to them. Let God damn them and judge them forever.

You remember what happened. From the king down to the most menial servant, the people of Nineveh repented and sat in sackcloth and ashes. They even took sackcloth and covered their beasts of burden, and they cried to the Lord and asked Him to forgive their sins. God looked down from heaven and heard their plea. We read in Jonah 3 the conclusion of the story:

> And God saw their works, that they turned from their evil way; and God repented of the evil, that he had said that he would do unto them; and he did it not (v. 10).

What an amazing thing! God changed His heart. He changed His mind. When Nineveh repented, God repented. When Nineveh changed, God changed.

You see, the character of God does not change. God is unchanging in the sense that His heart does not change. His love and His mercy never change. He is the same forever. But when a man changes, God changes. A man is going down a road that leads straight to damnation and hell, and if that man will turn around and change, God will bless his life with everlasting grace and goodness. That is what happened in Nineveh. When the Ninevites changed the Lord saw it and in mercy forgave them.

This made Jonah angry and he sat under a vine on a hillside and pouted: "Lord, isn't that the reason why I didn't want to go to Nineveh? I knew you were a God of mercy and that you would forgive. And now you have forgiven them and they are all saved and are going to heaven."

The Lord asked: "Jonah, Jonah, why are you not happy? Why are you not glad that they changed? Why are you not rejoicing in your spirit that these heathen have gotten right with Me? There are 120,000 children in the city of Nineveh that do not even know their right hand from their left, and you sit up here on the side of the hill and pout because My damnation, My fire, and My brimstone have not fallen upon them."

I have said all of my life, and I believe it more with every passing day, that a man ought to preach the whole counsel of God. He ought to preach about judgment. He ought to preach about damnation. He ought to preach about hell. He ought to preach about the great assize when men stand before God. He ought to warn men of the terror of falling into eternal perdition. But when a man preaches about hell, he ought not to do it as though he were glad people were going there or he was rejoicing in the damnation of the lost. When a man preaches about hell, he ought to spend five times the time he ordinarily would on his knees, and when he preaches about damnation and hell he ought to do it with a broken heart. We do not rejoice that people are damned. We do not rejoice that people are lost. We do not rejoice that people are on their way to perdition. Jesus died to save the lost and He has sent us as witnesses in the world to point the way of life everlasting. That is the Spirit of God. The Spirit of the Lord is always one of inclusiveness. It includes you and it includes the whole world. Some people are yellow. Jesus died for them. Some people are black. Jesus died for them. Some people are red. Jesus died for them. Some people are white, and Jesus died for them. But the sovereign compassion of God is poured out upon all men everywhere.

To belong to a kingdom like that and to preach a gospel like that is the most precious and enriching of all the revelations to be found in God's Book. There are no excluded people now in the presence of the Lord but all of us are sinners alike and all of us can be saved alike. All of us are dear in the presence of the Lord Jesus who died to save us. That is the Gospel that was affirmed in the first Jerusalem council. That is the Gospel delivered to the churches of Judaea, Galatia, Macedonia, and Achaia. That is the Gospel that is delivered to us today. All men everywhere are invited to come to take the water of life freely, to eat the manna from heaven, to be fellow-heirs in the kingdom of our Savior. That is why we are Christians today.

There were missionaries in generations past who preached the gospel to the white savages in Ireland, Scotland, and in England. There were pioneer preachers who crossed the Alleghenies and preached the gospel to my people who were in West Texas. In one of those revival meetings, my father, who was a cowpoke in West Texas, twenty-seven years of age, was converted. I can remember as a little child the messages of those pioneer preachers. They were uneducated, but they were strong in the faith and in the Word of God. They were preeminently evangelistic, calling men to repentance and faith in the blessed Jesus. In one of those services I was saved.

There is an all-inclusiveness about the love of God that is immeasurable and is extended even to men who are low and vile. The Lord Jesus died for them and the whole world is in His grace. His sovereign, compassionate love includes even us.

Bless His name! God be praised that His love reached even to me!

26

The Holy Spirit As One of Us

For it seemed good to the Holy Ghost, and to us . . . (Acts 15:28)

A verse that has always stayed in my heart is Acts 15:28: "For it seemed good to the Holy Spirit, and to us. . . ." What an amazing text! The Holy Spirit and man are together—thinking, deliberating, and deciding. One is God the Holy Spirit. The other is a man made out of dust. Yet, there is comradeship and communion between them. Could this be? Could it be that the Holy Spirit is actually and really God?

THE DEITY OF THE HOLY SPIRIT

1. There is no question but that the Bible presents the deity of the Holy Spirit. The great baptismal formula found in Matthew 28:19 says, "baptizing them in the name of the Father, and of the Son, and of the Holy Spirit. . . ." "The name" is singular, not plural. The full name of Deity is Father, Son, and Holy Spirit. In Christian experience, expressed in baptism, we know God as triune, Father, Son, and Holy Spirit. God the Father thought our salvation. The Son of God brought our salvation. The Holy Spirit wrought our salvation. God the Father so loved us that He sent His Son for us. Christ so loved us that He suffered and died and was buried for us. The Holy Spirit so loved us that He raised up Christ from the dead to ascend into heaven where the Lord intercedes for us. The same Holy Spirit shall also raise us up. We know God as triune in Christian experience.

2. The presentation of the one true God in the Bible is triune, three

203

in one. An example is the beautiful benedictory sentence of 2 Corinthians 13:14, "The grace of the Lord Jesus Christ, and the love of God, and the communion of the Holy Spirit, be with you all. Amen." There are always three.

3. Whatever can be said of God can be said of the Holy Spirit.

    (1) He is eternal. Hebrews 9:14 says, ". . . Christ, who through the eternal Spirit offered himself without spot to God. . . ."

    (2) He is omnipotent. Genesis 1:2 says, "And the Spirit of God moved upon the face of the waters."

    (3) He is omniscient. He knows all that the Father knows. First Corinthians 2:10-11 states, "For the Spirit searcheth all things, yea, the deep things of God . . . even so the things of God knoweth no man, but the Spirit of God."

    (4) He is omnipresent. He is everywhere; all of Him is present everywhere at the same time, at the same instant. The beautiful Psalm 139 says:

Whither shall I go from thy spirit? or whither shall I flee from thy presence?
If I ascend up into heaven, thou art there: if I make my bed in hell, behold, thou art there.
If I take the wings of the morning, and dwell in the uttermost parts of the sea;
Even there shall thy hand lead me, and thy right hand shall hold me.
If I say, Surely the darkness shall cover me; even the night shall be light about me.
Yea, the darkness hideth not from thee; but the night shineth as the day: the darkness and the light are both alike to thee (vv. 7-12).

    (5) He is the Spirit of holiness (Rom. 1:4).

    (6) He is the Spirit of life (Rom. 8:2).

    (7) He is the Spirit of truth (John 14:17).

    (8) He is the Spirit of God who lives in the temples of our bodies (1 Cor. 6:19).

He is to be worshiped, adored, loved, obeyed. We are on most holy ground, thus speaking of the Holy Spirit of God. The truth involved is most sacred and precious.

THE WORKS OF THE HOLY SPIRIT ARE LITERALLY THE WORKS OF GOD

1. The Holy Spirit is the author of the holy Scriptures. The Bible was written over a period of 1,500 years by more than forty different writers in the sixty-six different books, yet it is one book. Its unity is undeniable. It has one author, the Spirit of God.

Second Timothy 3:16 says, *"Pasa graphe theopneustos,"* which literally means, "All Scripture God-breathed." Every part of the Bible is the product of the breath, the Spirit, the *ruach* (Heb.) the *pneuma* (Greek) of God.

Second Peter 1:20, 21 says:

> . . . no prophecy of the scripture is of any private interpretation.
> For the prophecy came not in old time by the will of man: but holy men of God spake as they were moved by the Holy Ghost.

Let me translate that literally, word for word: "Every prophecy of Scripture of its own origination did not come into being, for not by the will of man was brought forth at any time a prophecy, but by the Holy Spirit being borne, spoke the Holy men of God."

Scripture did not originate in the mind of the writers. The moving Spirit of God is the author of every word that is written in the Bible. This is illustrated in the life of David.

Second Samuel says:

> Now these be the last words of David. David the son of Jesse said, and the man who was raised up on high, the anointed of the God of Jacob, and the sweet psalmist of Israel, said,
> The spirit of the Lord spake by me, and his word was in my tongue (23:1-2).

What he said, David is avowing, were not his words, but what the Holy Spirit of God guided him to say.

In Psalm 22:16 we read, "they pierced my hands and my feet." Psalm 22:18 says, 'They part my garments among them, and cast lots upon my vesture."

Did David ever actually experience that? No. No one ever pierced his hands and his feet. No one ever cast lots over his garments. Then why are those words in this psalm? The Holy Spirit of God moved him to write it as a prophetic description of the Lord Christ.

Thus it came to be written in Acts 1:16, ". . . the Holy Ghost by the mouth of David spake . . . ," then it quotes from the Holy Spirit.

This is also illustrated in the life of Ezekiel. Ezekiel 2:2 says: "And the spirit entered into me when he spake unto me, and set me upon my feet, that I heard him that spake unto me." Then Ezekiel wrote the glorious and heavenly vision.

The author of the Bible is the Holy Spirit of God. Its revelation comes from the Holy Spirit and its inspiration; that is, its recording without error, also comes from Him. The revelations written in the Bible were given by the Holy Spirit; that is, the disclosures of things past that no man could ever know and the disclosures of things future that no man could ever see. These are the revelations of the Holy Spirit.

Inspiration refers to the transmission of the truth. The correctness of the record, the inerrancy and infallibility of the written word, are the work of inspiration by the Holy Spirit.

2. He is the great Teacher and Illuminator. John 14:26 says, "But the Comforter, which is the Holy Ghost, whom the Father will send in my name, he shall teach you all things. . . ."

John 16:13 says, "When he, the Spirit of truth, is come, he will guide you into all truth. . . ."

It is a wonderful thing to sit at the feet of a teacher or to listen to a pastor who has studied and prepared the message he delivers. But ultimately, the truth of God that means life for us comes from the Holy Spirit. Look at the Scriptures for yourself. Never take the word of a man alone, no matter who he is. Take God's Word, let the Holy Spirit guide you into its truth, and He will respond. He is that great Teacher and Illuminator.

3. He is the instrument of our regeneration. He convicts us of sin. John 16:8 avows, "When he is come, he will reprove [convict] the world of sin. . . ."

He regenerates the soul. John 3 says:

> Jesus answered, Verily, verily, I say unto thee, Except a man be born of water [the Word] and of the Spirit, he cannot enter into the kingdom of God.
> The wind bloweth where is listeth . . . so is every one that is born of the Spirit (vv. 5, 8).

It is the work of the Holy Spirit of God to give us a new heart. He regenerates our souls. We are new in Him. "If anyone be in Christ, he is a new creation." That is a work of the Holy Spirit of God.

Titus 3:5, 6 tells us:

> Not by works of righteousness which we have done, but according to his mercy he saved us, by the washing of regeneration, and renewing of the Holy Ghost;
> Which he shed on us abundantly through Jesus Christ our Savior.

If the gospel has power, if it is effective, if it is the instrument of God to our salvation, that is the work of the Holy Spirit.

Zechariah 4:6 avows: "Not by might, nor by power, but by my spirit, saith the LORD of hosts."

First Corinthians 2:4 says: "And my speech and my preaching was not with enticing words of man's wisdom, but in demonstration of the Spirit and of power."

In 1 Thessalonians 1:5 we read, "For our gospel came not unto you in word only, but also in power, and in the Holy Ghost, and in much assurance. . . ."

We cannot convert anyone, not even the smallest child. We can only witness and pray. The work of regeneration is the work of the Holy Spirit of God. If you have been saved, it is the Spirit of God who saved you.

4. He is the Comforter in the Christian life. He comforts; He strengthens God's people.

John 14:16, 17 says:

> And I will pray the Father, and he shall give you another Comforter, that he may abide with you for ever;
> Even the Spirit of truth; whom the world cannot receive, because it seeth him not, neither knoweth him: but ye know him; for he dwelleth with you, and shall be in you.

He helps our infirmities. Romans 8:26 says, "Likewise the Spirit also helpeth our infirmities. . . ."

The Holy Spirit helps us in prayer. Romans 8 says:

> . . . for we know not what we should pray for as we ought: but the Spirit itself maketh intercession for us with groanings which cannot be uttered.
> And he that searcheth the hearts knoweth what is the mind of the Spirit, because he maketh intercession for the saints according to the will of God (vv. 26b-27).

Sometimes I think we never really pray until we cannot utter the words in syllable and sentences. We become so burdened or so filled with agony that God, who searches the hearts, hears the voice of the groans of the Spirit, and He answers from heaven.

5. The Holy Spirit speaks to the churches. Revelation 2 frequently says, "He that hath an ear, let him hear what the Spirit saith to the churches."

Are we so busy, so worldly, that we cannot hear the voice of the Spirit of God? There is a place in worship and in personal, private devotion to be quiet and to listen to the voice of the living God.

6. Many verses speak of the Holy Spirit in creation: e.g. Psalm 33:6; 104:30; Job 26:13; 33:4.

There are also many verses which speak of the Holy Spirit in the life of the believer and the working ministries of the church.

At the time of our regeneration by the Holy Spirit, we were baptized by the Spirit into the body of Christ: "For by one Spirit are we all baptized into one body . . ." (1 Cor. 12:13). The baptizing work of the Holy Spirit is seen in our addition to the church, the body of Christ. When I was saved, at that moment, the Holy Spirit took me and joined me to the body of Christ. *That only* is the baptizing work of the Holy Spirit.

When we teach correct doctrine, every mosaic in the pattern will fit beautifully. When we teach the entire truth of God, the teaching corroborates and complements itself. We are not added to the body of Christ then amputated off, then possibly added again. Such a fanciful doctrine is alien to the mind of God and to the Holy Scriptures. When we are added to the body of Christ, we become His members forever. We can never be lost. No one can pluck us out of God's hand. That is the great doctrine of the perseverence of the saints: we will make it to heaven. If we are saved, we are not going to be lost. When we are saved, the Holy Spirit of God baptizes us into the body of Christ and we belong there forever.

The Holy Spirit endows different members of the church for different ministries. We do not choose them for ourselves; the Spirit of God selects them for us. In His sovereign grace and elective choice, each member of the church, the body of Christ, is given gifts for the strengthening and edification of the congregation (1 Cor. 12:7-11).

Yet, Even Though Deity, The Holy Spirit Is One of Us

An amazing characterization in the text is that the Holy Spirit is someone as you are someone. The Holy Spirit is a person as you are a person.

The word "person," used to describe the Trinity of the Godhead, was first used by Tertullian, the first and greatest of the Latin fathers, and by the churches in their controversies with Sabellius in about A.D. 200. Sabellius, who also was brilliant and able, looked upon the Holy Spirit as just one of the modes, expressions, or manifestations of God. He looked upon the Holy Spirit as an energy, an effulgence of Deity. In controverting Sabellius, the best word Tertullian and his fellow Christian apologists could find was the word "person." The Holy Spirit is a person in the same sense that God the Father is a person, that God the Son is a person. In the history of the christological and theological controversies of the church, it is plainly seen that a denial of the personality of the Holy Spirit always ensues in a denial of the Trinity.

According to the Scriptures, the Holy Spirit is a full-orbed personality: He is Someone who can think (has mind and understanding), who can feel (has emotion and sensibilities), who can will (has volition, choice, and purpose), who can do, and who works in the world.

1. The Holy Spirit thinks. He has mind and intelligence. First Corinthians 2:11 says "For what man knoweth the things of a man, save the spirit of a man which is in him? even so the things of God knoweth no man, but the Spirit of God."

2. The Holy Spirit feels, is sensitive. In Ephesians 4:30 we read, "Grieve not the holy Spirit of God, whereby ye are sealed unto the day of redemption."

3. The Holy Spirit wills, chooses, and purposes, for 1 Corinthians 12:7 and 11 avow, "But the manifestation of the Spirit is given to every man to profit withal. . . . But all these worketh that one and the selfsame Spirit, dividing to every man severally as he will."

4. The Holy Spirit works and moves, as we have previously discussed in this study of the Spirit:

He moved the writing of the Holy Scriptures.

He regenerates our souls.

He strengthens us in our Christian life.

He raised Jesus from the dead.

He bestows spiritual gifts.

He speaks to the churches.

THE RELATIONSHIP BETWEEN THE PERSONS IN THE GODHEAD

1. There are two lines of teaching found in the Bible. One is that God is one, that God is a unity. The Bible insists upon the unity of the Godhead. The tremendous *shema*, which is the basis of the Judaic religion, is found in Deuteronomy 6:4; "Hear, O Israel: the LORD our God is one LORD."

The same avowal is found in the New Testament in 1 Corinthians 8:4-6: "There is none other God but one."

2. At the same time and in the same breath and sometimes in the same sentences, there is another line of revelation in the Bible revealing to us distinctions, separations, in the Godhead. In the Old Testament, Exodus 23:20, 21 says, "Behold, I send an Angel before thee. . . . Beware of him, obey his voice, provoke him not, . . . for my name is in him."

Genesis 48:15-16 says "The God which fed me . . . the Angel

which redeemed me from all evil. . . ." There is a capital "A" in the word Angel, who is identified with God Himself. In the New Testament we see it in the passage we have already read in the baptismal formula and in the beautiful benedictory sentence in 2 Corinthians 13:14: "The grace of the Lord Jesus Christ, and the love of God, and the communion of the Holy Ghost, be with you all."

God is triune. He is One. But there are three persons in the Godhead. We know Him in Christian experience as our Father. We know Him as our Savior who died for us. We know Him as the Holy Spirit who lives in our hearts.

3. The great and mighty work of the Holy Spirit is to glorify the Lord Jesus, to testify, to witness to Him. John 16:13-14 says: "He shall not speak of himself . . . he shall glorify me. . . ."

The Holy Spirit does not call attention to Himself, but points to the Lord Jesus. If I could place in the mouth of the Holy Spirit an exact definition, it would be this: "Not I, but Christ." Any time you hear a man of God deliver the message of God, that is the way he will speak, "Not I, but Christ."

He is called the Spirit of God in Matthew 3:16.

He is called the Spirit of Christ in Romans 8:9.

He is called the Spirit of Jesus in Philippians 1:19.

The Holy Spirit takes the place of the resurrected, glorified, ascended Lord Jesus in our hearts and lives. If Jesus were here in the flesh, He would show us, teach us, guide us, inspire us, encourage us, every moment of the day, every step of the way. But Jesus is ascended into heaven, there to make intercession for us at the right hand of the Father. With us, in us, by us, for us, in the Holy Spirit of Jesus as Jesus Himself. When we have the Spirit of Jesus in our hearts and in our lives, we have the Lord and Savior Himself. According to the words of Scripture in describing our human experience, it is impossible to distinguish between them.

We read in 1 Corinthians 6:19, "Your body is the temple of the Holy Spirit which is in you. . . ."

Galatians 2:20 says, "Christ liveth in me. . . ."

What is given to us by the Holy Spirit is Christ—Christ transcendant, unlimited, and gloriously victorious. We are given all of Him forever and ever. The gift of the Holy Spirit of God to us is Christ in our hearts, Christ in our lives, Christ walking by our side, and Christ raising us from the dead some triumphant hour!

27

What God Can Do Through a Woman

Now when they had gone throughout Phrygia and the region of Galatia, and were forbidden of the Holy Ghost to preach the word in Asia,

After they were come to Mysia, they assayed to go into Bithynia; but the Spirit suffered them not.

And they passing by Mysia came down to Troas.

And a vision appeared to Paul in the night; There stood a man of Macedonia, and prayed him, saying, Come over to Macedonia, and help us.

And after he had seen the vision, immediately we endeavoured to go into Macedonia, assuredly gathering that the Lord had called us for to preach the gospel unto them.

Therefore loosing from Troas, we came with a straight course to Samothracia, and the next day to Neapolis;

And from thence to Philippi, which is the chief city of that part of Macedonia, and a colony; and we were in that city abiding certain days.

And on the sabbath we went out of the city by a river side, where prayer was wont to be made; and we sat down, and spake unto the women which resorted thither.

And a certain woman named Lydia, a seller of purple, of the city of Thyatira, which worshiped God, heard us: whose heart the Lord opened, that she attended unto the things which were spoken of Paul.

And when she was baptized, and her household, she besought us, saying, If ye have judged me to be faithful to the Lord, come into my house, and abide there. And she constrained us. (Acts 16:6-15)

Frequently in the Book of Acts we come to a great turning point, a watershed in human history. We certainly stand at one of those continental divides as we read the story in chapter 16.

Paul had it in his heart to turn eastward through Asia, through

211

Mysia and Bithynia. But the Holy Spirit forbade him to go eastward, guiding him westward until finally Paul came down to the Aegean Sea. In the nighttime there appeared to him the vision as told in our text. A man of Macedonia said, "Come over the Hellespont and help us." Assuredly believing that God had intended that the gospel be preached to Europe, they crossed over into the new continent to bring the message of Christ to the people of the West.

ACTS 16 IS SO MEANINGFUL IN OUR LIVES

Think of the turn in religious history, culture, and civilization in this directive of the Holy Spirit of God! Had Paul turned East, it would have been Asia, China, and India who were sending missionaries to the white savages in Europe and America. But as it was, the Holy Spirit of God guided Paul and his three companions to preach the gospel to the West, so the whole turn of history is found in this brief story. How silently, how unobtrusively, how unannouncedly does the story continue! No blare of the trumpets, no marching of a great army with banners, but just this quaternion of men—Timothy, Silas, Dr. Luke, and Paul—coming to the city of Philippi. That unobtrusive appearance is of more importance and significance than all the exploits of Philip of Macedon, the father of Alexander the Great, for whom this town is named.

PHILIPPI

Philippi was a Roman colony; that is, it was settled by a group of Roman soldiers. In this instance the soldiers had fought and marched under Augustus Caesar. As their reward for bravery and faithfulness, each one was given a section of land which helped to build this colonized community of Philippi. The people of Philippi had their own government and they were free from taxation as they built a miniature of the eternal city.

Philippi was built alongside a small stream. The contour of the wall surrounding the city followed that little river. There were not enough Jews in Philippi to have a synagogue. Possibly there were no Jews at all. But the group of women in our text met outside the wall on the side of the river for the ablutions that accompanied ancient Jewish ceremony.

"AND ON THE SABBATH"

On the Sabbath Day the little group of women were gathered by the river in prayer and worship. You may feel you can worship God at home as well as you can at church. You can pray at home. You can read the Bible at home. You do not need to go to church. I understand. There is private prayer, but there is also public prayer. There is private worship, but there is also public worship. There is private reading of the Word of God, but there is also public expounding of the Holy Scriptures. We need each other. The church is called a *koinonia*, "a commonality," translated in the Bible "a communion," "a fellowship." If we love God and He speaks to us in our hearts in private, the first and natural desire we have in our souls is to share the goodness, the glory, and the greatness of our Lord with one another. We gather together in prayer. We gather together in song. We gather together in the opening of the Holy Scriptures. We gather together in intercession and worship. We gather together to make appeal for the faith of the Lord. People who love God love to be together.

There is not a more beautiful passage in the Bible than in the third chapter of Malachi:

> Then they that feared the LORD spake often one to another: and the LORD hearkened, and heard it, and a book of remembrance was written before him for them that feared the LORD, and that thought upon his name.
>
> And they shall be mine, saith the LORD of hosts, in that day when I make up my jewels; and I will spare them, as a man spareth his own son that serveth him (vv. 16-17).

We read again in Psalm 122:

> I was glad when they said unto me, Let us go up into the house of the LORD (v. 1).

On the Sabbath Day (to us, a Christian Sabbath Day, a Lord's Day), the little group was gathered together in prayer and intercession. While they were meeting, behold, someone came whose name was Paul. He was accompanied by three wonderful brethren. In that little prayer meeting by the riverside was a woman named Lydia. She was from Thyatira, and was a seller of purple crimson goods, of piece goods. She lived in a country that had been famous for its fabrics for a millennium. Croesus was the king of Lydia in the years gone by. Homer speaks of the beautiful fabrics that were woven and dyed in Lydia. Thyatira, a city in the Roman province of Asia, also a part of ancient Lydia, was no less famous because of the goods that were woven and dyed there. Lydia was a businesswoman who was a seller of piece goods which were manufactured and dyed in Thyatira.

She was a remarkable woman. She was not an idolatrous woman.

She was, as described in the Scriptures, "a woman who worshiped God," the word for "proselyte." She had turned aside from her pagan religion and empty idolatry to accept the Mosaic legislation. She had come into the knowledge of the true God, and in the pagan colonized city of Philippi, she had gathered around her a group of women who also called upon the name of the Lord. Lydia was worshiping God in an unusual way in the midst of a world filled with idolatry.

Lydia was worshiping God on the Sabbath Day. She had closed her shop and was by the riverside with a company of women. I wonder if Euodias and Syntyche, mentioned in the fourth chapter of the Book of Philippians, belonged to her household. One of the most marvelous things that any businessman or any businesswoman can do is to place God first in their lives. Lydia had given herself to the eternities, not to the temporalities; to the unseen, not to the seen; to the spiritual, and not to the material. As such, she was calling upon the name of the Lord, closing up her business on the Sabbath Day, that she might share with others a period of worship and intercession. Do you think God will bless a man who would do that, who would place Him first in his life, close up his business on Sunday, keep the day sacred for God? Would God bless a man who would place the Lord first in his life?

I remember a young fellow who was an attractive and successful salesman. He represented a great national packing company and had a clientele that was most affluent. One day the salesman was converted. God changed his heart and life and I baptized him. After he had been a Christian for three or four months, he came to me and said: "Pastor, I do not know where to turn. I do not know what to do. Something tragic has overwhelmed me in my life. In the days when I was not a Christian and I called on my clients, I had a deck of cards in my pocket and we played poker. I had a flask in my other pocket and we drank. I had the biggest time in the world and the customers were glad to see me come. They gave me big orders and I was making lots of money. Now that I am a Christian, I do not think that it is right for me to gamble. It is not right for me to drink. So when I am invited to sit down with the cards, I refuse. When I am invited to drink or to serve liquor, I refuse. As such, they do not like me anymore. They do not buy from me anymore. I am having a hard time."

I said to him: "Young fellow, if God does not see you through and if God does not bless you because of your dedication to Him, then I do not believe there is a God. Let us pray."

We knelt down and I asked God to strengthen the young salesman and to give him firm resolve and commitment in the life that he had found in Christ Jesus. The months passed, and some time later he came back to see me. This is what he said.

"Pastor, do you remember the conversation that we had and the prayer of dedication in which you led? I stood up from my knees and said: 'God help me. I will be true to You if I starve to death and lose every client I have.' Do you know what happened? It is almost inexplicable. The men began to call one another and say: 'You know, that young fellow tells you the truth. You can count on what he says. When he describes the product that he is selling us, it will be exactly as he says it is. He does not lie to us. He does not deceive us. He tells us honestly. He is a Christian. You can count on him.' Pastor, I have more customers and business now than I ever had in my life! I have never been so blessed as I have been in these last several months."

Do you believe that? Do you believe that God can do that for a man? I do! I do not think a man ever lost anything when he gave his heart to Jesus and it became known that he was a Christian. He will tell you the truth. It is exactly as he describes the product to be. Thus it was with Lydia. So it is with any businessman or any businesswoman who will do right by God and leave the result to Him.

When I was in India, the thing I missed the most was our Sunday. Friday, Saturday, Sunday, and Monday are all the same. They do not have a day of worship and they do not stop their activities. Everything continues on just the same. I did not realize what a Sunday, a Christian Sabbath does to the heart and what a difference it makes in culture, life, and civilization. On the Jewish Sabbath Day Lydia was worshiping God with the women who had gathered around her. One cannot help but admire a woman like that.

In 2 Kings, there is a passage in the fourth chapter that says that Elisha passed by Shunem where there was "a great woman" who constrained him to come in and eat bread. We think of Miriam, of Deborah, of Ruth, and of Hannah. We remember Abigail, who, in her wisdom, guided David. We think of Elizabeth and Anna, of Mary and Priscilla, and of Phoebe, Lois, and Eunice. Christianity seemingly would have gone under many times had it not been for a great and noble woman.

PAUL AND THE MAN OF MACEDONIA

Let me point out something in our text. The Scripture says:

And a vision appeared to Paul in the night; There stood a man of Macedonia, and prayed him, saying, Come over into Macedonia, and help us (Acts 16:9).

Paul, confident that God had called him to preach the gospel to the Europeans, crossed the Hellespont and went to answer the Macedonian call of this man. Paul was looking for that man outside the city. What he found instead was a woman. He had seen a *man* of Macedonia in the vision, but when he crossed into Europe to preach the gospel, what he found was a woman. How would one interpret that?

We can imagine that had Paul been someone else, when he saw a woman and not a man, he would have registered unhidden disappointment and would have said in his heart; "I am going back to Mysia and to Asia and to Bithynia. A woman? I had a vision of a man." Is that what he did?

No, for when he saw that the answer to the vision was a woman, he sat down with her and the little group of women around her and preached the gospel of the grace of the Son of God.

I have been asked a number of times, both by the faculty and by the students in a seminary of another denomination to whom I lectured, "Do you have a woman on your staff?"

I say: "Yes. I tell them that two-thirds of the leadership of our staff is women." They were overwhelmed by the thought of a woman on the staff. But that is the Christian faith. It is hard for us to realize that there was a time when it looked as though the whole Roman empire would be worshiping Mythra. But today, whoever heard of Mythra? One would have to be a student of ancient history and religion even to have heard the name. Why did not the religion succeed? Because no woman was allowed into any of the worship, any of the mysteries, or any of the convocations of Mythra. On the other hand, in the Christian church a woman was treated with great love, deference, and acceptance. In the Christian faith the women made the difference. It is our mothers, our wives, and the women in the church who often have kept it alive. Woman by woman, child by child, family by family, loving the Lord Jesus, the world is won.

Was this not true in the life of our Savior? At the well in Samaria, when the disciples returned from Sychar, do you remember the passage, "And they were amazed to see him speaking to a woman"? The Greek translation means "*a* woman," not "*the* woman." Out of the marvelous testimony of the Samaritan woman, I think, evolved the great Samaritan revival under Philip in Acts 8. What God can do through a woman!

"Whose Heart the Lord Opened"

Look at the conclusion of our story:

> And a certain woman named Lydia, a seller of purple, of the city of Thyatira, which worshiped God, heard us: whose heart the Lord opened, that she attended unto the things which were spoken of Paul.
> And when she was baptized, and her household, she besought us, saying, If ye have judged me to be faithful to the Lord, come into my house, and abide there. And she constrained us (Acts 16:14-15).

There is not a sweeter experience on earth than that. The Lord opened her heart, and "she attended unto the things which were spoken of Paul." To have someone come and sit in my study with a hungry heart is absolutely one of the sweetest experiences in life. That is the kind of a world in which I live all the time. A man comes, a woman comes, a child comes, wanting to know what God says, wanting to know the will of the Lord for his or her life, hungry-hearted, so interestedly listening. As I open the Scriptures and speak of the revelation of the mind of God in Christ Jesus, I see the fullness of the Spirit of faith and belief that leads to salvation and some day to heaven.

Attending to the things spoken by Paul, Romans 10 avows:

> So then faith cometh by hearing, and hearing by the word of God (v. 17).

How precious to find someone who wants to know about Jesus! It is like heaven itself.

So Lydia opened her heart and became a Christian. She opened her home and it became a church. She opened her life and it became a living shrine of praise and glory to the blessed Jesus. It is thus with us today. It can be thus with you. Open your heart to the Lord.

On the shield of the coat of arms of John Calvin was a hand raising a flaming heart to God. Likewise, may our prayer be: "Lord, I open my heart heavenward, Godward, and Christward. Come into my life."

28

The Man of Macedonia

Now when they had gone throughout Phrygia and the region of Galatia, and were forbidden of the Holy Ghost to preach the word in Asia,

After they were come to Mysia, they assayed to go into Bithynia: but the Spirit suffered them not.

And they passing by Mysia came down to Troas.

And a vision appeared to Paul in the night; There stood a man of Macedonia, and prayed him, saying, Come over into Macedonia, and help us.

And after he had seen the vision, immediately we endeavoured to go into Macedonia, assuredly gathering that the Lord had called us for to preach the gospel unto them. (Acts 16:6-10)

In this chapter we want to discuss the fellowship, communion, direction, and inspiration of the Holy Spirit. Notice how conversant the men in our text are in fellowship and communion with the Holy Spirit of God. They were forbidden by the Holy Spirit to preach the Word in Asia, for when they wanted to go into Bithynia, the Spirit changed their minds. The Holy Spirit and these faithful followers of the Lord seemed to be companions for this was the age of the Holy Spirit, the age of His infallible wisdom and direction. These men seemingly lived in close intimacy with the Holy Spirit.

Today we have trouble believing something like that. We stumble at the thought that the Holy Spirit could infallibly lead us, that He can direct us, give us wisdom, inspiration, and guidance from heaven. We are so materialistic and so secularly minded that it is difficult for us today to walk in the same intimate fellowship and communion with the Holy Spirit.

WE CAN ACCEPT MATTER AFFECTING MATTER

Somehow it is easy for us to believe and to see that matter can affect matter. For example, when I drop an object, it falls down. Why does it not fall up or to the side? It falls down because of gravity. No one knows or even shall know what gravity is, but we accept gravity with great commonality and experience.

The planets in their orbits are guided by that unseen, and undefinable force called gravity. We accept gravity without debate, though it is as mysterious to us as any spiritual revelation ever presented in the Bible. We do not have any problem seeing and believing that matter affects matter.

We can take a white piece of paper and sprinkle steel filings on it. Taking a magnet, underneath or above the paper, we can move those steel filings in any configuration. We can accept matter affecting matter.

One time I stood in Panama and watched the tides of the Pacific Ocean rise over nineteen feet high. On another occasion I stood on the shores of Nova Scotia in the Bay of Fundy and was overwhelmed by what I saw. The tides in the Bay of Fundy will reach seventy feet high. Can you imagine the power that could pull the Pacific Ocean nineteen feet high or pull the Atlantic Ocean seventy feet high? The rising of the tide is caused by the influence of the moon.

WE CAN ACCEPT MIND AFFECTING MIND

We have no trouble seeing and believing how mind affects mind, how personality affects personality. A man was decrying and ridiculing the thought of the healing miracles of our Lord, the fact that He could cause blind eyes to see, deaf ears to hear, and the skin of the leper to become clean. Someone pointed to him and said, "Sir, there is no one who could know what might happen in the presence of the personality of Jesus Christ of Nazareth!" That is God's truth. We can accept personality affecting personality.

How well I remember listening in World War II to Sir Winston Churchill as he encouraged the nations of Europe against the onslaught of Hitler's Nazi Germany. When it seemed that all would be lost and destroyed, Winston Churchill strengthened the hope of the world for a better day.

Napoleon, though a man of small stature, could take an army and inspire them beyond death itself.

The most explosive thing in the earth is not an atomic bomb, a hydrogen bomb, a neutron bomb, or any other kind of bomb. The most explosive thing in this earth is an idea. It is the effect of a mind upon mind. Just think of what has happened in the world since Karl Marx wrote *The Communist Manifesto*, an idea! We have no trouble accepting personality and mind affecting personality and mind.

WE STUMBLE AT THE LEADERSHIP OF THE HOLY SPIRIT

But when it comes to the leadership of the Holy Spirit of God, we stumble. Could there be an infallible direction, a source of wisdom and power and grace and glory that is as real, as sensitive as matter or personality in life?

The answer to that depends on the level of life on which we live. If we live on the level of animality, then all that governs our life is physical passion and motivation.

Or, we can raise the level of our life and live on the level of being an intellectual or an academician. We can be an infidel and an atheist. All the motivations and explanations of his life will be found in the materialistic secularism of the world.

But there is a third level of life that is as real as any of the other levels below and that is the life of the Spirit, the life combined with the holy presence and power of God. That is the life of the holy men of whom we read in the Bible, directed by the Holy Spirit of God.

Paul and his companions wanted to go East, but the Holy Spirit forbade them. They tried to turn north to Bithynia, but the Holy Spirit forbade them. They tried to turn back to the province of Asia, but the Holy Spirit forbade them. So guided by the Spirit, passing through Mysia, they finally came to the sea. Since they were unable to go north, south, east, or west, what were they to do? Then the Holy Spirit gave them a vision. In the night the Holy Spirit gave to the apostle Paul the vision of a man of Macedonia crying and saying, "Come over and help us."

THE CRY OF THE MAN OF MACEDONIA

We now look at the cry of the man in Macedonia. He stands in a country that is almost incomparable. This is the land of Philip who was king over Macedon. This is the land of his noble son, Alexander the Great, and his world-wide Greek empire. This man of Macedonia represented all of Greek culture and life. He is the man standing in the homeland of the Greek Empire asking, praying, and pleading for this emissary of heaven to come over and help them.

It would seem to me that the Greek world lacked nothing. There has never been a culture or a civilization that has even begun to rival that of the ancient Greeks, not today, not in all ages of the past. For history, the Greeks had Herodotus, Thucydides, and Xenophon. For government they had Solon, Pericles, and Aristides. For oratory they had Demosthenes. For drama they had Aeschylus, Euripides, and Sophocles. For poetry they had Phidias and Praxiteles. For science and mathematics they had Euclid and Pythagoras. For philosophy they had Socrates, Plato, Aristotle, Zeno the Stoic, and Epicurus. I read that a man looked through the catalogue of Oxford University in England and cited four hundred courses offered on Aristotle alone.

There has never been a culture, a civilization like the Greeks.

Look at the Greeks religiously. It was the most impressive religion the world had ever seen. Look at their temples, their houses of worship. The Parthenon in Athens, though today just a remnant of what it was, is still an architectural wonder of the world. One of the seven wonders of the world was a Greek temple of Artemis in Ephesus.

Have you ever seen the ruins in Baalbek? Located there are the remains of a Greek temple for the worship of Jupiter (Jove). There were no people like the Greeks.

They had many gods in their worship. Athens alone had 30,000 gods. They had gods for every facet of human life.

When we read the King James Version, the passage says that Paul, standing in the Areopagus, said, "Men and brethren, I see that in all things you are very superstitious." To have asserted that a cultured Athenian was superstitious would have been an insult. What Paul actually said was, *"Deisidaimonesteroi,"* "You are very reverent." Then ancient Greeks were very religious, and their religion was beyond anything the world had ever known. Their priests, their vestments, their pageantry, their hymns, and all the ritual and ceremony that attended the Greek religion were beautiful in the extreme.

The man from Macedonia represented the entire Greek world and he was crying to the emissary from Jesus Christ, "Come over into Macedonia and save us." He was praying for the followers of Christ to come. Why? The answer is patent. True soul-saving religion is never identified with pageantry, architecture, priesthood, vestments, festival days, or any other accouterments created by man. It is never conditioned upon culture or philosophy. It lies in a different world. The man of Macedonia cried, saying, "We have all the attendants, concomitants, and paraphernalia, but we do not have the regenerating power, we do not have the truth of God, we do not have the breath from heaven, the inspiration and the presence of the Holy Spirit of the Almighty."

In the first five verses of 1 Corinthians 2 Paul describes the message that he preached for he came preaching the Lord Jesus "that your faith should not stand in the wisdom of men, but in the power of God."

The truth and the reality of the religion of God is never found in its outward manifestations, but true religion is found in the moving presence of the Spirit of God.

THE CRY FOR A SPIRITUAL RELIGION

We cry for a spiritual religion in the services of the church, in the convocation of God's people, in the holy hours when we are gathered together in His name. The Pentecostal difference was this: Heretofore the Holy Spirit was seen at various times in various places. Sometimes it was seen as a fire flashing out in destructive judgment, sometimes as a pillar of smoke by day, sometimes in the shekinah glory of God within the tabernacle. Thus the Holy Spirit appeared to men. The Pentecostal difference is that after Pentecost the Holy Spirit took up a new abode. He now lives in the temple of man's heart. He lives in the glorious *ekklesia*, the communion and fellowship of the gathered saints of God in the church. The Holy Spirit has a new home. He lives in our hearts and he lives in the convocation of the church. He moves among the people. He comes to church in my heart and He comes to church in your heart. When all of us are gathered in a church that is given to the presence of God, we feel the Holy Spirit in our midst in the services. The Holy Spirit ought to be felt and recognized in the church service. He ought to be as real as the pastor standing before the congregation or as the one seated by your side. The stained glass window has nothing to do with it. The carpet on the floor has nothing to do with it. The ecclesiastical architecture of the church has nothing to do with it. We could have the Spirit of God with us just as well if we were meeting in a cave, in a home, on a sawdust floor, or in a warehouse. The difference lies in the presence of the Holy Spirit of God. That is real worship and a real church is where God dwells and where the Spirit moves.

We cry for the Holy Spirit of God in the ministries of the church. The heavenly assignment of the church is fulfilled when we are conscious of and responsible for the care of human souls, especially within our area. We should have spiritual ministries such as John writes in his gospel about Peter in Chapter 21: "The Lord said to Simon Peter, Lovest thou Me? Feed My lambs. Take care of My children. Lovest thou Me? Shepherd My sheep." When a man is spiritually minded, he will respond: "Lord, I will be responsible."

Let me illustrate. In 1912 one of the greatest tragedies of the sea occurred. The *Titanic*, the largest ship the world had ever seen, was on her maiden voyage from Belfast, Ireland, to New York City. In the middle of the night, the ship was speeding toward the West. The man operating the wireless telegraph knew that the ship was in a sea of ice and vast icebergs, and though he knew it, he removed his earphones and went to sleep. Five minutes after he removed his earphones, the *Titanic* at full speed rammed into a gigantic iceberg. When that happened, the American ship, *California*, was just twelve miles away. On the vast Atlantic, twelve miles is but a short distance. While the *Titanic* was sinking, carrying to a watery grave 1,625 souls of the leaders of the cultural, political, and industrial life of Britain and America, the *California* went on its way oblivious, unknowing of the tragedy that had just happened nearby. Why? Because of the irresponsibility of the man who should have been faithful at his post with his headphones.

A spiritual church is one that has recognized and accepted the responsibility for souls, for lives, for homes, and for families. These are our people, they breathe our air, they speak our language, they live our lives. Many of them are our dearest friends. They are our families, our sons and our daughters, and what it is to have a spiritual, Holy Ghost-led church is to accept from God a responsibility for their care.

O that God would give us a spiritual mind; one that is not engrossed in all the passions of the cheap and passing world! O that God would make us sensitive to the high calling of the winning of lost souls to Christ Jesus! Do you need a Sunday school teacher? I will study and try. Do you need someone to knock at the door? Call on me. Do you need someone to pray? I will ask God for His help and direction. Do you need someone to open the window or the door? Do you need someone to make a telephone call? That is what it is to have a spiritual church.

O God, that the pastor, the deacons, the numerous organizations, and the entire church would have that sensitivity for the Holy Spirit! We are not dealing in freight. We are dealing with souls—immortal, eternal lives. I believe that God, in looking at a people and a congregation like that, will pour out a double portion of His Spirit upon them. We would see gladness instead of sadness. We would see light instead of darkness. We would see people saved instead of being lost. We would see the glory of God in our presence!

29

The Preaching at Philippi

And it came to pass, as we went to prayer, a certain damsel possessed with a spirit of divination met us, which brought her masters much gain by soothsaying:

The same followed Paul and us, and cried, saying, These men are the servants of the most high God, which shew unto us the way of salvation.

And this did she many days. But Paul, being grieved, turned and said to the spirit, I command thee in the name of Jesus Christ to come out of her. And he came out the same hour.

And when her masters saw that the hope of their gains was gone, they caught Paul and Silas, and drew them into the market-place, unto the rulers,

And brought them to the magistrates, saying, These men, being Jews, do exceedingly trouble our city,

And teach customs, which are not lawful for us to receive, neither to observe, being Romans.

And the multitude rose up together against them: and the magistrates rent off their clothes, and commanded to beat them.

And when they had laid many stripes upon them, they cast them into prison, charging the jailer to keep them safely:

Who, having received such a charge, thrust them into the inner prison, and made their feet fast in the stocks.

And at midnight Paul and Silas prayed, and sang praises unto God: and the prisoners heard them.

And suddenly there was a great earthquake, so that the foundations of the prison were shaken: and immediately all the doors were opened, and every one's bands were loosed.

And the keeper of the prison awaking out of his sleep, and seeing the prison doors open, he drew out his sword, and would have killed himself, supposing that the prisoners had been fled.

But Paul cried with a loud voice, saying, Do thyself no harm: for we are all here.

Then he called for a light, and sprang in, and came trembling, and fell down before Paul and Silas,

And brought them out, and said, Sirs, what must I do to be saved?

And they said, Believe on the Lord Jesus Christ, and thou shalt be saved, and thy house.

And they spake unto him the word of the Lord, and to all that were in his house.

And he took them the same hour of the night, and washed their stripes; and was baptized, he and all his, straightway.

And when he had brought them into his house, he set meat before them, and rejoiced, believing in God with all his house.

And when it was day, the magistrates sent the sergeants, saying, Let those men go.

And the keeper of the prison told this saying to Paul, The magistrates have sent to let you go: now therefore depart, and go in peace.

But Paul said unto them, They have beaten us openly uncondemned, being Romans, and have cast us into prison; and now do they thrust us out privily? nay verily; but let them come themselves and fetch us out.

And the sergeants told these words unto the magistrates: and they feared, when they heard that they were Romans.

And they came and besought them, and brought them out, and desired them to depart out of the city.

And they went out of the prison, and entered into the house of Lydia: and when they had seen the brethren, they comforted them, and departed. (Acts 16:16-40)

We are in Acts 16, and we will take this portion verse by verse and follow it through.

And it came to pass, as we went to prayer, a certain damsel possessed with a spirit of divination met us, which brought her masters much gain by soothsaying (Acts 16:16).

The Greek word for "soothsaying" is an interesting characterization. A certain damsel was possessed with (in the King James Version) "a spirit of divination." The Greek word that is used is, with a *python* spirit. The origin of the use of the word comes from the oracle at Delphi, where years ago people worshiped a serpent, a python, which was a symbol of wisdom. Thereafter the priestesses at Delphi who delivered the oracular answers to questions brought to them were called Pythian priestesses. So the word *python* came to refer to people who were fortune tellers. They were soothsayers.

The girl in Philippi in our text was afflicted with a demoniacal spirit. In her words and cries of torment, the hearers found messages for the future unfolding in the days that lay ahead. Her masters used the poor girl for much gain. They were always present to make money from the mad sayings of that demented girl.

The men in Philippi took this poor, demented girl and were using her to make money for themselves. Seeking to turn her cries and agony into Pythian priestly soothsayings and fortune telling, she brought much gain to her masters.

She followed Paul, the Bible says, and cried, saying,

> These men [Paul, Silas, Timothy, Dr. Luke, and others] are the servants of the most high God, which shew unto us the way of salvation. And this did she many days (Acts 16:17-18).

Returning from prayer, she followed them, and the demon in her cried out the truth of the character of these strangers in this Roman colony of Philippi.

RECEIVING THE DEVIL'S MONEY

What do you think about receiving support from the devil? What do you think about taking money from those who have gained it by murder, terror, robbery, drunkenness, or embezzlement? I know there are churches and ministers who are happy to receive it. I remember one preacher, who, taking money for his church from gamblers and the liquor traffic, in order to cover over the immoral deception of the stipend, said: "This money had served the devil long enough. Now we are going to put it to use in the kingdom of God."

Paul refused such testimony and stipend.

> Paul, being grieved, turned and said to the spirit, I command thee in the name of Jesus Christ to come out of her, and she was delivered the same hour (Acts 16:18b).

Now look what happened.

> And when her masters saw that the hope of their gains was gone, they caught Paul and Silas, and drew them into the market-place unto the rulers,
> And brought them to the magistrates, saying, These men, being Jews, do exceedingly trouble our city,
> And teach customs which are not lawful for us to receive, neither to observe, being Romans (Acts 16:19-21).

What unabashed, outright liars! They never mentioned their gains. They never referred to the stipends, the money they received from that poor, demented girl. Now they are champions of the morality of the community. They are representatives of excellent citizenship and they seize Paul and Silas as men who have brought into the community customs and traditions that demoralize the civic life of the people. Infuriated by these leaders who had lost their gains,

> The multitude rose up together against them: and the magistrates rent off their clothes, and commanded to beat them (Acts 16:22).

A Roman way of beating was with a bundle of rods, the rods being a type of authority, a Fascist bundle.

> And when they had laid many stripes upon them, they cast them into prison, charging the jailer to keep them safely:
> Who, having received such a charge, thrust them into the inner prison, and made their feet fast in the stocks (Acts 16:23-24).

Therefore we see these preachers in an inner dungeon, fast in the stocks, beaten, their backs literally a pulp, and lying in their own blood on the floor.

> And at midnight Paul and Silas prayed, and sang praises unto God: and the prisoners heard them (Acts 16:25).

At midnight Paul and Silas prayed and sang, turning the prison into a church house, turning the midnight into midday, turning the cell into a sanctuary. What a thrilling picture: Paul and Silas thrust into an inner dungeon with their feet fast in the stocks, lying in their own blood, living in faith, not in circumstance, praising God. No rude, crude hand could touch their spirit of victory. If they could not pray in the house of Lydia, then they would pray in the prison of Philippi. If they were not to pray at midday, then they would pray at midnight. The whole world became a sanctuary of God before them. What a marvelous, incomparable victory! Just think of the thoroughfares of the city being turned into aisles of the church! However the circumstances and wherever the Christian is, he praises God and prays to the Lord in a spirit of exuberant victory.

The passage says, "And the prisoners heard them." No wonder! All that the prisoners had ever heard in those prison cells was imprecations, violent speech, cursing, and damnation, yet Paul and Silas were praising, praying, and glorifying God. It is almost beyond anything the heart can imagine.

We Never Know Who Is Watching and Listening to Us

You see, we do not go to church alone. The angels look down on us and watch us. We do not know how many others besides are listening when we are singing and praising God. One never knows.

When I was a student in Southern Seminary at Louisville, Kentucky, I lived in Mullins Hall, the single men's dormitory, a large, spacious, and beautiful building, built in the form of a U with a courtyard facing the campus of the seminary. One spring morning, I walked out into the courtyard. I felt wonderful. I was so happy in my soul, I felt like a million dollars. Like a mockingbird on the limb of a tall tree, I stood on the top step of the courtyard and began to sing at the top of my voice. This is what I sang:

> It pays to serve Jesus,
> It pays every day,
> It pays every step of the way.
> Though the pathway to glory may sometimes be drear,
> You'll be happy each step of the way.

At graduation time, a classmate came to me and said: "Criswell, I want to tell you something. A year or two ago I was in my room in Mullins Hall so despondent because there was trouble in my family at home and I was having so much difficulty in my work here at the seminary. I was so discouraged and downcast that I had resolved to leave school and go back home in despair and defeat. As I sat there in my room in the depths of discouragement, suddenly I heard someone singing in the middle of the courtyard. I got up, went to the window, looked down, and there you were on the top step in the middle of the courtyard singing: "It pays to serve Jesus every step of the way. Though the pathway to glory may sometimes be drear, You'll be happy each step of the way." I went back into my room, knelt down by the side of my bed, and gave myself to the Lord all over again. Now I have completed my work at the seminary, I am being graduated, and I just wanted you to know." I later learned that he became the pastor of one of the finest churches in the state of Virginia.

We do not know who is watching, who is listening, or who is being affected by our walk and our talk.

And suddenly there was a great earthquake, so that the foundations of the prison were shaken: and immediately all the doors were opened, and every one's bands were loosed.

And the keeper of the prison awaking out of his sleep, and seeing the prison doors open, he drew out his sword, and would have killed himself, supposing that the prisoners had been fled (Acts 16:26-27).

When Paul saw him, he said, "We are all here. Not one of us has fled. Not one has escaped." That jailer, after having heard Paul and Silas preach the gospel, facing execution and now suicide, came in with a torch, fell down before the disciples, and said, "What must I do to be saved?"

> And they said, Believe on the Lord Jesus Christ, and thou shalt be saved, and thy house.
> And they spake unto him the word of the Lord, and to all that were in his house.
> And he took them the same hour of the night, and washed their stripes; and was baptized, he and all his, straightway.
> And when he had brought them into his house, he set meat before them, and rejoiced, believing in God with all his house (Acts 16:31-34).

When a Man Tries to Dry Tears He Has Caused, He Has Christ in His Heart

Whenever you see a man washing wounds he has inflicted, whenever you see a man binding up hearts he has broken, whenever you see a man drying tears he has caused, there you will find a man with Jesus Christ in his soul. He is a born-again Christian, he is a new man. Such was the keeper of the prison.

I ran into such a circumstance in one of the most poignant experiences of my life. Going to preach to an evangelistic conference, I had to change planes in a city. In the airport, just walking around waiting for my next plane, I noticed a fine-looking, well-dressed man who was with a woman crippled with arthritis. His kindness and deep affection for her made an impression upon my heart. He tenderly bade her good-by, kissed her sweetly and preciously, then he took his place in line to get on the plane. To my surprise, he came up to me in the line and asked, "Would you mind if I sat by your side on the plane?"

I said, "I would be delighted to have you."

So we sat side by side on the plane. To get acquainted with him, I started talking to him, saying: "I noticed your unusual affection and kindness to that crippled woman in the airport. Is she your wife?"

He said, "Yes, she is my wife."

I said: "I think your attitude and solicitude toward her, the evident affection and love that you have for her is beautiful. Where are you going?"

He named the city.

I said, 'I am going there also."

Then he said: "That is why I am going, because you are going to be there. Whenever you come to the eastern part of the United States, I always go to hear you preach. When I heard that you were going to preach at the evangelistic conference, I made plans to attend."

I could not help but be impressed so I asked him, "Why do you do that?"

He told me that he was prospering in a business. He had a beautiful wife and a lovely house. He was most affluent. Then he started drinking and became an alcoholic. He started gambling and became addicted to it. He said that he broke the heart of his wife who begged him to stop and prayed for him. He lost his business and they lost their beautiful home. Finally, he became so vile in his life that his wife went back to her father's home. He said, "I was left penniless in drunkenness and debauchery, living in a cheap room in the city."

He continued: "In those days of my misery, you came to the city to hold a revival meeting. Out of sheer desperation in the depths of my misery, I went to hear you preach. Listening to you preach, I found the Lord as my Savior. I was born again."

The man said, "After the passing of days to make sure that I had really been born again, I made my way back to my wife's father's house. She came to the door. I told her that I was a new man, that I had been saved, that I had been born again. I asked her if she would come back home. She did."

He rebuilt his home. Not only that, but God blessed him. He said: "I now own an entire chain of stores. We have a beautiful home. God has aboundingly blessed us."

But then he added, "When my wife came back home, I saw that through the years of my drunkenness and debauchery I had destroyed her life. Everytime I see her, I feel that I caused it. What I am trying to do is somehow make up for the hurt that I caused."

Drying tears we have caused, mending hearts that we have broken, washing wounds that we have inflicted. When you see a person who does that, you are looking at a person who has Christ in his soul, trying to make amends, trying to redeem. Thus we see this Philippian jailer washing stripes, setting meat before Paul and Silas, and rejoicing, believing in God with all of his house. That is what it is to be a Christian. The Christian faith is not gloomy and it does not bring darkness. The Christian faith is joy, gladness, hope, and rejoicing. It is the sweetest pilgrimage one could ever make.

Now let us look at the magistrates.

> And when it was day, the magistrates sent the sergeants, saying, Let those men go (Acts 16:35).

The evil man, the lost man, has a ghost in front of him, behind him, to the right of him, and to the left of him. The wicked flee when there is none to pursue. The way of the transgressor is hard. God Himself works against those who do evil. Heaven is against an evil man. God is against him. The whole future is against him. The earth is against him. When a man lives evilly and wickedly, the whole universe conspires against him. These magistrates never gave Paul and Silas a hearing. They never gave them a fair trial. All they did in their violence and wickedness was to beat them and force them to enter the prison. Now fearful, they say, "Let these men go."

> But Paul said unto them, They have beaten us openly uncondemned, being Romans, and have cast us into prison; and now do they thrust us out privily? nay verily; but let them come themselves and fetch us out.
> And the sergeants told these words unto the magistrates: and they feared, when they heard that they were Romans.
> And they came and besought them, and brought them out, and desired them to depart out of the city (Acts 16:37-39).

What with earthquakes, converted jailers, Roman citizenships, and everything else, they were happy to be rid of the preachers. That is one of the truths of life that we often forget. We think that the wicked have the good time, we think the lost man has glory in his worldliness. My brother, it is the opposite. It is diametrically opposite. It is only the man who walks in the will of God who walks in the light of the Lord; only the man who loves Jesus has in his heart the peace that passes all understanding.

> And they went out of the prison, and entered into the house of Lydia: and when they had seen the brethren, they comforted them, and departed (Acts 16:40).

Paul and Silas called the brethren and comforted them. But one would have thought the brethren would have been comforting Paul and Silas. They were the ones who were beaten and thrust into an inner dungeon with their feet locked in the stocks. It is Paul and Silas, beaten, who encourage the brethren.

You will find that true in every Christian life. It is the man who has suffered and it is the man who has the sentence of death upon him, it is the man who knows sorrow, trouble, and tears who will encourage you and see you through. My friend, if you ever need someone to say precious, spiritual, and strengthening words to you, do not go to the man who is on top of the world. Go to the one who has known what it is to be crushed, to weep, and to be defeated. If you listen to him, you will find strength, help, and encouragement from the depths of the sorrow he has known in his life.

Sometimes I think the Lord leads us through these valleys that we might be prepared and ready for heaven. May God help us to lean on Him for the strength and encouragement to live triumphantly.

30

The Doctrine of Salvation

And at midnight Paul and Silas prayed, and sang praises unto God: and the prisoners heard them.

And suddenly there was a great earthquake, so that the foundations of the prison were shaken: and immediately all the doors were opened, and every one's bands were loosed.

And the keeper of the prison awaking out of his sleep, and seeing the prison doors open, he drew out his sword, and would have killed himself, supposing that the prisoners had been fled.

But Paul cried with a loud voice, saying, Do thyself no harm: for we are all here.

Then he called for a light, and sprang in, and came trembling, and fell down before Paul and Silas,

And brought them out, and said, Sirs, what must I do to be saved?

And they said, Believe on the Lord Jesus Christ, and thou shalt be saved, and thy house.

And they spake unto him the word of the Lord, and to all that were in his house.

And he took them the same hour of the night and washed their stripes; and was baptized, he and all his, straightway.

And when he had brought them into his house, he set meat before them, and rejoiced, believing in God with all his house (Acts 16:25-34).

Wherever in the Bible God tells us how to be saved, He does it in one simple, monosyllabic sentence. Not once in the Word of God does the Lord take even two sentences to tell a man how to be saved. Our text describes the conversion of the Philippian jailer when he asked, "What must I do to be saved?"

And they said, Believe on the Lord Jesus Christ, and thou shalt be saved (Acts 16:31).

A NEED

Three things are necessary for a man to become a child of God. First, there is always a felt and an expressed need. No one can be saved who does not feel a need to be saved. No one can be forgiven his sins unless he has the burden and the consciousness of sin upon his heart. That is why a small child can take a step toward God. But to be converted, to be forgiven—the experience of regeneration—is in an altogether different world. If Jesus is the Savior, He must always save us from something. That something is the guilt and the condemnation of our sins. Salvation always begins in a felt need. I am not what I ought to be, I am not what I can be, I am not by the grace of God what I shall be. Being lost and the consciousness of being lost brings us to the Savior.

The Philippian jailer is down on his knees. He is facing execution in disgrace and shame, so much so that he attempts to take his own life with his sharp Roman sword. In abject misery, he asks the question of deepest human need, "What must I do to be saved?"

When a man finds himself needing God, he is near the kingdom, I do not care who he is, what he has done, or his status in life.

I remember eating dinner in a country home in which the family had invited the hired hand, a most untutored, untaught, and ignorant boy. The young fellow sat right across the table from me. I began talking to him and asked him if he knew the Lord, if he was a Christian.

He replied: "Sir, I ain't no Christian. I am a lost sinner."

I replied to the young fellow: "Son, you are near the kingdom. In these days of revival, I predict that you will be wonderfully saved." He was.

The beginning of salvation is in a need in our hearts and in our lives.

A SAVIOR

Second, there is a Savior to whom we can make appeal who was sent into the world to save us from the judgment and condemnation of God upon our sins.

When the Bible was written, all the names of the people had deep and everlasting significance. The word "Jesus" in Hebrew is *Joshua*, the word for "Savior." "Christ" is the anointed One of God. "Lord" refers to His deity. This is God's Son sent into the world to pay for our sins. He died as our substitute. "The wages of sin is death," and "the soul that sins shall die." If I have no advocate, no Savior, no intercessor, no mediator, or no substitute, then I die.

I die in two ways. I die physically and I die spiritually. My body dies. My soul dies. How shall I live if the judgment of death is passed upon me because of my sins?

God made a way in His love and grace. He sent the Lord Jesus to die in our stead, to pay the penalty for our sins. Therefore, in Christ, we never die. The dissolution of man's body of clay is but the entrance into heaven against the hour when God will give us a new and a resurrected body. The soul is regenerated and goes to be with Jesus in the hour of His translation and coronation. Jesus is our Savior and He delivers us from the penalty of physical death, which to us now is an entrance into heaven, the second death which we shall never face. We are delivered in the goodness and grace of the Lord Jesus Christ.

A RESPONSE

Third, a man must respond. All God asks from us is a response, an acceptance. Believe, accept, trust in, commit your life to the Lord Jesus Christ, and you will be saved. God has so made it that the grace of the Lord Jesus is not mediated to me unless I accept it. A pardon is not a pardon by American law, expressed by the Supreme Court itself, unless one accepts it. That is the law of God. If I am pardoned, I must receive and accept the pardon. It is that simple. "Whosoever believeth"—but I must believe. "If thou shalt confess with thy mouth the Lord Jesus"—but I must confess. When I respond, God does some marvelous thing for my soul and my life.

Years ago, the young Count Zinzendorf who was rich, noble, personable, gifted, and worldly, used his wealth for his own personal enjoyment and amusement. One day, walking through the Düsseldorf Gallery in Germany, the young count stood transfixed before a picture of the Lord Jesus, crowned with thorns, suffering for our sins. Underneath was printed the Latin caption, *"Hoc faci pro te, Quid facis pro me?"* The translation is, "This have I done for thee. What hast thou done for me?" The young count in the art gallery gave his life to Christ. That began the greatest world-wide missionary movement we have ever known.

There must be a response in our hearts as there was in the conversion of that young, rich nobleman. There must be a commitment, an answer to God from our hearts and lives.

As Isaac Watts wrote:

> Was it for crimes that I have done
> He groaned upon the tree?
> Amazing pity! grace unknown!
> And love beyond degree!
>
> But drops of grief can ne'er repay
> The debt of love I owe;
> Here, Lord, I give myself to Thee,
> 'Tis all that I can do.

The doctrine of salvation is a need, "I am a lost sinner"; a Savior, found in the Lord Jesus; and a response, "I accept Him and trust Him for all that He said He was and for all He promised to do."

SALVATION IS NOT A MATTER OF WORKS

The obverse, what salvation is not. First, salvation is not a matter of works. It is not something that I work for and God gives to me because He owes me a debt. I do not work for it. Ephesians 2 tells us:

> For by grace are ye saved through faith; and that not of yourselves: it is the gift of God:
> Not of works, lest any man should boast (vv. 8-9).

When I get to heaven, I will not pat my hand and say, "That won for me my salvation." Nor will I pat my foot, saying, "My foot gained for me salvation." Nor shall I tap my head and say, "My head gained for me my salvation." No. When I get to glory, it will be, "Worthy is the Lamb that was slain, who hath washed us and redeemed us by His own blood, and made us kings and priests unto God forever and ever." Salvation is all of grace. It is nothing of works. As Paul wrote in Titus 3:

> Not by works of righteousness which we have done, but according to his mercy he saved us, by the washing of regeneration, and renewing of the Holy Ghost (v. 5).

Salvation is all of God. It is not anything that a man does. We are not saved by baptism, by the ordinances, or by a ceremonial ritual in the church. It is the grace of God that saves us.

SALVATION IS NOT A MATTER OF WORTH

Second, salvation is not a matter of worth. I am not saved because I deserve it or because I am good enough to attain it. How could any man ever say that he deserves the suffering, the sacrifice, and the cross of the Son of God? We cannot be good enough and we do not deserve salvation.

When the Lord died, He did not die just for the best of us. He also died for the worst of us. If a man seeks to make himself worthy of the love and grace of God in Christ Jesus, he will never attain it.

> Come ye sinners, poor and needy,
> Lost and ruined by the fall;
> If you tarry till you're better,
> You will never come at all.
>
> I will arise and go to Jesus,
> He will embrace me in his arms;
> In the arms of my dear Saviour,
> Oh, there are ten thousand charms.

Salvation is not a matter of worth. It is a matter of God's grace and love and our acceptance in Him. We are never good enough for it.

SALVATION IS NOT A MATTER OF TEMPORALITIES

Third, salvation is not a matter of temporalities. It is not something for a moment, then it evanescently fades and passes away. Salvation is forever. John 10 tells us:

> I give unto them eternal life; and they shall never perish, neither shall any man pluck them out of my hand.
> My Father, which gave them me, is greater than all; and no man is able to pluck them out of my Father's hand.
> I and my Father are one (vv. 28-30).

Salvation is a matter of eternities. When a man gives his heart to Christ, he is changed. He is someone new. He is someone else. Salvation is forever.

One time a boy at a youth camp asked me about the doctrine of being saved forever. I think in his young experience he had come across Christians who were not quite as he thought they should be. In any event, he was asking whether they were genuinely saved or not.

I replied to him: "Christians can live carnal lives as anyone else can, but this is the difference: When a man is not saved, he is lost, he is a man of the world. When he goes out in the world and lives in iniquity, in wickedness, and in sin, he will enjoy living it up. But if he is saved, if he is a Christian, he may get out in the world, but he will be miserable and unhappy. He is where he ought not to be. He is doing things that he ought not do. His heart condemns him. You see, he is a child of God. He has been saved. The seed of the Lord stays in his soul forever. He is someone else. He has been changed."

When a pig falls in the mud, he wallows in it and likes it. When a sheep falls in the mud, he struggles to get out of it. That is a child of God.

God says that we are born again. We are born children into the kingdom of God. One cannot unborn his children. That is the way it is in the kingdom of God, for 2 Corinthians 5:17 says, "Therefore if any man be in Christ, he is a new creature. . . ." God has touched us and He has promised that He will be with us to see us through and bless us forever. Some day He will take us to heaven. Some day He will open wide the doors of glory and welcome us in.

That is what it is to be saved, that is what it means to trust in Jesus, and that is what God does to our hearts when we look in faith to Him.

31

Saving Faith

And brought them out, and said, Sirs, what must I do to be saved?
And they said, Believe on the Lord Jesus Christ, and thou shalt be saved, and thy house.
And they spake unto him the word of the Lord, and to all that were in his house.
And he took them the same hour of the night, and washed their stripes; and was baptized, he and all his, straightway. (Acts 16:30-33)

Let us discuss a little more the story of the conversion of the Philippian jailer. Paul and Silas were beaten, cast into an inner dungeon, their feet fast in the stocks, and at midnight they prayed and sang to God. Then the Lord shook the whole earth and the foundations of the prison trembled. The prisoners' bands and stocks were loosed. The prison doors were thrown wide open. The jailer, who was keeper of the prison and was responsible for the lives of his prisoners, thinking they had all fled since the doors were wide open, took a sword and prepared to plunge it into his heart rather than face an ignominious execution before a Roman tribunal. Paul, seeing it, cried with a loud voice: "We are all here. Do thyself no harm." The jailer, calling for a torch, came and fell down before Paul and Silas and asked that famous question, "Sirs, what must I do to be saved?" They answered an equally famous reply:

Believe on the Lord Jesus Christ, and thou shalt be saved, and thy house.

Then the narrative continues.

And they spake unto him the word of the Lord, and to all that were in his house.

And he took them the same hour of the night, and washed their stripes; and was baptized, he and all his straightway.

And when he had brought them into his house, he set meat before them and rejoiced, believing in God with all his house (Acts 16:31-34).

A man could be asked, "Are you a Christian?"

He could reply: "Why, certainly. Do you think I am a heathen, that I am an infidel, that I am a Mohammedan? Of course, I am a Christian."

But there is more to being a Christian than belonging to a certain stratum of cultural life or national identification, such as an Indian who would doubtless be a Hindu, a Thai living in Thailand would doubtless be a Buddhist, or someone in America would doubtless be a Christian. Living in America does not make one automatically a Christian.

Or the man could reply: "Why, surely, I am a Christian. I believe that Jesus was a great teacher. I believe He was a fine, noble, ethical pioneer. I believe He was a historical person who carried forward in His life a great social reformation."

There are many degrees to the acceptance of Jesus Christ. But that is not what this refers to nor is it the subject of this passage in Acts 16. What is it to be a Christian and what is it to have saving faith? Let me answer that question. When Paul avowed, "Believe on the Lord Jesus Christ, and thou shalt be saved," he meant two things.

AN ACCEPTANCE OF THE WITNESS CONCERNING JESUS CHRIST

To be a Christian is to receive. It is to accept. We must receive the testimony of God concerning His Son as it is recorded in the Holy Scriptures—what He was, what He did, and what He is able to do for us.

For example, in Acts 10 Peter, preaching to the Gentiles in Caesarea, said:

To him give all the prophets witness, that through his name whosoever believeth in him shall receive remission of sins. (Acts 10:43)

Peter said that all of the Old Testament prophets witness to the Lord Jesus.

The last verse of John 20 says:

But these are written, that ye might believe that Jesus is the Christ, the Son of

God; and that believing ye might have life through his name (v. 31).

Thus the New Testament is a witness to the saving grace of God in Jesus Christ.

Therefore, to be a Christian, means you receive the witness of the Father. "This is my beloved Son, in whom I am well pleased; hear ye him" (Matt. 17:5). We also receive the witness of the Son Himself. John 6 tells us:

> And this is the will of him that sent me, that every one which seeth the Son, and believeth on him, may have everlasting life: and I will raise him up at the last day (v. 40).

We must also receive the witness of the Holy Spirit to Jesus. Romans 1 avows:

> [Jesus is] declared to be the Son of God with power, according to the spirit of holiness, by the resurrection from the dead (v. 4).

This is what it is to be a Christian, receiving the witness of the triune God concerning the Son, receiving the testimony of the Holy Scriptures. The Scriptures say that we are all lost and that, dying, we face inevitable judgment. The Bible tells us that Christ died for our sin according to the Scriptures. The Scriptures say also that whosoever accepts Him and believes in Him shall have eternal life. I accept that. Being a Christian is accepting the witness of the Scriptures to the Lord Jesus, accepting the pardon that the Scriptures offer to us in Christ. I accept the free gift of eternal life and the remission of my sins in Him. The Lord promises it, and I receive it.

There was a famous case several years ago of a man who was to be electrocuted, but the governor of the state pardoned him. However, the man refused to accept the pardon and wanted to be electrocuted. It caused confusion and consternation in the law courts of the state. The case was finally brought to the Supreme Court of the United States which declared, "A pardon is not a pardon until it is accepted." The man died in the electric chair according to his wish.

So it is with being a Christian. A pardon is not a pardon until I accept it. God in His Holy Scriptures witnesses to eternal life given to us in the remission of our sins, and if I accept it, it becomes for me forgiveness, remission, salvation, and eternal life. Saving faith is an acceptance of pardon and life from the hands of our Lord.

John 1 avows:

But as many as received him, to them gave he power to become the sons of God even to them that believe on his name (v. 12).

I receive life in the world to come. John 14 tells us:

> I go to prepare a place for you.
> And if I go and prepare a place for you, I will come again, and receive you unto myself; that where I am, there ye may be also (vv. 2b-3).

To become a Christian, I must receive saving faith from the hands of God, accept the pardon from the goodness and grace and love of our blessed Jesus. Ephesians 2 tells us:

> For by grace are ye saved through faith; . . . it is the gift of God (v. 8).

SAVING FAITH IS A COMMITTAL

Saving faith is a commital. One time I bowed my head in prayer and asked, "Dear Lord, what does it mean when the Bible says, 'Believe on the Lord Jesus Christ, and thou shalt be saved'? What is it when the passage tells us, 'For whosoever believeth in him shall not perish, but have everlasting life'? What is saving faith?" James says the devils believe and tremble. The devil knows about the Lord, beyond what we know or understand, but the devil is not saved. What is saving faith?

An answer came to my heart in that prayer:

> . . . for I know whom I have believed, and am persuaded that he is able to keep that which I have committed unto him against that day (2 Tim. 1:12).

There is the word, believe. This is the definition: "I am persuaded that he is able to keep that which I have committed unto him against that day." Saving faith is a committal. I commit my soul and my life to Jesus.

I looked closely at the Greek word *epi*, the word for "on" in the passage, "What must I do to be saved? And they said, Believe *on* the Lord Jesus Christ, and thou shalt be saved." *Pisteuo* is the Greek word for "believe." The word translated "on" is *epi*. *Pisteuo epi*, "Believe on" the Lord Jesus Christ. *Epi* is also the word for "upon," like the Greek word *epidermis*; *epi*, upon, *derma*, skin, so *epidermis* is the word for the outer layer, the outer skin. Wherever you see the word *epi*, "upon" is the meaning. It is used in numerous instances in the Greek New Testament.

> *epibaino*—to go upon, as a ship
> *epiballo*—to cast upon, as *epiblema*, an English word

epiblepo—to look upon
epiopteuo—to look upon
episkeptomai—to look upon
epigrapho—to write upon, *epigraph, epigram*
epikathizo—to sit upon
epikaleo—to call upon
epikeimai—to lie upon
epilambano—take hold upon, *epilepsy,* a seizure
epioikodomeo—to build upon
epipipto—to fall upon
epirrapto—to sew upon
epistepho—to turn upon
epitithemi—to lay upon, to place upon; *epithet* comes from that
epiphaino—to shine upon, *epiphany* comes from that
epiphero—to bring upon
epicheo—to pour upon
epichpio—to spread upon, to anoint
epistello—to send upon, *epistle* comes from that

Always in those forms, *epi* refers to casting oneself upon, leaning upon, committing oneself upon. That is what it is to become a Christian, to commit yourself, to lean upon, to depend upon the Lord Jesus.

Look what the passage says: The jailer was not told to cast himself upon, to lean upon, *pisteuo,* the church. We do not look to the church for salvation. We do not look to ordinances for salvation. We do not look to the preacher for salvation. We do not look to the deacons for salvation. We do not look to ourselves for salvation. The passage says *pisteuo epi,* "Believing upon, casting ourselves upon, depending upon," the Lord Jesus. Times change, circumstances change, feelings change, but Jesus does not change. Depend upon man, anchor your hope upon the church, and inevitably there will be a time in your life when you will be disillusioned and discouraged. We look to Jesus and He is all right. There may be many things wrong with the church, with the members, with the preacher, with the officers in the congregation, and with all human aspects of the church, but there is nothing wrong with Jesus.

SALVATION IS AN OBJECTIVE COMMITTAL

That means that our salvation is objective, it is outside of ourselves.

It is not something on the inside of us. It is beyond us. Whenever you start looking at yourself, and especially with regard to your salvation, you are going to be the most discouraged follower of Jesus in the world: Did I repent right? Did I believe right? Am I doing right? When you look inside yourself, you will be filled with tears, trepidation, and all kinds of discouragement by the weaknesses in your life. We are all alike. We may look at someone and say, "What a tower of strength he is!" or "What a wonderful woman she is!" If you knew everything about everyone there would be no one of us who would be standing with his head up before you. If you were to take a film of all of the secret thoughts and imaginations of your life and put it on a screen, you would bow your head in shame and walk out the door. Do not ever think that we are not all alike. We are. We are all sinners alike. We are all lost alike. We are all dying alike. We all face the judgment day of almighty God alike. When we compare ourselves with each other, some of us, we think, may be better than others. But before God and the holiness of the Lord God, we are all alike. That is why the Bible presents our salvation as being objective. Our salvation is brought for us outside of ourselves.

Let me illustrate. In the days of the flood, salvation was outside of Noah, outside of Shem, Ham, and Japeth, outside of their wives, outside of their families. Salvation was outside of themselves in the ark. When they were in the ark, the storm roared, the rains fell, the lightning flashed, the thunder split the sky, and the whole world lay in destruction. But in the ark, there was safety, assurance, quiet. Salvation was outside of Noah, in the ark; objective salvation was outside of themselves.

In the days of the death terror over Egypt, the angel passed over every home and every firstborn in the land of Egypt was to die. What a night of horror! If you had one child, that child would die. If you had two children, the eldest would die. The firstborn of everything of man and beast died under the judgment of God that night. But the Lord said, "If you will take the blood of the lamb, and sprinkle it in the form of a cross on the lintel and on each side of the doorposts, you will be saved." Get under the blood, wait, and rest in the Lord. All they were to do was just to rest in the promise of God and the death angel would pass over. It is an objective salvation, outside of themselves.

Look once again. In the days of the wilderness wanderings, when there were fiery serpents everywhere, any man who was bitten by a snake would fall into convulsions, would swell, would die. In the middle of the camp, Moses raised a serpent of brass. If anyone dying would but look at the serpent of brass, he lived. Salvation was outside of himself. In himself there was fever, venom, convulsion, agony, and death. But outside of himself there was salvation, life, strength, and length of days.

Our salvation is like that. It is not in ourselves. It is in Jesus. As long as I keep my eyes upon the Lord, I am all right. Whatever happens around us does not matter. We are to depend upon, trust, love, and serve the Lord Jesus.

Do you remember Peter walking on the water? As long as he kept his eyes on the Lord, he walked on the water. But when he took his eyes off the Lord and began to look at the winds and the waves, he began to sink. We are that way. If we get our eyes off the Lord and begin to look at all the people around us, we will be so discouraged, we won't know what to do. If we keep our eyes upon the Lord, everything will be all right. He is not going to fail. He will not be discouraged. He will not let us down. He will see us through. What a Savior!

Let me give an illustration. In 1950 the Foreign Mission Board of the Southern Baptist Convention sent me, with Dr. Duke McCall, on a preaching mission around the world. In those days, the type of aircraft that was used to cross the ocean was a DC-4, a big, heavy, awkward plane with four big propellers. On the trip from Tokyo to Wake Island over the Pacific Ocean, we ran into a terrible hurricane. It was as black as midnight inside that hurricane. The sun was completely blotted out. The plane was tossed as a leaf blown by the wind. One cannot imagine how I felt, seated there in that plane, absolutely helpless. I do not know anything about flying an engine, and certainly not in an awesome storm like that. While we were in the hurricane, the pilot spoke over the public address system. He said: "Do not be afraid. This plane is strong and is made for a storm such as this. In a little while, we will be out of it." Suddenly, we burst out of the storm into the pure, heavenly sunlight. In a second, we passed from the darkness into the light.

That experience came to my heart as a poignant illustration of what it is to rest in Jesus. Our salvation is in His hands. He sees us through. The old Negro spiritual avows:

> When the storms of life are raging,
> Stand by me.

When the hosts of hell assail,
And my strength begins to fail,
Thou who never lost a battle,
Stand by me.

When the world is tossing me
Like a ship upon the sea,
Thou who rulest wind and water,
Stand by me.

Rest, *epi*, upon the Lord. *Pisteuo epi*, Believe *upon* the Lord. It is remarkable what happens to your heart when you do. However the wind and storm of life, however the frustrations and exigencies that befall us there in the midst of the storm, we just lean on Jesus, trust in Him, depend upon Him, believe in Him. That is what it is to be saved. That is what it is to be a Christian!

32

The New Life in Jesus

And they said, Believe on the Lord Jesus Christ, and thou shalt be saved, and thy house.

And they spake unto him the word of the Lord, and to all that were in his house.

And he took them the same hour of the night, and washed their stripes; and was baptized, he and all his, striaghtway.

And when he had brought them into his house, he set meat before them, and rejoiced, believing in God with all his house. (Acts 16:31-34)

Paul and Silas were two preachers, men of God. They did not desecrate a temple. They did not rob a corporation. They did not do violence to the government. They were not guilty of treason against Caesar. They were men who had preached the gospel of the grace of the blessed Jesus. But this hardened jailer, far beyond any sense of duty, far beyond any necessity of confinement or incarceration, treated those men as though they were vile and dangerous criminals. He presided over their flogging. He cast them into the innermost part of a cruel dungeon, and then, as though that were not enough, he fastened their feet in the stocks. That meant, of course, that they had to lie flat on their backs on the floor of the prison. They were lying in their own blood as they had just been ruthlessly and unmercifully beaten. The cruel, hardened jailer had wrought these deeds against Paul and Silas.

HE WASHED THEIR STRIPES

But after the jailer received salvation, he took the disciples to his home and washed their wounds. This illustrates one of the tremendous characteristics of the Christian faith. Christianity makes a man sensitive to human suffering. Before the jailer was saved, he thought about flogging those men, about cruelly incarcerating them, about fastening their feet in the stocks. He thought nothing about placing them in the innermost cell of that dark prison, for he was a hardened sinner. But after he opened his heart to the preaching of the gospel of the Son of God, he immediately became sensitive to human suffering. So he washed the disciples' wounds.

As I look at history and at the whole world, there is nothing more characteristic, more typical of the Christian faith, than sensitivity to human suffering. In the day of the Philippian jailer, in all the Roman empire there was not one house for the poor, not one hospital, not one orphans' home, not one place for the care of the leper, not one institution in which the deranged could be ministered to. Before Jesus Christ, and before the preaching of the gospel of the Son of God, the heart of the world was harsh, cruel, and hard. The biggest difference made in human history has been made by the loving, tender, and compassionate Jesus. Wherever the gospel is preached, there will you find a new hope, a new day, a new comfort, a new ministry, and a new home for the poor, for the sick, for the disabled, for the deranged, for those who are hurting and suffering. Let me illustrate.

In the story of the mission of our Lord in the land of the Gaderenes, lived a man who was demented. Where did he live? The Bible says that he lived in the tombs, in the cemeteries, pushed out of society. He lived wherever he could find an escape from the harsh judgments of a cruel and merciless culture. His home was in the tombs.

Look again. In the story of the man who fell among thieves on the road to Jericho, who passed him by on one side? A priest. Who passed him by on the other side? A Levite. Who left him to die in his own wounds and in his own suffering? Those who were supposed to represent the kingdom of God. The whole world was like that. Suffering, bleeding, and wounding all were a part of someone else, but never a charge to us.

Another example is found in the story of the lepers of that ancient day. Where did they live and what were they commanded to do? The lepers were cast out. They were not allowed into the villages or into the cities. They were not allowed where people were. Wherever the leper went, he was to place his hand over his mouth and cry as he walked, "Unclean, unclean!" That is why in the story in Matthew 8 when the

Lord was surrounded by a great throng, the passage says, "And, behold, there came a leper and worshipped him" (v. 2). How could the leper just walk up to Jesus? The answer is apparent. As he walked with his hand over his mouth crying, "Unclean, unclean!" immediately a great circle opened before him and he just walked up to the blessed Jesus. It was a day in which men were insensitive to human suffering. All of the great institutions of ministry, tender care, thoughtfulness, and love are the fruits of the Christian faith, of the preaching of the gospel of the Son of God.

One of the most poignant memories I have took place in Africa. With Dr. Goldie, one of the missionaries of our Southern Baptist Convention, I drove in his little English car to visit the clan settlements of lepers which he had established. Dr. Goldie had gathered all of the lepers together because in any pagan society the leper is pushed out to die of exposure and starvation. He gathered them and was ministering to them in those clan settlements. As I watched him working with the people, I thought in my heart: Who sent out that missionary? We did. Who bought that medicine? We did, we who love the Lord Jesus. Who made it possible to gather that flotsam and jetsam of humanity together and teach them the Word of God and minister to their healing? We did, who love the Lord Jesus. That is one of the sweetest characteristics of the Christian faith. "He took them the same hour of the night, and washed their stripes." The Christian faith has been doing that ever since. The culture of our modern western world has been framed and created by the preaching of the gospel of the Son of God.

He Was Baptized

The second thing that the Philippian jailer did after he was saved was to be baptized, "he and all his, straightway." Sometimes I see people hesitate before being baptized. It seems to me that being baptized is such a precious privilege to follow our Lord's example. Jesus did not need to be baptized, but He was, and His obedience pleased the Father. We read in Matthew 3:

Then cometh Jesus from Galilee to Jordan unto John, to be baptized of him.
But John forbad him, saying, I have need to be baptized of thee, and comest thou to me?
And Jesus answering said unto him, Suffer it to be so now: for thus it becometh us to fulfil all righteousness. Then he suffered him.
And Jesus, when he was baptized, went up straightway out of the water: and,

lo, the heavens were opened unto him, and he saw the Spirit of God descending like a dove, and lighting upon him:

And lo a voice from heaven, saying, This is my beloved Son, in whom I am well pleased (vv. 13-17).

To follow the Lord in baptism is one of the sweet privileges of life. There is not much I can do for Jesus. He said: "If I were hungry, I would not tell thee. The gold and the silver are mine, the cattle on a thousand hills are mine." There is not much we can do for God. But what we can do, we ought to do, and by God's grace, let us do. The Lord asked that we be baptized on a confession of faith. He Himself sets the beautiful example, holy and pure, in His own baptism in the Jordan River.

Every disciple in the New Testament thereafter followed our Lord in the likeness of that holy and heavenly ordinance. In Acts 16 when Lydia opened her heart to the gospel, the first thing she did was to be baptized.

We follow the story of the Ethiopian eunuch in Acts 8:

And as they went on their way, they came unto a certain water: and the eunuch said: See, here is water; what doth hinder me to be baptized?

And Philip said, If thou believest with all thine heart, thou mayest. And he answered and said, I believe that Jesus Christ is the Son of God.

And he commanded the chariot to stand still: and they went down both into the water, both Philip and the eunuch; and he baptized him.

And when they were come up out of the water, the Spirit of the Lord caught away Philip, that the eunuch saw him no more: and he went on his way rejoicing (vv. 36-39).

Praise the Lord! There is always a fullness of heavenly reward when a man follows the mandates and the commandments of God.

The Philippian jailer, immediately after he had washed their stripes, was baptized. The members of his household, who also were presented the plan of salvation, were saved and baptized, following the jailer's precious example.

HE REJOICED, BELIEVING IN GOD

The jailer did one more thing after he was saved: "And when he had brought them into his house, he set meat before them, and rejoiced, believing in God with all his house." What a remarkable thing! The jailer washed their stripes, was baptized, and now is rejoicing, believing in God with all his heart.

In my reading I began to follow the life of one of the world's great preachers named Thomas Chalmers. There were two mighty preachers from Scotland. One was John Knox and the other was Thomas Chalmers. Chalmers was born in 1780 and died in 1847. He was one of the most illustrious Scotsmen of his day. Prime Minister Gladstone of England wrote this about the wonderful preacher, "The world can never forget his warrior grandeur, his unbounded philanthropy, his strength of purpose, his mental integrity, his absorbed and absorbing earnestness, and above all, his singular simplicity; he was one of nature's noblemen."

Thomas Carlyle wrote a sentence about him: "Thomas Chalmers was a strong featured man and of a very beautiful character."

Having introduced him, I want to show you what happened to him. He was called of God and licensed to preach at the age of nineteen. He became pastor of the little church at Kilmany in Scotland. For eight years the brilliant, oratorical, and forensic young man stood before his little congregation. Every Sunday he denounced them for their sins. He preached on the Ten Commandments and he delivered his message in such a way as though all the members of the little church had broken all ten of them every day of the week. Once in awhile there was an exception in which he would deviate from that tone of thundering denunciation of the congregation and he would speak about the evil designs of Napoleon Bonaparte. He would denounce the ravages of the French tyrant over Europe. His little congregation, recognizing the academic superiority and the brilliant gifts of their young pastor, were as bewildered at his denunciations of the congregation as they were when he turned aside and denounced Napoleon Bonaparte. How would Napoleon know what he was doing at that little church in Kilmany as he flagrantly, openly, and violently condemned the atrocious designs of the French general? Chalmers preached in that manner for eight years without a break.

Then something happened. The people were more bewildered than they were before. After eight years of vigorous denunciation, suddenly they did not recognize him. For the next four years in Kilmany, instead of thundering against crimes and sins, and instead of expatiating upon the iniquities of the Napoleonic crusades, Sunday after Sunday with tears in his eyes, he pleaded with men about the grace of God in Christ Jesus, preaching the cross and the love of the Lord, asking men to come to Jesus and receive Him as their Savior. It is recorded in his biography that many times when he rose to pronounce the benediction, he would start all over again and plead with the men to accept Jesus as their Savior. The congregation could not understand what had happened. A revival broke out. People were saved. It was a new day and a new rejoicing.

What had happened was that in the thirty-first year of his life, Thomas Chalmers was converted! He had an experience of regeneration. For the first eight years of his ministry at Kilmany, his message was one of thunder and denunciation. Then for the last four years his message was, "Turn and be saved."

Chalmers' biographer writes of the change and he puts it like this, "Before, he preached 'Do and live,' but now he preached, 'Believe and be saved'."

In his farewell message at Kilmany before going to the great city pulpit in Glasgow, and finally to the University of Edinburgh, he spoke of that change, how God had turned his heart, his soul, and his message to a new gospel, to a new faith, and to a new commitment.

My brethren, we all know that we ought to do good. There is not a criminal in the land who does not know that he ought to do good. The problem lies in our human nature. When we would do good, evil is present with us. How does one find strength to serve God? How can a man be different from what he is? As long as the preacher preaches, "Do and live," the people will listen, leave, and find themselves weak and helpless. But when the preacher preaches, "Believe and be saved," the people go out and find in Christ a new hope, a new strength, a new presence, a new blessing, a new prayer, a new vision, a new day, a new life. It is the difference between Mount Sinai, which, if a man touched, he had to be struck through with a dart, and Mount Calvary, to which anyone might ascend. Anyone can kneel at the cross. Anyone can look up into the face of Jesus. Anyone can believe and be saved. That means us. That means you and your family. We do not have to be as we are. Jesus can change us. We can find fulfillment, achievement, presence, and blessing in the Lord Jesus.

The Philippian jailer was rejoicing, believing in God. The gospel message is never, "Do and live." The gospel message is always, "Believe and be saved," "Wash and be clean," "Look and live." It is in His omnipotent and gracious hands that we find strength for the way. That is what it is to look in faith to the Lord Jesus!

33

How Can I Know That I Am Saved?

And brought them out, and said, Sirs, what must I do to be saved?
And they said, Believe on the Lord Jesus Christ, and thou shalt be saved, and
thy house. (Acts 16:30-31)

How can I know that I am saved? Our Lord asked, "What would it
profit a man if he gained the whole world and then lost his own soul?"
What would it profit a man if he gave his life to frolic and entertainment, and then died and fell into hell? What would it be for a man if
he achieved every worldly purpose in heart or imagination, then spent
an eternity in darkness, condemnation, and damnation? There could
be no question comparable to "What must I do to be saved?" The
incomparable revelation of God's grace and mercy toward us reveals
that the answer is not found in us but in the Lord: "Believe on the Lord
Jesus Christ, and thou shalt be saved" (Acts 16:31).

MAN IS LOST WITHOUT GOD

First, let us discuss the concept of our being lost. The secular world,
which is the world we see in the modern, panoramic scene, denies that
it is lost. Secularists themselves deny that they are lost. Do you remember the campaign which was carried through so many of the great
cities of America in which people placed on their car bumpers a
placard which read, "I Have Found It!"? Later one could see cars
which had placards stating, "I Never Lost It." The secularist avows: "I
am not lost. I have no need of salvation. I do not face any judgment for

my sins. I will walk into God's presence with my head lifted high, make my own defense and apology, and stand in my own righteousness. When the hour of my death comes, I will be sufficient to deliver myself. I am not lost."

The concept of being lost was the crux of the preaching of John the Baptist. In Matthew 3, when the ministry of the great forerunner of the Lord is presented to the world, John says to the leaders of Jerusalem:

> O generation of vipers, who hath warned you to flee from the wrath to come? And think not to say within yourselves, We have Abraham to our father: for I say unto you, that God is able of these stones to raise up children unto Abraham (vv. 7b, 9).

That is the response of the entire secular world. They feel they do not need to be saved. They are already right with themselves, right with the world, right with God. They will face eternity, death, and judgment in their own strength.

Congratulations! However, the starkest tragedy I know in human life and in human history is this: that mankind is lost without God! We are fallen in all of our faculties. We are fallen in all of our emotions. There is no part of human life in which we do not see the wreckage and the lostness of our souls.

I see it in every area of life. I see our fallen nature in the movie industry which presents films that are increasingly salacious, iniquitious, and sinful. The modern movie is not increasingly exalting but is increasingly debasing.

I see it in our television programs. The language used and the stories portrayed are increasingly violent and immoral.

I see it in our literature. The language and the illustrations are increasingly evil.

I see it in the political life of nations. There is so much terrorism and violence that finally people live in fear, hopelessness, and helplessness.

I see it in the academic world. Humanism and secularism is increasing in our schools; that is they are leaving God out of the picture. Not only do they leave God out by the presentation of other factual material, but they leave God out by law and by constitutional judgment. The whole world is lost, and however one wishes to say it— sociologically, psychologically, philosophically, or theologically—the world of humanity is lost without God. Individually we all face the judgment upon our own sins and inevitable death.

WHO CAN SAVE US?

Who can save us? Can we save ourselves? Would to God that we could. Would to God there was a political system that could deliver us. Would to God there was an academic system that could save us. Would to God there was a philosophical proposition that could be delivered to us, thereby obviating the consequences of our fallen minds, fallen natures, and our inevitable death. But our helplessness before our lostness is seen in a description of us in the Word of God.

The first verse of Ephesians 2 says that we are dead in trespasses and in sins. What can a dead cadaver do to save himself? When I am dead, what can I do to save myself?

My mother can save me. My mother loved me, watched over me, and gave me every material care that could be poured out upon a boy. My mother can save me. But my mother is dead!

My father can save me. My father was a fine, humble, honest, and hard-working man. He can save me. But my father is dead! My father and mother are buried together and we have wept many tears over their tomb.

The pastor who baptized me can save me. But the pastor is dead.

The wonderful man who stayed in our home and preached the revival meeting and talked to me every night after church will save me. But he is dead. The whole generation that I knew in those days is dead. How can they save me when they are dead? How can I finally save myself when I am dead? "The wages of sin is death" and "the soul that sins shall die," our Bible proclaims.

Can I win salvation for myself? I can follow a program of improvement and self-amelioration. I can dress up my life. I can reform. I can rid myself of the things which drag me down. I can purify my soul and heart. I can live righteously before God, and then some day I can present myself, having made of me a beautiful and perfect life.

My problem is that I do not achieve perfection, and God demands holiness and perfection. Without holiness, no man shall see God. My righteousnesses in His sight are as filthy rags. The Lord says that in His holiness and in His presence I am unclean, dirty, a lost sinner. I am helpless.

But maybe if I cultivate the divine spark that is in me, I can achieve salvation. You see, the image of God is inside of me. I am made like Him. The image of the Lord is stamped upon my soul. If I will just cultivate that spark of divinity, then I can achieve perfection and salvation.

But however I achieve any measure of the likeness of God, I shall still have sinned and I still die. I face being a dead corpse.

Maybe in a great sacrifice, maybe in some heroic laying down my life for a noble cause, maybe for my country, maybe I could just give myself to great and holy things. Maybe if I beat my body as Martin Luther did, maybe then I can be just and stand in the presence of God self-delivered.

But the more I face any kind of heroic sacrifice, the more certainly am I conscious that I shall surely die.

Death is written in all of my members. It is written in the very color of my hair. It is written in the lines on my face. It is written in the aging of my physical frame. It is written in the years of my life I have already lived. I face a certain inevitable judgment of death. Who can deliver me? How can I be saved?

MAN IS SAVED BY GOD ALONE

My salvation lies over and beyond me. It is achieved by One outside of me. I am saved by God and God alone. Salvation is a display of His grace, mercy, and love. It is He who does it—all of it. When we arrive with the redeemed in glory and sing our song of praise and redemption, we shall sing to Christ alone. Worthy is the Lamb, to receive riches, and honor, and glory, for He has redeemed us from our sins by His own blood. He has made us kings and priests to God, and we shall reign forever and ever. All glory to Christ! While I was a corpse, He quickened me. He spoke me into life. He raised me up. In His mercy He washed me from my sins. He made me to stand in His presence. Our salvation is in God.

GOD DEALS WITH THE SIN QUESTION

There are two things that God does. First, He deals with the sin question in our lives. How do we stand in the presence of God being sinners with the judgment of death in our physical frame and in our spiritual souls? Who can deliver us from so great a condemnation? How can God forgive us and at the same time be true to His own nature in bringing judgment upon sin? How can God be just, how can He be righteous, and at the same time justify the unrighteous? How can God judge sin and at the same time forgive us? If God overlooks our sin, pays no attention to it, then His whole moral universe collapses. God has to uphold His law and righteousness. He has to deal with the sin question in our lives. How does He do that?

In the most merciful way that the mind could imagine. God took all our sins and placed them at the account of His only begotten Son. He took all our debts that we owe and laid them at the feet of the Lord Jesus. Jesus paid it all. He took our sins and He became sin for us. He suffered in our stead. He paid the full penalty of our sins. Had there never been anyone else living in the world, He would have died just the same for you. He took your sins and bore them in His own body on the tree. Every sin brings its full measure of judgment and condemnation. Jesus paid the price, the debt, the judgment, the suffering on the tree. That is how God dealt with the sin question.

GOD DEALS WITH THE QUESTION OF FREE MORAL AGENCY

Second, how does God deal with the question of free moral agency; that is, how does God not violate my own personality? God made me free. He gave me choice. He cannot coerce me, cannot force me, and at the same time let me be free. How does God face the question of my free, moral creation and not violate my freedom of choice and my personality?

This is the way God does it. He lays in His goodness and grace the plan of salvation before me and then He gives me an ultimate choice. I can look or not look. I can believe or not believe. I can accept, or not accept. I can trust, or not trust. I can come to Him, or refuse. The choice is up to me. God honors my personality, my freedom, and the way He made me. His appeal is always one of wooing, of inviting, of pleading, of opening the door, of welcome. That is the choice for you.

Let me illustrate the best I can. Let us think of a great sovereign king, all-powerful, in the day when the king ruled with absolute omnipotence. In his kingdom there are men who are seditionists and revolutionists. They say, "We will not have this man reign over us!" They rebel, take up arms, and war against the king. But in their revolution they are frustrated and lost. They face inevitable execution. The king is powerful and they are guilty of rebellion, sedition, revolution, and bearing arms against him.

Then the king in his great mercy and goodness decrees, "Universal amnesty is granted to anyone who has rebelled if he will just come and receive forgiveness and pardon."

The revolutionaries talk among themselves. Some say: "Do not believe that. Do not trust him. That is a ruse, a deception. You lay down your arms and surrender and ask pardon from his hands and he will seize you and execute you. You cannot trust his word. You cannot believe in him."

But one revolutionary says: "I believe that he will keep his word. I am going to lay down my arms of rebellion. I am going to surrender to him and ask for pardon. I believe he will keep his promise of amnesty."

A second revolutionary says: "Maybe I cannot trust him. Maybe I cannot accept him for what he said. But I am going to see if he keeps his word and if he will forgive and pardon me."

A third revolutionary says: "These years of my rebellion have brought nothing but misery to my life. I am so unhappy in the way I have been living, I do not know what to do. I am going to see if he will help me, if there can be a change in my life from this rebellion, fear, and failure. I am going to see if he will help me."

A fourth revolutionary says: "I am a dying man. I am going to see if he will raise me."

All four of them come before the great king. First there is the revolutionary who has laid down his arms, surrenders, and says: "I believe your word when you say that there is amnesty, pardon, and forgiveness. I believe you will keep your promise. I trust in your mercy and goodness."

The second revolutionary comes before the great king and says: "Lord, I do not know whether you will keep your word or not, but I am going to try. Here I am, Lord. I am asking for forgiveness and pardon. We will see if you keep your word."

The third one stands and says: "Lord, my life is so incomplete and broken. I want your help, your strength, your wisdom, and your direction."

The fourth one says: "Lord, just strengthen me to lift up my face. I am dying. Lord, is there life in you?"

You tell me. Do you think the great king will be merciful? Do you think he will keep his word?

The Lord says, "He that cometh unto me, I will in no wise cast out" (John 6:37).

> Come, ye sinners, poor and needy
> Lost and ruined by the fall;
> If you tarry till you're better,
> You will never come at all.
>
> I will arise and go to Jesus,
> He will embrace me in His arms;
> In the arms of my dear Saviour,
> Oh, there are ten thousand charms.
>
> I heard the voice of Jesus say,
> "Come unto Me and rest;
> Lay down, thou weary one,
> Lay down thy head upon My breast."
>
> I came to Jesus and I was,
> Weary and worn and sad,
> I found in Him a resting-place,
> And He has made me glad.

All four revolutionaries stand before the great king justified, for-given, and pardoned. Why? Because God will keep His word. "Whosoever believeth in him shall not perish, but have everlasting life." If I can find it in my heart just to believe in His unchanging promise, I am saved forever!

34

The Pulpit Preacher

Now when they had passed through Amphipolis and Apollonia, they came to Thessalonica, where was a synagogue of the Jews:

And Paul, as his manner was, went in unto them, and three sabbath days reasoned with them out of the scriptures,

Opening and alleging, that Christ must needs have suffered, and risen again from the dead; and that this Jesus, whom I preach unto you, is Christ.

And some of them believed, and consorted with Paul and Silas; and of the devout Greeks a great multitude, and of the chief women not a few.

But the Jews which believed not, moved with envy, took unto them certain lewd fellows of the baser sort, and gathered a company, and set all the city on an uproar, and assaulted the house of Jason, and sought to bring them out to the people.

And when they found them not, they drew Jason and certain brethren unto the rulers of the city, crying, These that have turned the world upside down are come hither also;

Whom Jason hath received: and these all do contrary to the decrees of Caesar, saying that there is another king, one Jesus.

And they troubled the people and the rulers of the city, when they heard these things.

And when they had taken security of Jason, and of the other, they let them go.

And the brethren immediately sent away Paul and Silas by night unto Berea: who coming thither went into the synagogue of the Jews.

These were more noble than those in Thessalonica, in that they received the word with all readiness of mind, and searched the scriptures daily, whether those things were so.

Therefore many of them believed; also of honourable women which were Greeks, and of men, not a few. (Acts 17:1-12)

With this chapter we begin our discussion of Acts 17. Acts 16 closed with Paul and Silas beaten and in prison. As they prayed and glorified

God and sang hymns, the Lord shook the jail and the entire town. Thereafter the Philippian jailer was wonderfully converted. Then the authorities of the city, having beaten Paul and Silas without trial, were most happy to have them depart from the colony city of Philippi.

Now in Acts 17 Paul and Silas walk the distance of thirty-three miles from Philippi to Amphipolis, but they do not preach. We might at first think they have ceased their battles for the Lord. They have laid down their arms. The persecution, the flogging, and the imprisonment that they met in Philippi were too much. They have renounced the faith. They go through Amphipolis and there is no message. Then they walk the thirty miles to Appolonia and again there is no preaching. Surely they have ceased their preaching in order to anoint their wounds and to lick their stripes.

Then they walk thirty-seven miles further and come to the capital of the Roman province of Macedonia, Thessalonica. Ah, in Thessalonica there is a synagogue of the Jews. It was this synagogue in Thessalonica that the apostles were seeking. These who had been grounded in the law of Moses and who knew the writings of the prophets were seeds which God could germinate into a fruit to the glory of Christ.

As His Manner Was

With his heart burning within, the apostle Paul enters the synagogue, "and as his manner was, went in unto them, and three sabbath days reasoned with them out of the scriptures." This is a magnificent portrayal of the habits of a man. "As his manner was," he went to church.

The same pattern can be found in the life of the Lord Jesus in Luke 4. "As his custom was," He went into the synagogue and took up the scroll of the prophet Isaiah. Unrolling the scroll, He read to them out of the prophecy of that glorious messenger from heaven.

We will find, when we study the life of the early Christians, that they lived in the church. They were not casual visitors. They did not come inadvertently, but they attended the services with great dedication, purpose, and habit.

So it should be for Christians today. It should be second nature for those of us who name the name of Christ to walk into the door of the house of God and to sit down with His people. It should be our way of life.

So Paul, "as his manner was, went into them for three sabbath days." This is an excellent portrayal of the acceptance of the rabbinical learning and the marvelous preaching of Paul. For three consecutive sabbath days in a synagogue in which he was a stranger, he delivered a message of the Lord, reasoning with them out of the Scriptures.

I think this is one of the finest definitions of what true preaching ought to be, "reasoning with them out of the scriptures." The preacher with an open Bible in his hand stands in a mighty fortress, one that has been fashioned by the Lord God Himself. If the preacher invents his own sermon, he stands in a tower of paper. Any little flame will burn it up and any tiny breeze will blow it away. But the preacher who stands with the Word of God in his hand stands upon an immovable and impregnable rock.

This is what the apostle Paul did as he went into the cities of Palestine, Asia, and Europe. He carried with him a message from heaven, not one he invented, but one that was written out for him in the Holy Word.

I stumbled into an unusual experience in visiting with a young husband whose wife was a faithful member of our church. In obedience to her earnest appeal, I talked to the young fellow about the Lord, about coming to church. He said, "Would you like for me to be honest with you?"

I answered, "Why, certainly."

He said: "I will tell you exactly why I do not come to church. I do not like to hear you preach."

I replied, "That is surely honest and frank and I appreciate it, but just for interest, why is it that you do not like to hear me preach?"

He replied: "I will tell you exactly why. I have been there several times with my wife and every time all you have done is preach out of the Bible."

I asked, "What do you expect me to do?"

He answered: "When I go to church, I like to hear a preacher talk about politics, economics, and about current events. But all you preach is the Bible."

I said: "Young fellow, I do not blame you for not liking to hear me preach, because when you come to my church, you will never come just to hear a lecture on economics, politics, or transient current events which are headlines in the daily newspaper. It will be a message from the Book."

I think that is what the preacher is called to do. He is an echo. He does not invent his sermon. It is written out for him in the Holy Scriptures and he is a voice crying in the wilderness.

OPENING AND ALLEGING

"Paul, as his manner was, went in unto them, and three sabbath days reasoned with them out of the scriptures, opening and alleging . . ." (Acts 17:2-3a).

We have in this verse two interesting words: *dianoigo*, which means "to fully disclose, to open fully" and *paratithemi*. *Para* means "alongside," *tithemi* means "to place." *Paratithemi* means "placing alongside," translated here, "alleging"; that is, the apostle Paul brought proofs for the deity, the kingship, and the Saviorhood of the Lord Jesus. "Opening and alleging, that Christ must needs have suffered, and risen again from the dead; and that this Jesus, whom I preach unto you, is Christ" (Acts 17:3).

Let me show you a use of that word *dianoigo* in Luke 24.

On the way to Emmaus, a stranger got in step with Cleopas and another disciple and began to talk to them about the Word of God. When the disciples came to their home in Emmaus at eventide, they invited the stranger to eat with them. We follow the story:

And it came to pass, as he sat at meat with them, he took bread, and blessed it, and brake, and gave to them.

And their eyes were opened, and they knew him; and he vanished out of their sight.

And they said one to another, Did not our heart burn within us, while he talked with us by the way, and while he opened to us the scriptures? (vv. 30-32).

There is that word *dianoigo*, "opened."

To a child of God, that is the most moving and fulfilling of all the experiences of life, to listen to the "opening" of the Scriptures, the deep, wonderful, marvelous, heavenly, sayings of God!

THIS JESUS IS CHRIST

You see, the sword has a point to it. The sermon has an appeal in it. Paul is preaching for a verdict, "opening and alleging . . . that this Jesus, whom I preach unto you, is Christ."

God be praised for a man who delivers his message with an appeal for belief in the Lord Jesus! God be praised when the Holy Spirit sanctifies and hallows the Word and the man answers, "My Lord and my God!" That is the purpose of preaching. That is the purpose of our assembling in worship that lost people might come to know the Lord. It is as John the apostle closed his gospel, "But these are written, that ye might believe that Jesus is the Christ, the Son of God; and that believing ye might have life through his name" (20:31). That is marvelous!

There is a story that I have heard many times. It must be true because I have heard it repeated from several sources. As you know, there were two glorious, world-famous preachers in London in the last century. One was named Joseph Parker, who was one of the most brilliant men who ever lived. His messages scintillate and sparkle. The other, of course, was Charles Haddon Spurgeon, whom I read all the time.

A man went to hear Joseph Parker and left, saying, "What a great and mighty preacher!" Then the same man went to hear Charles Haddon Spurgeon and went away, saying, "What a great and glorious Savior!"

That is the purpose of preaching, that we might exalt the Lord Jesus, so that when people leave the service they may say in their hearts, "Is it not wonderful who Jesus is, what He does, what He means!"

ANOTHER KING, ONE JESUS

Continuing in our story, those who did not believe the gospel preaching of Paul and Silas created a turmoil and a trouble in the city. Not finding Paul and Silas, they took Jason (the Greek way of spelling "Joshua"; I suppose he was a Jew). They assaulted his house because he had opened it to Paul and Silas, and not finding them, they hailed Jason before the politarchs, the rulers of the city. They said, "These all do contrary to the decrees of Caesar, saying that there is another king, one Jesus."

We have heard that before. When the Lord was arrested and brought before Pontius Pilate, his accusers said, "This man is a traitor and he is guilty of sedition, for he says that he is a king; and we have no king but Caesar." Then Pilate, looking at that thorn-crowned, bloody, beaten, despised, spat-upon, and outcast Nazarene turned to Him and said, "Art thou a king?"

The Lord replied, "Thou sayest that I am a king," the strongest affirmative that the Greek language is capable of avowing. "Yes, thou sayest that I am a king; to this end was I born, for this purpose came I into the world."

Jesus lived and died a king. The superscription they placed over His cross read, "This is Jesus, the King."

When Paul preached in Thessalonica, he wrote in 1 and 2 Thessalonians what he preached. Every chapter ends with the second coming of the Lord. Every chapter discusses the kingly return of our Savior, the Lord Jesus. He is not a King of sedition. He is not a King of insurrection. He is not a King of devastation and destruction. He is a King of glory, of salvation, of truth, and of peace. He is Jesus, the King.

The People of Berea Were More Noble

When the Jews had taken security of Jason, they made him post bond for the good conduct of his guests. The brethren took Paul and Silas by night and sent them unto Berea, fifty miles away. The passage states that the people in Berea "were more noble than those in Thessalonica, in that they received the word with all readiness of mind" (17:11). They were more noble, not referring to their birth or their breeding, but more noble in that they listened intently, eagerly, and hungrily.

No one ever had a silver tongue who first did not have a golden ear. To listen is a gift from God. It takes two to make a sermon, someone to preach, and someone to listen. Expectancy turns into inspiration. It is the quiet, earnest, hungry listening of a congregation that brings the best out of a preacher.

The people in Berea received the word eagerly and searched the Scriptures daily, to see whether what was said, was true. "Therefore many of them believed" (Acts 17:12), having searched the living Word of God.

If your faith is built upon the personality of the preacher, and you have been swept away by oratory, by the fame of the evangelist, or by some other human denominator, then your faith is a rope of sand. It dissolves so quickly. But if your faith is built upon Christ and in the Word of the living God revealed in the Holy Bible, whoever the minister or the evangelist, it is like cables of steel. It anchors you to God forever and ever. "The flower fadeth, the grass withereth, but the Word of God shall stand forever."

What a wonderful thing to build your life, your faith, your destiny, and your every tomorrow upon the infallible, unchanging, inspired Word of the living God!

35

What the Scriptures Say

These were more noble than those in Thessalonica, in that they received the word with all readiness of mind, and searched the scriptures daily, whether those things were so. (Acts 17:11)

There is one great theme to be found in all of the Bible, and we shall discuss that now.

And Paul, as his manner was, went in unto them, and three sabbath days reasoned with them out of the scriptures,

Opening and alleging, that Christ must needs have suffered, and risen again from the dead; and that this Jesus, whom I preach unto you, is Christ.

These [Bereans] were more noble than those in Thessalonica, in that they received the word with all readiness of mind, and searched the scriptures daily, whether those things were so.

Therefore many of them believed; also of honourable women which were Greeks, and of men, not a few. (Acts 17:2-3, 11-12)

What do the Scriptures say? They point to Jesus. They lead us to the Lord. They present to us our Savior. They build in us a great faith in the Lord of our salvation.

Notice how the Scriptures discuss the entire ministry of Paul and Silas. What do they do in this tremendous missionary journey? How do they carry through their effort? They do it around the Word of God. They continue it throughout their second misssionary journey, the third, and the last. The entire effort of these disciples who represent the courts of heaven is bound up in the Holy Scriptures. They love the Word of the Lord.

267

In his last letter, Paul writes to Timothy, "Come quickly." He is in the Mamertine Dungeon facing immediate execution, it is in the cold of winter, and he tells Timothy to bring "the cloak that I left at Troas with Carpus, and the books, but especially the parchments" (2 Tim. 4:13). The parchments were the scrolls, the Holy Scriptures. In his last moments, Paul wants the Bible in his hand.

The passage tells us that the noble Bereans searched the Scriptures daily. What a magnificent description of their nobility!

In preparing this chapter I read of the life of a brilliant and able man, a successful businessman and a noted civic leader, who was a marvelous witness for the Lord. He said that his mother died before he was old enough to read. His father died soon thereafter. At twelve years of age he left his uncle's home to go out into the world to face life for himself. He said that just before he left his uncle's home, his older sister took him into a room so they could be by themselves. She had in her hand a little pocket Bible out of which she read to him. Then they knelt down, and with many tears and with her arms around her brother, she prayed for him and commended him to the Lord. When they stood up after the prayer, she placed that little Bible in his hands with a promise exacted from him that he would read it every day. He said that he kept that Bible with him through the years and read out of it every day. That is a wonderful, glorious testimony!

What does the Bible say to us? It tells us of the Lord Jesus. It points to the blessed Savior. That is so beautifully illustrated in all of the New Testament for when the Lord came to the synagogue in Nazareth, He read out of the scroll of the prophet Isaiah. Then placing the scroll down, He said, "This day is this scripture fulfilled in your ears" (Luke 4:21).

The Scriptures point to the Lord Jesus.

We read in Luke 24, that as the Lord walked with the two disciples on the way to Emmaus, He opened to them the Scriptures and pointed out to them the things concerning Himself.

Later, before His ascension, as He met with the twelve apostles, He opened their understanding, beginning at Moses, the prophets, the writings, and the Psalms. He showed them the things concerning Himself.

When Peter stood up to preach before the Gentiles in Caesarea, he said, "To him give all the prophets witness, that through his name whosoever believeth in him shall receive remission of sins" (Acts 10:43).

In Acts 8 the evangelist Philip is seated in a chariot by the side of the treasurer of Ethiopia. The treasurer is reading Isaiah 53 when he asks, "Of whom does the prophet speak?" The Bible says that Philip, beginning at the same Scripture, preached unto him Jesus. The Scriptures point to Jesus.

In the description of the magnificent preacher of the Christian faith, Apollos of Alexandria, the last verse in Acts 18 says that "he mightily convinced the Jews . . . shewing by the scriptures that Jesus was the Christ" (v. 28).

I think that same Apollos of Alexandria wrote the Book of Hebrews. Whoever wrote it was an Alexandrian and an eloquent man, I think the most eloquent who ever lived. In the Book of Hebrews he quotes a passage, "Lo, I come [speaking of Christ] (in the volume of the book it is written of me,) to do thy will, O God" (10:7). The Scriptures point to the Lord Jesus.

In Revelation 10, John sees an angel with one foot on the sea, one foot on the land, and in his hand an open book. And the angel proclaimed out of that book, "This do all the prophets declare from the beginning of the creation, the Lord Jesus." What do the Scriptures say? They lead us to the Savior.

I believe that I could summarize the entire Bible under three categories. One, Someone is coming; two, Someone is here; and three, Someone is coming again.

SOMEBODY IS COMING

Someone is coming is the theme of the entire Old Covenant. In promise, someone is coming.

Genesis 3:15 refers to "the seed of the woman." What an amazing description! The woman never had seed. It is the man who has seed. The old rabbis poured over that story and did not understand the beginning of its meaning. The seed of the woman shall bruise, shall crush Satan's head. This was the Protevangelium, the first gospel before the gospel. Someone is coming.

IN PROMISE

We read in Genesis 49 that Jacob turned to Judah, his fourth son, and said:

The sceptre shall not depart from Judah, nor a lawgiver from between his feet, until Shiloh come; and unto him shall the gathering of the people be (v. 10).

Someone is coming, and to Him shall the gathering of the people be. In 2 Samuel 7 God told King David that he would have a son who would sit upon the throne forever, and of his kingdom there would be no end, to establish it for ever and ever. Someone is coming.

The Old Covenant closes with Malachi in chapter 3:

Behold, I will send my messenger, and he shall prepare the way before me: and the Lord, whom ye seek, shall suddenly come to his temple, even the messenger of the covenant, whom ye delight in: behold, he shall come, saith the LORD of hosts (v. 1).

Someone is coming. All of the prophets of the Old Testaments declare His appearance.

IN TYPE

Chapter 9 of the Book of Hebrews presents the tabernacle as a type of the Lord Jesus. The altar speaks of Jesus, the laver speaks of Jesus, the shewbread speaks of Jesus, the lampstand speaks of Jesus, the golden altar of incense speaks of Jesus, the veil speaks of Jesus, the propitiatory speaks of Jesus, the mercy seat speaks of Jesus, the cherubim speak of Jesus. All of the types of the Old Testament speak of the Lord Jesus. You see, God had to teach us the language of heaven so that when time came for us to look upon the sacrifice for our sins, we would know what sacrifice means. When God spoke to us of an altar, of a sacrifice, of atonement, we could understand the words by the type that prefigured the reality. In all of the ritual, ceremonial worship services of the Old Testament, God is teaching us, so we might understand when Jesus comes, what God is doing for us through Him, making an atonement for our souls.

IN DESCRIPTION

Not only is Someone coming in promise and in type, but in that Old Covenant He is described in meticulous detail. Psalm 22 is written in the first person. David, who wrote it, never experienced anything such as he writes in that Psalm, yet he writes it in the first person. What is he doing? He is describing the Lord Jesus as though he stood by the cross.

In Isaiah 52 and 53 it is as though Isaiah was standing at the cross, watching every moment of that tragic and sorrowful day when Jesus died and was buried. Yet Isaiah lived 750 years before the day of the cross.

Zechariah describes the wounds of the Lord's hands and feet, he speaks of the fountain of a cleansing opening for Israel, and all of the things which pertain to the blessedness of the Lord Jesus. The prophet says He is coming as a King, riding upon the foal of an ass, and He shall speak peace to the nations of the world. His dominion shall be from sea to sea and His kingdom shall last forever. That is the Old Covenant. Someone is coming.

Someone Is Here

The second part of the Bible states that Someone is here.

Standing in the study of a church in Moscow, I saw on the wall a painting of a throng of people. There in the midst of the throng was the great John the Baptist. Just beyond stood the Lord Jesus. John has his hand raised to proclaim, "Behold, the Lamb of God that taketh away the sin of the world." That is the gospel. Someone is here.

Matthew tells the story of Jesus the Messiah Christ, the fulfillment of all Old Testament prophecy.

Mark tells the story of the intensive miracle-working ministry of our Lord with signs confirming His mission in the earth.

Luke tells the story of Jesus as the compassionate Savior of the world.

John tells the story of Jesus as the appearance of the veritable Son of God, "Whom our eyes have seen, our ears have heard, and our hands have handled," the very Word of God. He closes his Gospel with the avowal, "These [signs] are written, that ye might believe that Jesus is the Christ, the Son of God; and that believing ye might have life through his name." Someone is here.

Someone is with us forever. "If I go away, I will send the Holy Spirit that he may abide with you forever." In the Spirit of our Lord we have Him, all of Him, wherever we are in the earth. If you are shut in a room of prayer in your house, Jesus is there. If you are on the other side of the sea, bowing with a group of God's sainted people, Jesus is there. When we gather together in our worship services, Jesus is there. Someone has come.

Someone Is Coming Again

Someone is coming again. Paul calls the promise "the blessed hope." Christ's return is the concluding theme of the Holy Scriptures. Our Lord spoke to the apostles in John 14:

> Let not your heart be troubled: ye believe in God, believe also in me.
> And if I go and prepare a place for you, I will come again, and receive you unto myself; that where I am, there ye may be also (vv. 1, 3).

Someone is coming again. More tears of hope have fallen on John 14 than upon any other leaf in human literature. "I will not leave you comfortless; I will come for you." Someone is coming again.

In Acts 1, as the Lord ascends into heaven, angels appear to the grief-stricken apostles who are left in a hostile and perverse world. The angels say, "Ye men of Galilee, why stand ye gazing up into heaven? this same Jesus . . . shall so come in like manner as ye have seen him go into heaven" (v. 11). He is not coming just in death. He is not just returning in the diffusion of the gospel. He Himself is coming again. This same Jesus in like manner shall descend on clouds of shekinah glory. Someone is coming again.

The apostle Peter preaches in Acts 3, "Whom the heaven must receive, until the times of restitution of all things . . ." (v. 21a). He shall come and this world will be turned back again into the Garden of Eden in peace, simplicity, and holiness. Sorrow and sighing shall flee away. There shall be no more death, no more tears, no more crying, and no more pain. These things will pass away when He comes again. It is the theme of the apostle Paul. We read in 1 Thessalonians:

> But I would not have you to be ignorant, brethren, concerning them which are asleep, that ye sorrow not, even as others which have no hope.
> For if we believe that Jesus died and rose again, even so them also which sleep in Jesus will God bring with him.
> For the Lord himself shall descend from heaven with a shout, with the voice of the archangel, and with the trump of God: and the dead in Christ shall rise first:
> Then we which are alive and remain shall be caught up together with them in the clouds, to meet the Lord in the air: and so shall we ever be with the Lord (4:13-14, 16-17).

The brother of our Lord, Jude, writes, "Behold, the Lord cometh with ten thousands of his saints" (v. 14). Someone is coming again.

The whole climactic word of the Scriptures is that Jesus is coming again. *Apocalypse* is the first startling Greek word of the Revelation, the unveiling of Jesus Christ. Its subject, its theme, its text is Revelation 1:7, "Behold, he cometh with clouds; and every eye shall see him." The Lord shall descend in the shekinah glory of God. A cloud received Him out of their sight, and when He comes back, it will be in the same glorious manner. The Revelation closes with that last and final promise, Someone is coming:

> I Jesus have sent mine angel to testify unto you these things in the churches. I am the root and the offspring of David, and the bright and morning star.
>
> And the Spirit and the bride say, Come. And let him that heareth say, Come. And let him that is athirst come. And whosoever will, let him take the water of life freely.
>
> He which testifieth these things saith, Surely I come quickly. Amen. Even so, come, Lord Jesus (22: 16-17, 20).

If we know our hearts, we are ready. Any day, Lord, any time, come. That is what the Scriptures say, Someone is coming again.

Oh, the precious and heavenly commitment that we have in our Lord Jesus!

36

To the Unknown God

Now while Paul waited for them at Athens, his spirit was stirred in him, when he saw the city wholly given to idolatry.

Therefore disputed he in the synagogue with the Jews, and with the devout persons, and in the market daily with them that met with him.

Then certain philosophers of the Epicureans, and of the Stoics, encountered him. And some said, What will this babbler say? other some, He seemeth to be a setter forth of strange gods: because he preached unto them Jesus and the resurrection.

And they took him, and brought him unto Areopagus, saying, May we know what this new doctrine, whereof thou speakest, is?

For thou bringest certain strange things to our ears: we would know therefore what these things mean.

(For all the Athenians and strangers which were there spent their time in nothing else, but either to tell, or to hear some new thing.)

Then Paul stood in the midst of Mars' hill, and said, Ye men of Athens, I perceive that in all things ye are too superstitious.

For as I passed by, and beheld your devotions, I found an altar with this inscription, TO THE UNKNOWN GOD. Whom therefore ye ignorantly worship, him declare I unto you. (Acts 17:16-24)

The story in our text is one of the most amazing situations that the mind could imagine. Paul, the preacher of Jesus, had come to the far-famed university city of Athens. How did he fare? Let us take a look.

Before Paul came to Athens, four disciples had crossed the Hellespont into Macedonia for the first time to preach the gospel in Europe. They were Paul, Silas, Timothy, and Dr. Luke, the beloved physician, who had been left in Philippi. Timothy stayed in Thessalonica. Silas was left in Berea, later joined by Timothy. Paul is alone in the great university city of Athens waiting for Timothy and Silas to join him. While in Athens, walking through the streets of the city, the text says that "his spirit was stirred in him, when he saw the city wholly given to idolatry" (Acts 17:16). His spirit was *paroxuno*. The English derivative is "paroxysm," which means "to be greatly stirred, agitated."

It has been said that it was easier to find a god in Athens than it was to find a man. Wherever there was a niche into which a marble statue of a god or goddess could be placed, there it was placed. Everywhere, down every street, on every hill, in every shrine, in every temple, gods and goddesses could be found. Paul's spirit was greatly stirred in him when he saw the city wholly given to idolatry.

Modern Idolatry

Lest we think that the Athenians gave themselves to the worship of false gods, but that we today have advanced beyond their cultural and intellectual life, it might be good to look at ourselves. In so doing, we may find that there are more false gods worshiped today in Paris, London, New York, Los Angeles, and in Dallas than there were in ancient Attica and its capital city of Athens. You see, we give ourselves to the same false worship. We just call it by a different name, but it is no less ruinous and catastrophic. We do not say that we worship the god Mammon. What we see is the devotion of life to riches, wealth, success, achievement, and advancement. We do not say that we worship the god Bacchus, but the people no less give themselves to drunkenness, to drugs, and to debauchery. We do not bow before the goddesses Astarte, Aphrodite, or Venus, but we no less give ourselves to promiscuity and the cheap, terrible degradation of the human body and the human spirit. We do not speak of the god Mars, but the whole world winces before power politics, a false nationalism, terrorism, and the threat of confrontation and war. We are no less preparing for confrontation in the free world than are the communists in their world. We have not advanced over the ancient Athenians.

Athens Was the Cultural and University Center of the World

Is it not amazing that this intellectual, cultural city of Athens could be given to idolatry? There has never been a civilization that has produced the quality of scientists, philosophers, artists, and sculptors who even approach the Greek world. And yet, the very heart and center of that cultural life was given to idolatry.

Here again, lest we look upon the Greek university system in scorn as though we had advanced far beyond them, we must look at our university centers in the western world. How do they fare in idolatry? Do they bow before the true God and do they exalt the great Lord who created heaven and earth? No. They do not. They worship images and gods that are no less devastating to the human spirit. They are just called by different names. They do not say "God"; they say "Nature." They do not say "Bible"; they say "Manuals of Science." They do not say "Salvation"; they say "Inevitable Progress—Evolution." They do not say "Altar"; they say, "Experiment." They do not say "Savior"; they say "Culture and Education." They do not say "Heaven." What they say is the fuzziest, most ephemeral of all the assumptions in human life. They speak of some political, transient, and philosophical utopia. That is modern humanistic vanity, worse than ancient idolatry. They give themselves to a vast denial of the revelation of God who made heaven and earth and before whom we are accountable. So whether it is Paul in Athens, or whether it is we in this great modern world, the worship of idolatry has not changed.

THE REACTION OF THE ATHENIANS TO PAUL

Paul spoke in the market place, in the Agora, with whomever would listen to him. He encountered certain philosophers, Epicureans, Stoics, and some of them said the most contemptuous sentence. Let me read it to you: *"Ti an theloi ho spermalogos houtos legein."* Did you notice the word *"spermalogos"*? It is an unusual word. The word means "seedpicker." They state that Paul is wasting time with trifles. "What will that seedpicker say if he has anything to say?" is a good translation of that sarcastic question. The translation in our text is "What would this babbler say?"

Others said, "You know, he seems to be a setter forth of strange gods," this because he was preaching unto them *Iesous* and *Anastasis*. Seemingly he spoke of two gods, *Iesous* and *Anastasis*, Jesus and the Resurrection. The Greek culture was familiar with the idea of gods in pairs, male and female. There was Jove and Juno, Venus and Adonis, Isis and Osiris, Baal and Astarte. *Iesous* is male, *anastasis* is female, so it seemed to them when Paul spoke of Jesus and the Resurrection that he was setting forth strange gods.

Our story says in verse 19 that they brought him to the Areopagus.

In verse 22 the Scripture says that Paul stood in the midst of Mars Hill. *Areopagus* is the Greek word for Mars Hill. *Areios* is the adjectival form of *Ares*, the Greek name for the Latin god, *Mars*. In the Greek the word is *Ares*, the god of war. *Areois* is the adjectival form of Ares. *Pagos* is the Greek word for hill. So *Areopagus* is Mars Hill. It referred to the highest court of the Athenians. Seven hundred and fifty years before Christ that court was sitting in session. Did you know that to this day the Supreme Court in Athens is called "The Areopagus"? Paul is brought before that distinguished court surrounded by all the Athenian listeners to speak of this new *doxa*, translated "doctrine," this new teaching of Jesus and the Resurrection.

The Areopagus is the place where the brilliant and the great of all Athenian history stood. Solon, the Athenian lawgiver stood there. That is the place where Pericles stood in the 400's B.C. delivering his matchless orations. That is the place where Demosthenes stood delivering his *Philippics*, stirring rebellion against the Macedonian king, Philip, the father of Alexander the Great. That is the place where the great philosophers stood. That is the place where Socrates was condemned to die. In the Areopagus surrounded by those Athenian listeners, Paul presented the Lord Jesus. Such a confrontation in human history!

The Athenians were already persuaded of much that Paul had to say. Practically all Athenians believed in the supernatural. There were very few of them who were persuaded, as our modern infidels are, that the world just created itself. Such a persuasion is the most outlandish, incredible, and impossible teaching of which the mind could conceive, yet that is the accepted teaching of our modern university system. Such incredible stupidity!

In addition, the people in Athens believed in the judgment upon evil, which they called a "nemesis." Practically all of the ancient Greek tragedies are built around the goddess Nemesis. The story of Greek tragedy presents a man who had dipped his hands in human blood or has done violence and wrong, then a nemesis follows, finally bringing the man to judgment. The Greeks believed there were rewards for good and evil and they believed in the government of gods.

In the King James Version Paul says, "I perceive that in all things ye are too superstitious." Paul did not insult the Athenians with the word, "superstitious." The Greek word, *deisidaimonesterous* should be translated, "I perceive that in all things ye are very reverent and very religious." It is a compliment to anyone anywhere to be called reverent. Thus, the wise man or woman, boy or girl, seeks after the true knowledge of God. As the proverb says, "The beginning of wisdom is the fear, the reverential awe before God." The Athenians were most reverent and religious.

MAN'S SEEKING FOR GOD NEEDS DIRECTION

The story of the human race from the beginning had been that man is incurably religious. We cannot remove from the heart of man the wondering after the great Lord God. What is needed is that the longing in the human heart to have fellowship with the Creator, the great God who made us, have direction that we might come into the true light.

Socrates was made to commit suicide by the court of the Areopagus because he was accused of taking away the mind of the youth from the true worship of deity, the gods. What we need is the light, the revelation from heaven, a word from the Almighty.

For those who have been introduced into the Masonic Lodge, there is a place in the initiation of the lodge where a blinded man cries, "I need light!" That is the cry of the human soul and the human spirit, that I might see, that I might come to know, that I might understand, that I might be guided.

So the apostle Paul, standing before the court of the Areopagus on Mars Hill, began to speak, "I perceive that in all things ye are very religious, very reverent." Paul says: "For as I passed by, and beheld your devotions, I found an altar with this inscription, *Agnosto Theo*, TO AN UNKNOWN GOD" (Acts 17:23). Then he began his address declaring to them this "Unknown God." With all the gods of their temples and marvelous shrines, there was still a longing, a yearning, a restlessness in their hearts. They had not found the truth which they were so earnestly seeking. So they erected an altar to an unknown god.

Is that not typical of human life that gives itself to the cheap emoluments of the world? Man seeks in self-chosen ways satisfaction for his soul, but somehow he never reaches it. One gives himself to anything worldly, name it—promiscuity, cheap pleasure, drunkenness, alcohol, drugs, fame, success, fortune, wealth, knowledge—and when he has achieved it, it turns to dust and ashes in his hands. There is an emptiness, a sterility, and a barrenness in the rewards of the world.

I often think of the Hollywood movie stars. Think of the money, the fame, and all of the success they have. But if I were looking for someone who uses drugs or for someone to commit suicide, I would look in their lives. The gains of this world are so empty and unsatisfying.

THE ADDRESS OF PAUL

Continuing in our story, the apostle pronounced and preached the glorious hope and revelation of the Lord God in Christ Jesus:

> Whom therefore ye ignorantly worship, him declare I unto you. God that made the world and all things therein, seeing that he is Lord of heaven and earth, dwelleth not in temples made with hands (Acts 17:23b-24).

I can see the apostle standing on Mars Hill. Even the remains of the Acropolis are dramatic and impressively beautiful today. Crowning the Acropolis is the Parthenon, doubtless one of the most magnificent pieces of human architecture the world has ever known. Inside is the statue of Pallas Athena, after whom the city was named. Her Latin name is Minerva, goddess of art and wisdom. As patron goddess she stands with her spear guarding the city. There are other magnificent temples to the Greek gods and goddesses nearby. With a gesture of his hand, the apostle stood and proclaimed, "God that made the world and all things therein, seeing that he is Lord of heaven and earth, dwelleth not in temples made with hands." Then he preached the blessed Jesus, how the Lord God, deity, took form and flesh, walked among us as a man, breathed our air, lived our lives, and suffered our troubles, heartaches, and fortunes. He died our death, and God accepted His atoning grace in our behalf in that He raised the Lord from the dead to be our Intercessor, our faithful High Priest, and our Mediator in heaven. He understands and cares for us. We can go to Him with our heartaches and troubles, with our tears and hurts, with our weaknesses and our sins. We can bow in His presence and He welcomes us, He speaks to us, He saves us, He blesses us, He fills our heart to overflowing.

Blessed be the name of the Lord! What a gospel! What a hope! How could anyone turn aside from the invitation of the blessed Jesus!

37

Just Passing By

For as I passed by, and beheld your devotions, I found an altar with this inscription, TO THE UNKNOWN GOD. Whom therefore ye ignorantly worship, him declare I unto you. (Acts 17:23)

In Acts 17:23 we find the Greek word, *dierchomai*, the participle of which is *dierchomenos*, which is the word translated here, "passing by." "For as I passed by, I saw your many devotions." Paul had felt in his soul the paroxysm, the agitation of seeing the whole city given to idolatry.

In the heart of Africa I am introduced to the king of a large tribe. He lives in a compound in which the entrance is a very impressive gate. All around the compound live his many wives and children. I see in front of the entrance to the compound, his home, a little house built right in the way. I ask the missionary, "What is the purpose of the little house?"

The missionary replies: "That house is a devil's house. There is a god that he worships who is fierce and awesome. The king worships the god because he is afraid of him, lest evil come to him and his house."

Passing by, I see an enormous kapok tree. Looking at it closely, I see that it is covered with blood. I ask the missionary, "Why is blood on the tree?"

He replies, "The people believe that the spirit of a god lives in the tree and they worship the tree, making sacrifices before the gods and covering the tree with the blood of the sacrifices."

I go further and see a large rock. Looking at it closely, I see that it is covered with blood. Again, the missionary says to me: "They believe that the spirit of a god lives in the rock and they worship it. They are animists. They worship the rock and offer sacrifices to it and cover it with blood." Just passing by.

Coming to Jerusalem, I see a large mosque on the Dome of the Rock. On the inside of the mosque is a very famous rock. The Muslim says: "See the footprint in the rock? That is the footprint left by the prophet Mohammed when he stepped from the rock onto his steed and was taken up into heaven. The vial, so sacred in our hands, contains a hair that fell from his head. We have it as a shrine and memorial to the translation of Mohammed the prophet." Just passing by.

Walking through one of the greatest cities of Africa, I see that the street is completely filled for two or three blocks with men dressed in white who are bowing in their prayer time toward Mecca. Just passing by.

Going through India, I see Sikhs with their long hair, knotted in the back in the fashion of a woman's bun. I also see a special group of holy men in Hinduism, mostly naked, walking up and down the streets. They never bathe. They have never bathed in their life. They are holy Hindus bowing before the gods. After they have bowed before the gods, they take their finger and make a dot on their forehead of an amber-colored substance. Just passing by.

In the Orient, the houses in China and Japan are built with an upward slant to the roof. If you ask, "Why is the roof slanted outward and upward?" the answer inevitably will be, "When evil spirits fall on the house, they could come in and do us harm, but when the roof is slanted upward on the edge, the evil spirits bounce off and go back into space and do not hurt us." Just passing by.

Through the Ages

Nor have the ages passed been any different. When one visits Mesa Verde in southwestern Colorado he sees where the cliff dwellers lived. In places of their dead he will see little pots and pans and evidences of vegetables and fruit buried also, because the dead were going on a long journey into a land they had never discovered. The cliff dwellers believed in the life that is yet to come and placed these instruments alongside the bodies to be used in the happy hunting ground. In some instances, the American Indian was buried with his bow and arrow for use in the world beyond the gates of death. For many centuries, the hieroglyphics in which the mummies in Egypt were buried were unknown to the western world, but the Rosetta Stone revealed that each one of those mummies was wrapped in what was called the Book of the Dead, that they might know how to do and what to expect in their journey that was yet to come.

Nor is it any different now. In the Old Testament the concern of Jehovah God for Israel was not that they would become atheist and infidels, but that they might worship the gods of the Ammonites, of the Hittites, of the Hivites, and of the Amorites.

When Elijah was on Mt. Carmel, he said, "If Baal be god, worship Baal, but if Jehovah be God, worship Jehovah." He did not say, "If Jehovah be God or if there be no God." It was Baal or Jehovah.

In Assyria when the northern kingdom of Israel was taken away and the Assyrians colonized the land, the government of Assyria sent a priest for Jehovah that he might teach the Assyrian strangers the god of the land.

When the storm hit the ship in which Jonah lay asleep, the captain of the ship awakened every man and said, "Cry to your god that we be saved."

It is the same through all of the centuries; just passing by.

When Paul waited in Athens, he was stirred in his soul when he saw the city given to idolatry. Just passing by this believing and worshiping world.

SHEER SUPERSTITION

I come to the place in my life when I say: To believe in God is intellectual vanity and inconceivable stupidity. I am not going to be caught in the web of all that worship. I shall live my life without the gods and I shall live my life scientifically. I shall live it intellectually. I shall live it academically. I have now achieved the place in my life where I am above any of the gods. Old gods like Baal and Astarte, new gods like Buddha and Krishna; I have no god in my life. I have come to a place in my intellectual achievement and progress where I do not need God and I do not believe in God. I am free and I give myself to my new liberated, intellectual, and scientific life.

Wonderful. So I am liberated and free. But there are some things along the way, just passing by, that nag at my heart and knock at the door of my spirit. I cannot hide my face from them.

BUT THERE IS MORE

First, through all the centuries there has been devotion to a god. It could be that man's idolatry and misunderstanding just point out the fact that there might be a real God. These are but false imitations of a true reality.

In Exodus 7, when Moses cast his rod down before Pharaoh and it became a serpent, the sorcerers cast their rods down and they became serpents, imitating what God had done. But it could be that imitation but points out that there was a real gift that the Lord gave as a sign to Moses.

It could be that when I see an imitation of a Raphael, it points to the fact that there is a real Raphael, a real painter. These imitations but avow that he really painted.

It could be that when I hear a man try to sing like Caruso, it just points out the fact that there was a real Caruso.

When I see an imitation diamond, it could be that the imitation but emphasizes the fact that there is a real diamond somewhere.

All of the false gods and ageless devotions could be the pointing out of the fact that there is a great reality and truth in deity and divinity.

I somewhere meet that reality down every road. I cannot hide myself from it. If I am intellectually honest, I meet it everywhere.

Being a pastor, I have lived no small part of my life in a hospital, visiting and praying with the sick. The surgeon sharpens the scalpel and intrudes into the human body. Then with sutures, the wound is placed together again. But who heals it? Does the doctor heal it? He is totally helpless. Someone heals. Someone makes well. Someone closes up the wound. Who is that Someone?

In reading the stories of human life and seeing the beauty that surrounds me, I see over and beyond some other Someone. I see Him everywhere.

I look at the stars which follow patterns and laws without a second variation through the untold ages. Who did that? Who promulgated the laws and who holds the universe in His hand?

In looking at history, it seems that life is struggling toward some kind of consummation. Who moves in nations, in continents, and in life?

I look at the science of biology. Take a little watermelon seed. It calls forth its architects and engineers, and it creates a watermelon 200,000 times its own weight. Its little architects and engineers get together and call in aroma, color, taste, and 500 other little things just like itself. Who made the watermelon seed? The whole world is filled with wonder and victory, the sign and signature of a great Someone.

IN HUMAN NEED

Most of all, the human heart has a need. There is a precious family who have a darling, flaxen-haired little girl. The child dies and lies in the casket at home. The mother says, "Just one more time, may I comb her hair?" As she combs the flaxen hair, the father turns his face away to hide the tears. Oh, that I knew Someone who could say, "Suffer the little children to come unto me, and forbid them not, for of such is the kingdom of heaven!"

But you see, I have dismissed Him. I do not believe in God. I have come to an intellectual plateau in my life where those who are devotees of God are stupid to me. I have risen above them.

But the longing lingers in my soul. Would to God I knew Someone who could say, "Come unto me."

The days pass, the years follow, and the life is almost spent. The silver cord is loosed, the golden bowl is broken. The pitcher is broken at the fountain, and the wheel is broken at the cistern. The valley seems long and there is no one in step with me. Would to God there was someone who would say to me: "The Lord is your shepherd. Though you walk through the valley of the shadow of death, you need not be afraid. The signs of His presence, a rod and a staff, will comfort you, and you will live in the house of the Lord forever and ever!"

But I have dismissed Him. I have come to an intellectual excellence where I do not believe in God.

But oh, my poor heart and soul! What shall I say of the sense of weakness, sin, and guilt! Would to God there was Someone who could say, "This is my blood of the new covenant shed for the remission of sins!"

In this long journey called life, would to God Someone could say: "I will never leave thee nor forsake thee. I will see you through!"

I MUST RETHINK MY FACTS

Maybe I have not considered all the facts. Perhaps I have overlooked some of the great facts of life.

One, the greatest fact in human history is the fact of God.

Two, the greatest fact in human story is the fact of Jesus Christ. He divided time, A.D. and B.C. Around Him centers the love and devotion of uncounted millions. Maybe Jesus is a fact as these other things are facts.

Is it not astonishing that men can study rocks and evolve a science of geology, and they can study stars and evolve a science of astronomy? They can study fossils and evolve a science of past history, but is it not strange that I should not be able to discover the great fact of Jesus Christ and find in Him an ultimate answer to all of the hurts and troubles of mankind? I can study the heavenly bodies and never be sensitive to the Creator who came down from glory.

Ah, Lord, that I might have that wisdom, not only to be sensitive to the ages of the rocks, but to know, love, and adore the Rock of the ages.

> Rock of ages, cleft for me,
> Let me hide myself in Thee.
> Let the water and the blood,
> From Thy wounded side which flowed,
> Be of sin the double cure,
> Save from wrath and make me pure.

Maybe God could give me the unusual sensitivity and capacity to see beyond the stars, the Bright and Morning Star, Him who said;

> I Jesus have sent mine angel to testify unto you these things in the churches. I am the root and the offspring of David, and the bright and the morning star.
> And the Spirit and the bride say, Come. And let him that heareth say, Come. And let him that is athirst come. And whosoever will, let him take the water of life freely (Rev. 22:16-17).

Maybe God will give me the intellectual capacity, the academic achievement, the sensitivity of understanding to find in the Lily of the Valley those botanical miracles that lead me to Christ; to find in a grain of wheat, Him who died that I might live—Bread of heaven, manna from above, the angels' food.

> Break Thou the bread of life,
> Dear Lord, to me,
> As Thou didst break the loaves
> Beside the sea;
> Beyond the sacred page
> I seek Thee, Lord;
> My spirit pants for Thee,
> O living Word.

It is a wonderful man, an intellectual man, a man of wisdom and spiritual achievement who sees God everywhere—who sees Him in the stars at night, who sees Him rise in the strength of the morning sun; who sees Him in the plants that grow; who sees Him in the very food that we eat; who sees His presence in the times of human sorrow; who sees Him as the moving Spirit in history; who sees Him in friendship and in love; who sees Him on the pages of the Bible; who feels His loving presence when he kneels in prayer. We can meet the Lord down every road and see Him in every created thing. A man's heart is happy in Jesus. Just passing by.

Back of all the phenomena that one sees in human life and history is God. Blessed is he who sees Him in Jesus Christ and finds the Lord precious to his soul!

38

Commanded Repentance

And the times of this ignorance God winked at; but now commandeth all men everywhere to repent. (Acts 17:30)

Verses 22 through 31 of Acts 17 present one of the tremendous addresses of human history when the apostle Paul stood on Mars Hill and spoke to the supreme court of the ancient cultural and academic life of Athens. We will look especially at verse 30: ". . . but now (God) commandeth all men everywhere to repent."

This is a command performance, something that God demands. No man shall enter the kingdom of God who has not repented before the Lord. No man can stand before God in his own righteousness, in his own holiness, in his own goodness, but our approach to God must always be in deepest contrition, humility, and repentance. The prophetic message to Israel always is one of repentance, of turning, of confession, of getting right with God. We read in Isaiah 59:

> Behold, the LORD's hand is not shortened, that it cannot save; nor his ear heavy, that it cannot hear:
> But your iniquities have separated between you and your God, and your sins have hid his face from you, that he will not hear (vv. 1-2).

Likewise, hear the call of the prophet Ezekiel:

> Have I any pleasure at all that the wicked should die? saith the LORD GOD: and not that he should return from his ways, and live? (18:23).

287

The appeal of the prophet Jeremiah was:

> Why will ye die, thou and thy people, by the sword, by the famine, and by the pestilence, as the LORD hath spoken against the nation that will not serve the king of Babylon? (27:13).

The Babylonians came in 605 B.C. and carried Daniel and some of the royal seed away. Jeremiah lifted up his voice and cried, "Repent; get right with God." The Babylonians came again in 598 B.C. and carried away Ezekiel, most of the priesthood, and many of the royal family. Again Jeremiah cried, "Repent, get right with God!" The Babylonians came the third time in 587 B.C. and they had no need to return, for this time they carried the nation into captivity, destroyed Jerusalem, broke down its walls, and burned the holy temple with fire. God commands that we repent, for there is no life beyond death without repentance. Our non-repentance spells judgment and death for us.

GOD APPEALS TO AMERICA TODAY

God addresses the same word to the nation of America today. I used to think of America as being a Christian nation. Our principles were godly. The background of our history was Christian. The founding fathers who came to the new world and gave birth to the nation were well-grounded in the Bible. They were disciples of the Lord Jesus and they came to build churches, Christian homes, and finally a Christian government. But for us to call America a Christian nation today would be a gross misjudgment and misnomer. Our nation today is secular, worldly, and materialistic. For the most part, our people live as though God did not exist. We have been led into that way of life by a difference in our dependence upon the bread we eat, the clothing we wear, and the shelter under which we abide. There was a time in the past when the people looked up to God for the blessings of life. It was from His hands that the gentle rain fell, that the seed germinated, that the crops were harvested, and that our lives were blessed and kept. We used to look up to God for all of the blessings which sustain and enrich our days. Somehow in our academic community and in the teaching of the younger generations, we have come no longer to depend upon God, but to depend upon science, machinery, and gadgetry. We may not admit or realize it, but we are still no less dependent upon the generous goodness of God for the blessings upon our nation than in any generation past or in any century gone by.

I saw that fact poignantly illustrated in a little poem that I read on the back of a church bulletin when I was preaching in London one time. It read:

> We plough the fields with tractors,
> With drills we sow the land;
> But growth is still the wondrous gift
> of God's almighty hand.
> We add our fertilizers
> To help the growing grain—
> But for its full fruition
> It needs God's sun and rain.
>
> With many new machines now
> We do the work each day:
> We reap the fields with combines,
> We bale the new-mown hay.
> But it is God who gives us
> Inventive skills and drives
> Which lighten labour's drudg'ry
> And gives us fuller lives.

With all our inventions, our machines, and our gadgetry, our lives are still dependent upon the generous remembrances of God. A nation that turns from the Lord inevitably turns to judgment and death. The cry of the prophets is the cry of God's true servants today. God commands all men everywhere to repent. But how can a nation repent? How can a city repent? How can an audience repent? How can a great aggregate of people repent?

WE REPENT ONE BY ONE

There is no such thing as a nation repenting, as an audience or a great aggregate of people repenting. We repent one by one, individually, as we appear before God. If a nation repents, it is because its people repent one by one. If a city repents, it is because its citizens turn to the Lord one by one. If an audience and a congregation repents, it is because one by one we repent. The nation cannot repent if I do not repent. The nation cannot turn to God if I do not turn. The nation cannot accept Christ if I do not accept Christ. The call to repentance is always to the human heart, to the human soul. God commands us to repent. This is God's way for our forgiveness, our deliverance, and our salvation, for no man shall ever come into the presence of the Lord except in deepest contrition, humility, and confession. This is what God leads us to see and to understand when he preaches to us the gospel of salvation and deliverance.

Let me illustrate. A man in a hospital was terminally ill. A Christian worker came by to see him. In his kindness and prayerful interest, the worker said to the man, "Sir, is there anything I can do for you?"

The man replied, "No, sir; thank you, nothing."

As the days passed, each time the worker would come by and say to the dying man, "Is there something that I can do for you?" the man would reply, "No, sir; thank you, nothing." The day came when the man finally faced the inevitable hour of death which we all shall face. The Christian repeated his question, "Sir, just once again, is there anything I can do for you?"

The man, looking up into the face of his visitor, replied humbly: "No, thank you, there is nothing that you can do for me. But oh, sir, would to God there were some things you could undo for me!"

What do you do when you come to the place of realization that we need Someone who can undo some things for us? As we look at the human family, we see them turn to many things as they seek to hide the guilt, the barrenness, the frustration, the disappointment, or the loss in their lives. Some of them turn to drink and drown their lives in drink. Some turn to drugs and seek a way out of the disappointments and frustrations of life in drugs. Some turn to all kinds of endeavors and seek to bury their lives in these worldly pursuits. In any event and each instance, the result is always one of ultimate and final despair. We will never find deliverance for our souls in drugs, in drink, in promiscuity, or in worldly pursuits and pleasures. There is just one way a man can find salvation and deliverance for his soul and that is in his coming before God in deepest contrition and humility, repenting of his sins. "God commandeth all men everywhere to repent."

WHAT REPENTANCE IS NOT

If my life and my salvation and my deliverance is dependent upon my repentance, what is repentance?

First, repentance is *not* remorse, sorrow, or regret. There is a play upon words in the Greek as it is used in the New Testament in 2 Corinthians 7:

> For though I made you sorry with a letter, I do not repent, though I did repent: for I perceive that the same epistle hath made you sorry, though it were but for a season.
>
> Now I rejoice, not that ye were made sorry, but that ye sorrowed to repentance: for ye were made sorry after a godly manner, that ye might receive damage by us in nothing.

> For godly sorrow worketh repentance to salvation not to be repented of: but the sorrow of the world worketh death (vv. 8-10).

The two Greek words which vitally affect us are *metamelomai*, which means "sorrow," "regret," or "remorse," and *metanoeo* which means "repentance," "turning," a "change of mind, attitude, and way." Now let me read the passage again.

> For though I made you sorry with a letter, I do not regret it, *metamelomai*, though I did *metamelomai*, regret it, for I perceive that the sorrow I caused you was for just awhile,
>
> But now I rejoice, not that ye were made sorry, but that ye sorrowed to *metanoeo*, to repentance, to a change of heart and mind.
>
> For godly sorrow worketh *metanoeo* to salvation not to be *metamelomai*, not to be regretted, but the sorrow of the world worketh death.

There is a *metamelomai*, there is a regret, a remorse, but this is not repentance. *Metamelomai* is the word that is used to describe Judas. When Judas saw what he had done, he repented, and went and hanged himself. That is what the New Testament says in English. But the word is *metamelomai*. When Judas saw that what he had done had resulted in the crucifixion of our Lord, he *metamelomai*—filled with remorse and regret, he took his own life. And that is not *metanoeo*; that is not repentance. As much as Judas had sinned in betraying innocent blood, had he returned, had he *metaneoeo*, repented, come to Jesus, and bowed down in His presence and said, "Lord, Lord, forgive me of this awesome thing that I have done in betraying You with a kiss," I know the heart of my Lord well enough to know that Judas would have been forgiven and he would have been saved.

But repentance also is not a catastrophic providence that overwhelms us, even a great religious experience.

Let me illustrate that. In a small town in which the church had just completed a revival meeting, a man was talking to a preacher. The man said, "You know, it just never did strike me."

The preacher said, "What do you mean, that it never did strike you?"

He replied, "In the great revival we have just been through, there were many who were saved, but it never did strike me."

He was telling the preacher that he attended the services, he listened to the gospel, and he expected God to do some unusual and earth-shaking thing for him. But as he sat there and no angel came and lifted him up to set him in the kingdom, or no light from heaven blinded him in the way, or no ball of fire burst over his head, no marvelous and catastrophic event overwhelmed him, therefore, he was not saved.

That is not repentance. Repentance is *not* some earthshaking experience that overwhelms you. I could pray that every one of us might have the experience of an apostle Paul, but there is just one apostle Paul. All of the rest of the apostles were saved just as I was, in a simple coming to the Lord Jesus.

Repentance is *not* a passive waiting for God to do something. We do not just sit, wait, and abide.

A man was talking to an old boatman. Looking down at the water by the pier, he said, "If I fell in that water, would I drown?"

The old boatman said, "No."

The fellow asked, "Well, what would it take for me to drown?"

The boatman replied: "It is not falling in the water that drowns you. It is staying there that drowns you."

That is exactly our passivity. It is doing nothing that damns us, that condemns us. One does not have to murder someone to be condemned, to be lost, to be judged. He does not have to commit a violent crime in order to face the judgment of God. He does not have to be guilty of a tremendous act of desperation and iniquity in order to be judged. By nature, we are sinners. We do not need to be taught to be sinners. We are born with the black drop of sin in our blood. As the days pass, we are sensitive and become conscious of dereliction, mistake, iniquity, sin, and lostness in our lives. To be lost is a state of being. By nature, we are children of wrath, dead in trespasses and in sins. In passivity, I can finally face the judgment of God still lost in my sin by just drifting into eternity without God.

WHAT REPENTANCE IS

Repentance is a volitional, conscious, decided turning toward the Lord. I have been walking one way, away from God, but then I change, I turn. I then go toward God. I had been walking away from the church and God's people, but then I turn and ask God to forgive my sin. That is repentance, *metanoeo*. I have changed my heart, my mind, my direction, and my attitude. I turn from the world and toward Jesus.

The rest of it is in God's hands. When I turn, when I ask God to help me, to save me and to forgive me, and He does not do it, then if I am lost it is His fault. Then salvation is up to Him. I cannot save myself. I cannot regenerate my soul. I cannot forgive myself. I cannot reborn myself. All I can do is repent, ask God, and then my salvation is in His hands.

> The soul that on Jesus
> hath leaned for repose,
> I will not, I will not
> desert to its foes;
> That soul, though all hell
> should endeavor to shake,
> I'll never, no, never,
> no, never forsake.

How do you know that? Because the Lord said, "He that cometh unto me, I will in no wise cast out." That is repentance. That is what it is to walk into the kingdom. "God commandeth all men everywhere to turn, to come, to believe, to repent." When I do it, when I come, when I turn, when I trust, when I commit my life to the blessed Jesus, my salvation is in His hands, and He never fails!

39

The Fixed Day of Judgment

Because he hath appointed a day, in the which he will judge the world in
righteousness by that man whom he hath ordained; whereof he hath given
assurance unto all men, in that he hath raised him from the dead. (Acts 17:31)

We are commanded to repent. It is not given to us by choice. We
are commanded to repent because God hath *estesen*, the first aorist
active indicative form of *histemi*, which means "to set," "to establish,"
"to sustain." God has firmly appointed, set, named a day, a time in
which He will judge the world in righteousness by that man whom He
hath *horizo*, "marked out," "designated." Our English word "horizon"
comes from the word *horizo* and refers to the demarcation line where
the sky above and the earth beneath meet. Christ Jesus is marked out,
designated as the One who will judge all mankind in a set day of the
Lord.

The fact is most plain and emphatic. According to the entire Word
of God, it is a day that we inevitably must face. All of us shall appear
before Christ as our Judge. As the Bible teaches, we shall be in two
groups. One group will be those who are raptured. We will be in the
presence of the judgment seat of Christ in heaven, called the Bema of
our Lord. All who are saved, who know Jesus, who have repented of
their sins, who have asked God to forgive them, who have accepted the
Lord as their Savior, shall appear before the Great Judge, the Lord
Jesus, after the resurrection of the righteous dead. And Jesus will
reward us according to our works.

Then those who do not accept the Lord as Savior will appear before the Great White Throne Judgment and will cry for the rocks and the mountains to fall on them. The very earth and heavens will flee away from His countenance on that awesome day, a set point in time in the sovereignty of God. All of us shall appear before Jesus, either in His gracious goodness to us as a friend in court, or as the awesome Judge, the wrath of the Lamb.

Paul says that we are to repent in view of the fact that God has appointed a day in which He will judge the world.

THE UNCHANGING GOD

If this is a set day of the Lord, then God is an unchanging God. However the providences flow and the events happen, the Lord God is unchanging in some of the commitments He makes and some of the words He says.

When we think of an unchanging God who sets events which are firmly established forever, then the question is asked: "You say God is unchanging; then why prayer? What is the necessity for prayer if these things are unchanging and established?"

People sometimes will say, if they know the Bible: "God changes. In Isaiah 38 God sent the prophet to Hezekiah and said, 'Set thy house in order, for thou shalt surely die and not live.' Hezekiah turned his face to the wall, prayed, and cried before the Lord. God turned Isaiah around and said, 'Go back and tell him, I have seen your tears, I have heard your prayers, and I have added to your life fifteen years.' God changed in that instance."

Sometimes a man will add, "Jonah preached the word of the Lord and said, 'Yet forty days and Nineveh shall be destroyed.' Then the king of Assyria, down to the lowest, menial servant in his palace, and even the beasts were clothed in sackcloth, and they repented before the Lord. When the Lord saw that Nineveh repented, He repented. When God saw that Nineveh changed, He changed. When God saw that Nineveh cried to Him in prayer for mercy, He changed. He did not destroy the city. Jonah pouted because God changed and did not do what He said He would do. If these events are true, then why do you preach about an unchanging God who sets and appoints days and judgments that are firmly established?"

Let me point out a fact in history. Hezekiah surely died. Assyria and Nineveh were surely destroyed. On God's slide rule, sometimes in His goodness and providence, the Lord will listen to a man's cry, will look at a man's tears, and in pity and mercy, do something else. But the unchangeableness of God lies in His character, who He is, and what He does in His sovereign lordship. He is Lord over all and forever. The Lord set days in His sovereign grace and guides all events in all history toward those set days.

We see an illustration of this in the set days when Jesus was born. Through the centuries God guided all history to that day when Jesus should be born.

The Greek Empire had no knowledge of the gospel at all, yet they taught the world the Greek language in which the gospel was preached and the New Testament was written. The Roman Empire built roads and drew the whole civilized world together so that the apostles could preach the gospel from one end of the Mediterranean to the other. The Hebrew people were in Jerusalem and Judaea where God said the Lord Jesus would be born. In the fullness of time, when all history conspired under the sovereign hand of God for that moment which was set by the Lord in heaven, Jesus was born.

He was crucified on a set day. He was raised from the dead on a set day. He is coming again on a set day. The Lord said, "I do not know that day, the angels do not know that day, but that day is known to My Father in heaven." There is an appointed day when Jesus will come and all the events of time and history will move toward that day. That is the unchangeableness of God.

THE SOVEREIGNTY OF GOD

Did you notice as you read the address of the apostle Paul on Mars Hill how he emphasized the sovereignty of God? Look at it carefully. Paul spoke of God as being the great Creator of the world and everything in it. Then he spoke of the sovereign God as being the One who sustains the world. He gives life and breath to all creation.

Then Paul spoke of the sovereign God as being the Governor, the Director, the Overlord of all the nations. In time and in space, He sets our destinies. What an amazing avowal! He determines the times and the bounds of our existence. The nations endure as long as God chooses that they endure. The space they occupy is the space God allots that they occupy. He is the great Sovereign of all the nations of the world.

Then Paul spoke of the Lord God as being the ultimate Judge of all mankind. He has appointed a day in which He will judge the world. This is the sovereignty of God.

Paul also avowed that the world and the whole course of history does not move by blind chance, by philosophical happenstance, or indifference. All of history, life, and time move according to the sovereignty of God who is Judge of all men. Paul never deviated from that. He spoke of election, of foreordination, of judgment, and of sovereignty. When one uses those words, he describes the Lord God in heaven.

THE LIMITS OF PERSONAL FREEDOM

If these things are true, then what of men who say: "I repudiate the doctrine. I absolutely refuse to believe that I am not completely free, completely at my own choice and in my own will. I deny the sovereignty of God. I am completely free. I am free for the working out of my own destiny. In no sense and in no way am I under the lordship and sovereignty of God."

Man is free in the sense that he can refuse to believe. He is free in that he can refuse to repent. He is free in that he can say No to God in His love and in His grace. But man is not free and he will never be free in the sense that God's sovereign hand rules in this world in which we live and in the destiny of history in which we are involved.

So man says: "I refuse to believe that God controls this world and controls my life and that some day I shall stand before Him in judgment. I am absolutely free."

Fine. Time marches on, and it carries man with it. However man may say he refuses to accept, to believe, time has him in its grasp and it marches on carrying him with it.

"But you do not understand. You see, I am going to stop the hands of the clock. I am not to be circumscribed and limited in my personal freedom. When the flood waters of judgment come, I will open my umbrella or I will paddle my little canoe, and I will be untouched by the floods and the maelstrom. You say that the house will burn down over my head? I refuse to see the flames. You say that the lightning of God's judgment will cross the livid sky? I will blind my eyes to it and I will not look."

But whether you try to stop the hands of the clock, whether you open an umbrella against the floods that are going to fall, or whether you blind your eyes to the lightning of the destiny that crosses the sky, you are caught in the vice of time and it carries you with it. You are caught in the hands of history and it carries you with it. You are caught in the universe on which planet you live, and as it moves, you move with it.

There are great facts in life over which we have no control. They are in the sovereign hands of God. The days pass and I get older and the years pass and I come to the grave. Death comes and I am helpless before it. It is nothing but the honesty of facing reality to understand and to see that there are great appointments and judgments set and established by the Lord God. I am like an infinitesimal speck in the great storm that blows.

So the apostle says that I am to repent, I am to bow, I am to give obeisance, I am to pray, I am to turn, I am to get right with God because He has appointed a day, a set day in which He will judge all the earth.

THE JUDGMENTS OF GOD

That is a teaching you can find throughout the Word of God. It is not unique or something unusual that the apostle is preaching to the Athenians. It is the whole Word of God. God judges the world. He judges men. He judges nations. He sets days of judgment.

Have you heard of the seven dispensations? That is a system of theology that is most powerfully presented by those who study the Word of the Lord. What gives rise to the teaching of those seven great periods in the Bible in God's dealing with men are the judgments of God in the destiny of men as it is revealed in human history. Each dispensation ends in a judgment. All of them are types and harbingers of the final Judgment Day of the Lord.

For example, there is a dispensation that is called innocence and it ends in a judgment. "In the day that thou eatest thereof, thou shalt surely die." That is set by the sovereign hand of God, for when man sins, he dies. "The wages of sin is death." In the day that Adam and Eve sinned, they died. Is it not a strange thing that no man has ever lived beyond a day on God's clock, which is a thousand years? That is a judgment of God.

In the days of the Antedeluvians, when righteous Noah preached, God said, "Yet one hundred twenty years and I will destroy this world." One hundred twenty years, a set day of the Lord, was a judgment day.

As long as the people of Israel were obedient to the Lord, they had the right to live in the land, but when they disobeyed, God said the judgment would come. In 587 B.C. they were carried away into captivity. When Jesus spoke to the people of Israel, His prophecy was that "this generation shall not pass" until the judgments from God would fall. In A.D. 70 the Roman legions came and destroyed the city and destroyed the nation. That is a judgment of God. All of these events are but harbingers of what God does in our day and in our time. Our day shall end in a great judgment; namely, the Day of Armageddon. The world moves toward that final day of the Lord. It is most unusual how the world is turning and shaping.

For example, it says in the Bible that there will be an army from the east of 200,000 men who are going to drive toward Israel, the Middle East. Did you know that as tourist groups are now beginning to visit China, if one had an Israeli visa in his passport, he could not enter Red China? What has Red China to do with that tiny country of Israel? Israel could be tucked away in a little corner of the 1,000,000,000 people who live in China. Why pick out that tiny land and say that if you have an Israeli visa in your passport, you cannot get into China?

That is the way God is moving in our generation. There is going to be a confrontation of the nations of the world in the Middle East. All of the communist nations will be together. Right now Russia and China are at odds, but it will not always be that way. That is temporary and just on the surface. The whole world is moving toward the great Judgment Day of almighty God. Man cannot disassociate himself from it. The little babe in the cradle, reaching up its tiny arm, is reaching toward the day of judgment. The youth, striding by with elastic tread, is striding toward the Judgment Day of almighty God. The poor man, dressed in rags, is walking toward the Judgment Day, as is the Christian pilgrim, with songs on his lips and praises to God on his heart. The lost sinner, doing despite to the Spirit of grace, saying No to God and No to the love of Jesus, is facing God's Judgment Day. Of that day, Jesus had more to say than anything else of which He spoke. Sometimes He would speak of it as sheep and goats; one on the right and one on the left. Sometimes He would speak of it in terms of two sleeping in a bed; one is taken and the other left. Sometimes He would speak of it as two men working in a field; one is taken away and one is left. Sometimes He would speak of it as two grinding at a mill; one is taken and the other left.

Thus it was that Paul preached in the light of this established day of the Lord. Let us repent, let us get right with God, let us ask forgiveness for our sins, let us receive the atoning grace and love of Christ for our souls. Let us walk in the pilgrim way and live, work, and die or be raptured, in the blessedness of the grace and love of the Lord Jesus.

Like Dionysius and Damaris who turned and believed, let us turn and repent, and then in the strength of His glory, let us live our lives triumphantly in this day and stand in the presence of the Lord Jesus, our friend and Savior in the day that is yet to come!

40

It Is Reasonable to Be a Christian

And when they heard of the resurrection of the dead, some mocked: and others said, We will hear thee again of this matter. (Acts 17:32)

He had been speaking with the people in the Agora, the market-place:

Then certain philosophers of the Epicureans, and of the Stoics, encountered him. And some said, What will this babbler say? other some, He seemeth to be a setter forth of strange gods: because he preached unto them Jesus and the resurrection.

And they took him, and brought him unto Areopagus, saying, May we know what this new doctrine, whereof thou speakest, is? (Acts 17:18-19).

The Supreme Court in Greece, then as now, is called the Areopagus. Paul stood in the midst of the court on Mars Hill. A group of Athenians and other learned philosophers listened as Paul spoke.

Delivering his message of the Creator who made heaven and earth, Paul spoke of the revelation of the one true God in Jesus Christ and spoke of Him as being the One by whom all the world will be judged. He is designated as such by the fact that He was raised from the dead. We continue reading in verse 32:

And when they heard of the resurrection of the dead, some mocked.

The Greek word translated "mocked" in the English language is a strong word, *chleuazo*. Do you remember reading in the second chapter of Acts when Pentecost brought down from heaven the outpouring of the Spirit of God? The believers were testifying to the grace

301

of our Lord in the languages of the people. The people who mocked, scoffed, and ridiculed the disciples are described by this word, *chleuazo*. In our story, the philosophers ridiculed, jeered, and mocked the apostle Paul as he presented the Lord Jesus' resurrection from the dead.

There were other men who were more gracious and bowed themselves out, saying, "We will hear thee again of this matter" (Acts 17:32b). We continue reading:

> So Paul departed from among them.
> Howbeit certain men clave unto him, and believed: among the which was Dionysius the Areopagite, and a woman named Damaris, and others with them (Acts 17:33-34).

We would like to discuss the two responses to the message of the apostle Paul, the response of the philosophers, and the response of those who accepted the message of the apostle and became followers of the Lord.

These philosophers were atheists. Two groups of them are named; the Epicureans and the Stoics. The Epicureans were named after Epicurus who lived a few years before and a few years after the date of 300 B.C. He was a brilliant and gifted academician. The Epicureans' explanation of the universe was atomic, which is as modern a teaching as one will find being taught by university professors today. The Epicureans accepted the atomic theory which was taught by Democratus, one of their philosophical predecessors. Democratus taught, and the Epicureans believed, that the universe was composed of atomic particles. The word *atom* in Greek means "uncut," the final, indivisible part of matter. They believed that the coarser atoms made the material world around them and that the finer atoms made up our spirits, our souls. The whole universe was the fortuitous gathering together and separating of atoms. There is no God, there is no purpose, there is no meaning. Life is altogether purposeless and aimless. They were hedonists who believed that one should get out of life the best he can because life on earth is all there is. They followed a modern philosophy proclaiming that there is nothing after life.

The Stoics were atheists of a different order, and were founded by Zeno. They were called Stoics because the philosopher Zeno taught in a *stoa*, the Greek word for "porch." They were pantheists. *Pan* is the Greek word for "all, everything"; *theos* is the word for God. They identified God with the material universe. There is no person in it, no personality in back of it. They believed that a thing just runs of itself impersonally. That is where the word "stoic" originated. A stoic is a man who accepts whatever providence there is in life and bows down before its fatalism.

These philosophers listened to Paul as he spoke of the one true God, a person who was revealed to us in Jesus Christ and was marked out as the Son of God by His resurrection from the dead. When they heard that proclamation of Paul, they scoffed, mocked, and ridiculed. Such inanity and non-intellectualness! But some of them believed, such as Dionysius, who evidently was well-known in the Christian community, as did a wonderful, gifted woman named Damaris.

What is remarkable is that there is no difference between the atheists then and those with us now. There are great university centers all over the world in which the same response to the gospel of the Son of God is expressed. There are the materialists, the atheists, the pantheists, the philosophers, the academicians, and men of pseudo-science who scoff at the idea of a personal God. Certainly they do not believe in the revelation of God in Jesus Christ.

Then there are men in their communities who accept the gospel. Some of the most learned scientists and teachers of all time have been humble and devout Christians. On every university campus and in every academic community, one will find both the atheist and the believer. Which one is correct?

There Is Intelligence in Creation

First, there is intelligence, which implies personality, in back of the universe and in back of everything that we see. It is not blind, fortuitous chance and circumstance which brought the creation into existence. It takes infinitely more faith to believe that creation just happened than to accept the spiritual revelation of God in Christ Jesus. I want to illustrate that with a little story.

A teacher of a junior Sunday school class took out his pocket watch and laid it on the table in front of his boys. He said: "Fellows, I have something to show you. Do you see this watch? It made itself. No one made it. It just happened. A watch case just plopped down. Then a number of wheels and springs came rolling along and they jumped in. Then a face plopped on along with a couple of hands. Then a crystal rolled up to it and jumped on. And there we have the watch. No one made it; it just happened."

A little boy looked at him in amazement and said, "Ain't you crazy?"

There is an intricacy in back of the timing of this universe that is almost incredible were it not that we are observing it. Just look at these facts of astronomy.

Our universe is tucked away in a corner of one of the smaller nebulae, one of the great Milky Ways. Around the central sun, which is about 846,000 miles in diameter, are the planets in their orbits. The nearest one is Mercury, revolving around that central sun. Mercury is 36,000,000 miles away and it takes eighty-eight days for it to make its orbit. Beyond Mercury is the planet Venus, which is 67,000,000 miles out in its orbit and it takes seven months to go around the sun. The next planet is Earth, which is 93,000,000 miles from the sun, and it takes a year to go around the sun. The next planet in its orbit is Mars, which is 141,000,000 miles from the sun, and it takes a year and a half to make its orbit. The next planet is Jupiter, the largest of the planets. It is 483,000,000 miles away from the sun, and it takes twelve years for it to make its orbit. Then the next planet is Saturn, which is 886,000,000 miles away, and it takes thirty years for it to make its orbit around the sun. The next planet is Uranus, which is 1,800,000,000 miles away, and it takes eighty-four years for it to make its orbit around the sun. The next planet is Neptune, which is 2,800,000,000 miles away, and it takes 168 years for it to make its orbit around the sun. Finally, we come to Pluto, the last planet in our solar system, which is 3,680,000,000 miles away from the sun, and it takes 248 years to make its orbit around it. In all the uncounted and endless ages of the ages, those orbital courses have never varied one second? It is a marvel, and it is just one of the infinitude of marvels of the Intelligence that lies in back of our universe. Elgin Watch Company used to boast, "We set our time by the stars."

At the World's Fair in Chicago in 1933 I saw a tremendous graph of creation. Right in the middle of it is man. The creation is as small in infinitesimal size below the man as it is large in infinitude above him. The macrocosm above us is no bigger than the microcosm below us. The atomic world has its systems just as this universe has its systems. It is a miracle, it is a marvel, it staggers the imagination. Only an intelligent God could create such a thing.

For a man to believe that all of creation, including man, just happened, is the same as believing that one could take the letters of the

wagons of art treasures, taken from Corinth, graced the triumphant procession of that Roman general through the streets of Rome. But Julius Caesar rebuilt Corinth in 46 B.C., and, as before, it immediately began to flourish.

Corinth was literally a meeting place of the East and the West. On each side of Corinth was a port, joining two great seas together in that one commercial city.

Corinth had a population of about 200,000 free men and 500,000 slaves, which represented approximately the same proportion of population in every ancient Greek city. It was famous in every area of artistic and cultural life. Athens was not the capital of Achaia, but Corinth was, and it had a place in the cultural world in its own right. Corinthian bronze was famous throughout the world. To this day, the most beautiful column that has ever been created is called a "Corinthian column."

The city worshiped at the altar of every vice and debauchery. The 1,000 prostitutes that were devotees of the temple of Aphrodite deepened the immoral and sinful life of the city of Corinth.

It was to that ancient city of Corinth that Paul now made his way alone. Timothy and Silas were in Macedonia. As Paul was alone in Athens, so he was alone in Corinth.

Coming to the city, he found a large colony of Jewish people who had recently been expelled from the city of Rome by Claudius Caesar. Suetonius speaks of that Claudian edict. He said that the expulsion of the Jews was because of the riot and tumult in Rome caused by one Chrestus, and he spells it with an *e*. Many scholars think that Suetonius did not hear the word correctly, and what he should have written in his history was that the tumult in the Jewish community was caused by Christus, the Messiah Jesus. Either way, the emperor expelled the entire community of Jews from the imperial city. Many of them came to Corinth, and among them were Aquila and Priscilla.

Aquila in Greek means "eagle." *Priscilla* is the diminutive form of *Prisca*, which is the name of one of the great families of ancient Roman history. Doubtless, she was connected in some way with that noble family. She must have been a gifted and cultured woman, for in this same chapter, in verse 18, they are named "Priscilla and Aquila." Six times in the New Testament the couple is mentioned, and half of the time she is named first.

In this chapter we also meet Apollos of Alexandria, who, I believe, wrote the Book of Hebrews. It is Priscilla and Aquila who instruct that brilliant Alexandrian in the deep things of the Lord Jesus. He becomes a flaming preacher, incomparable, greater than Paul, for the Corinthians wanted to follow Apollos, even though Paul founded the church.

They had become Christians in Rome, and in Corinth, when Paul sought out the Jewish community and other tentmakers like himself, he found this couple already Christians. When hand touched hand, it was as though they had known each other for an eternity. Paul stayed with them and worked with them as a tentmaker. The language of a tentmaker is seen in Paul's epistles.

At the Southern Baptist Seminary in Louisville, Kentucky, across the great porch of Norton Hall, the administrative building in the seminary, you will find inscribed these words: *Ortho tomounto Ton Logon Tes Alethesis*, which means, "Rightly dividing the word of truth." Literally, it is a tentmaker's speech. *Orthotomounto* means "rightly cutting," "straight cutting" the word of truth, and Paul had to make his tent panels correctly in order to make good tents.

So Paul was in Corinth, as he was in Thessalonica, at his trade, supporting himself with his hands as he preached the gospel of Jesus Christ.

What do you think of a minister who works at a trade and who also pastors a church and preaches the gospel? I know that your attitude is no different from mine. I inordinately admire and appreciate the man who does that. I have met men all over the world who minister where the church is too small to support them, so they work with their hands and preach the gospel.

I remember many years ago visiting in a little town in New Mexico, and on that Sunday, I attended the little Baptist church. When the pastor learned that I was there, he came to me and said: "I am ashamed to preach in your presence. Please, will you come and preach to my people?"

"No," I said. "I want to worship God with you and listen to you."

He said, "But I am untaught. I am not a man of the schools. I am ashamed to preach in your presence."

I said: "My brother, you will not have a more sympathetic listener than I. You stand up there where you ought to be and preach the gospel of Christ, and I will be praying for you. I will be the most blessed of anyone listening to the message you bring."

So he took his place and he preached. He preached like an unlearned man would preach, but he loved God, and he blessed my heart.

After the service was over, he explained to me: "You see, I am a carpenter and I was called into the ministry in later life. I had no opportunity to go to school and prepare for my work. As a carpenter, I go to little places where they do not have a church and I build it with my own hands. This church I have built with my own hands. You see that little moble home beyond the church? That is where I live. As I win people to Christ, baptize my converts, and build the church, I turn it over to a pastor. Then I go to another place where I build another church."

I said: "Our Lord was a carpenter just like you, and He worked with His hands. You have gifts I do not possess. I could not build a church. I would not know how to frame it. But the church you have built is beautiful, and God is honored in your devotion and dedication."

God's tentmakers are all over the world, working in areas where the people are too poor and the congregation is too small to support the pastor. But they work as Paul did, they preach the gospel, and God blesses them as He blessed the apostle Paul.

PAUL WAS ENCOURAGED BY SILAS AND TIMOTHY

Our text says that Paul, while in the city of Corinth when Timothy and Silas came down from Macedonia, was "pressed in the Spirit."

I know exactly how it feels when your spirit feels a great paroxysm of emotion, as Paul described in Acts 17. In Athens his distress was brought about by the vast idolatry of the city, in Corinth the people were given to vice and degradation.

When Silas and Timothy came from Macedonia, the spirit of Paul was stirred within him by the Word, by the preaching of the gospel, by the revelation of the Lord in Jesus Christ. He began to testify openly, vigorously, and powerfully through the grace of God. The Lord wonderfully blessed him.

Out of that preaching of the gospel came the conversion of Justus, a Gentile, a "proselyte of the gate," in whose home Paul stayed. Also came the conversion of Crispus, who was the chief ruler of the synagogue. "And many of the Corinthians *akouontes*," the word is present indicative participle, meaning that they continued hearing, they continued to believe, and they continued to be baptized. It was a wonderful outpouring of the Spirit of the Lord. The people were being saved every day, believing the gospel, and being baptized into the body of the Lord Jesus.

PAUL WAS ENCOURAGED BY THE LORD

Not only was Paul encouraged by the presence of Silas and Timothy, but he was also encouraged by the speaking of the Lord:

> Then spake the Lord to Paul in the night by a vision, Be not afraid, but speak, and hold not thy peace:
> For I am with thee . . . for I have much people in this city (Acts 18:9-10).

Evidently, Paul proposed to leave. Maybe the work was too difficult and the assignment too trying. He wrote in the first chapter of his letter to the church at Corinth, "To the Jews, the gospel message of Christ is a scandal, an offense to preach that this crucified, executed man is the Messiah of God." Then he says, "To the Greeks it is idiocy, it is foolishness." The Greek word that is used is *moronic*. The rabble rousers always were ready to persecute, to beat, to imprison, and to enslave. I suppose that these things had an effect upon the apostle Paul humanly. After all, the best of men have weaknesses, and Paul was a human being.

One of the most unusual things I have read about the life of Spurgeon is that he fell into deep depressions. It was almost an illness, yet he was the greatest preacher our Baptist people have ever produced.

When Paul thought of leaving, the Lord spoke to him and assured him. "Preach the gospel, the whole counsels of God, *all* of it."

It is such an easy temptation for a preacher to trim down his gospel message, to polish the sharp edges and make it attractive and palatable. The gospel message delivered to us from God presents the awesome condemnation that we are lost sinners. "There is none good, no not one," the Bible tells us. The gospel message delivers to us the awesome revelation of the judgment we face. Beyond the judgment is the wrath of God when we die in unforgiven sins. It is easy for the preacher to turn aside from the sharp edges of the Word of God and to accommodate his message to his so-called "cultured" audience.

The Lord encouraged Paul, saying: "Paul, speak the message of God, the revelation just as it is revealed to you from Jesus in heaven and on the pages of this sacred Book. Preach, for I am with you. Paul, do not look to yourself or to the Corinthians. Do not look to the rabble rousers who persecute and imprison. Paul, look to Me, for I am with you."

Blessed men, women, and young people who learn to do that, do not look to others, but look to Jesus!

"FOR I HAVE MUCH PEOPLE IN THE CITY"

God took a census and said, "These are mine. Speak to them, Paul, and they will respond."

That is the most marvelous promise I know in the preaching of the gospel to be found in God's Word. When Elijah said, "Lord, I am alone," the Lord replied: "Elijah, not so. I have 7,000 people in Israel who have not bowed to Baal."

When the pastor and the preacher stand up to deliver the message, God has His own. He has taken the census and He knows who and where they are. We read in Romans 16 that as Paul preached in Corinth his message entered the councils of the city. Erastus, the chamberlain (treasurer) of the city, was saved, as was his household. In that chapter, when Paul preached to the people in Corinth, Gaius, one of the noble citizens of Corinth, was saved. The church met in his spacious house. We also read in 1 Corinthians 16 that the household of Stephanus, Fortunatus, and Achaicus were saved. We read in Acts 18 that Crispus, the chief ruler of the synagogue, was saved, and all of his household. God blesses the preaching of the Gospel, He knows His own, and He gives us those whose hearts the Spirit has touched.

That is the comfort and the strength of the preacher of Christ. Not everyone will listen, the whole city will not respond, but God will always give us some.

Recently I was visiting with a couple who were so far removed from our church. He came from another communion and she from a different faith. Yet there they were, listening to a pastor. I said to them: "When I came to the church many years ago, I well remember kneeling down and praying, 'Dear God, if I faithfully preach the gospel and if I am true to Your Word, Lord, will you send us people?' I had the distinct conviction in my heart that God spoke to me, saying: 'If you will be faithful in preaching My Word, I will send you people. I will touch their hearts'." I said to the dear couple, "Here you are. I had no idea you live in the city. I never heard your name and never saw you before. Yet, you are asking me about the way of life and what it means to be saved and baptized."

The Spirit of God does that. Before the humblest child, we are so helpless and unable. We do not save anyone, much less regenerate or save a person's soul. God does it. The Holy Spirit of God saves a man when the message is faithfully preached.

Blessed be Jesus who so helps us, and blessed be the Spirit of the Lord who works with us. Blessed be the love of the Father who gives us such sweet harvests and such gracious response!

42

The City Church

For I am with thee and no man shall set on thee to hurt thee: for I have much people in this city. (Acts 18:10)

"Speak, for I have much people in this city." Paul was a tremendously astute and gifted missionary strategist. In his preaching of the gospel during the first days of the Christian century, he went from city to city. He preached in Ephesus, Thessalonica, Athens, Corinth, and finally, Rome. In the heart of each city he built lighthouses for Christ which changed the course of our civilization.

The Lord Is Always Interested in the City

When Paul preached the gospel in the cities, he but reflected the care, compassion, and love of our Lord for the city. Luke wrote frequently in the Book of Acts and in his Gospel of the deep interest and concern of our Savior for the city.

In Luke 9 it is said that our Lord steadfastly set His face toward the city. In chapter 13 of the Gospel we read that our Lord volitionally chose to die, to be crucified in the city. In Luke 19, our Lord is described as looking over the city and bursting into tears, weeping over its people. The same gospel writer also penned these words in the Book of Acts, and he no less depicted our Savior in heaven looking down upon the city, compassionately interested, for it was our risen and ascended Lord who spoke to Paul, saying, "Speak, I am with thee, I have much people in this city."

315

The Lord Encourages Paul to Stay in the City

The background of the address of our Lord to the apostle apparently is found in the discouragement and the obstacles which the apostle faced in Corinth. The people of Corinth were vigorously opposed to the gospel of Christ. Evidently, the apostle had it in his heart to leave. In an encouragement from the Savior, Paul was bid to remain and to speak, for the Lord said, "I have many in the city whom I am preparing to respond; they are Christians in the making, converts in the electing." So the apostle stayed in the face of these urban difficulties.

It is always difficult work to spread the gospel in the city.

Let us compare for a moment the preaching of the gospel in a rural area and in a city. I pastored in rural and village areas for ten years and became intimately conversant with the life of the people. Many of the rural churches were quarter-time churches; that is, they had services just once a month. The minister would come and preach the gospel on a Sunday, say, the fourth Sunday or the second Sunday of the month. For the rest of the month, the farmer who had heard the message, would think about the text and the sermon while he plowed in the field.

The village church, such as the one in which I grew up, was located in a small town where there was no theater (radio and television had not been discovered), and no entertainment at all. The most epochal event that could be announced was the coming of a revival meeting. Everyone attended, everyone listened, and everyone discussed, during the days of the week, the sermon that they had heard the day or night before. That was the rural and village life in which I grew up and in which I first began to minister.

Difficulties in the City

Compare that to city life today. Even between one Sunday and the next, there are thousands of things that reach into the heart and life of a man, things of the world, drowning out the message that he heard the Sunday before. City life moves at a fast and furious pace. There are so many distractions, interferences, and obstacles which arise, face, and confront the Word of God. But the city church is the most vital and significant of all the links in the kingdom of our Lord.

When I was a lad growing up, I turned my face toward the city. It never entered my mind that I would stay in a rural area. I had the dream of ministering in a city, and I am no different from any other young man or woman who grows up in a small town. They become educated and prepare themselves for an assignment in the city. By the thousands young people come to find home, life, and destiny in the city.

The cities govern and color the life of the whole nation. As the cities go, the nation goes. As the cities think, the nation thinks. As the cities vote, the nation votes. The whole cultural, political, economic, and educational life is determined by the city. Thus, the city church is vitally important to the gospel of Christ.

The Spirit of the Ministering City Church if It Lives

Let me point out some things that must characterize the city church life if it is to minister, if it is to be viable, and if it is to live.

First, the city church must of all things have in it the spirit of youth. It must never grow old and senile. So many of our city churches grow old through the years and become decrepit. They are finally buried in the great moving life of the vast metropolitan area. The church that is to live, the city church that is to minister, must ever keep the spirit of youth.

One time I stood on a city street in one of the great cities of America and looked at a used car lot. As I stood there, my mind went back to the days of my youth when I attended the church which used to stand on that lot.

The pastor was one of the dearest men I ever knew. His name was Carter Helm Jones. His father was chaplain to General Robert E. Lee in the Confederate Army.

When he was a little boy, his father sent him with a message to General Lee. Lee took Carter Helm Jones, placed him in the front of his saddle on his horse, Traveler, and took the little boy to his destination.

Pastor Jones was one of the most polished, cultured, and gifted of all of the pastors in the Southern Baptist Convention. He was lovable, gracious, and kind, but he presided over a church that had lost all its young people. There were no children or babies in it. The church was old and dying. Finally, it ceased to be.

A church must keep its vibrancy, viability, and youth if it is to live. Our faces may be wrinkled, but our hearts should never grow old. We are to stay young and alive.

In studying Browning, I remember reading the description of his funeral. Typical of funerals, it was sedate and slow.

Browning had an artist friend named Burne Jones who said: "As I sat there and listened to that dead funeral service, I thought of the intensive life of Robert Browning, who, all of his days down to old age, was alive and young in his heart and spirit. I just wished some man would come out of the triforium with a trumpet and blast the sound, raise the dead, wake the people, and speak of victory and resurrection!"

I thought: "That is great. Robert Browning did possess a vibrant and alive spirit." It was Browning who said:

> Grow old along with me
> The best is yet to be,
> The last of life, for which the first was made;
> Our times are in his hand
> Who saith, "A whole I planned,
> Youth shows but half; trust God; see all, nor be afraid!"

The church in the city that is to minister must keep its spirit of youth. It must remain vibrant, alive, and moving.

THE SPIRIT OF CONQUEST

The church that is to live in the city must be a church that marches, confronts, attacks, and moves. Depraved and evil are the times, but they are always that. This vile world is never a friend to grace. Every inch that we win for Jesus has to be fought over, just as God gave to Joshua and the children of Israel the land of Canaan for an inheritance. They had to fight for every inch of the land. It is no less true in the kingdom of God today.

When I first began my ministry, I once attended an associational meeting. Dr. Andrew Potter, our executive secretary, was attending the meeting. When a man stood up and delivered a woebegone message concerning the evil of the times, Dr. Potter replied: "My brethren, the times are always bad. Times were bad in the days of Noah, and of Abraham. They were lone believers in an idolatrous world. Times were bad in the days of Moses. They were bad in the days of Elijah and the great apostasy. They were bad in the days of Jesus, when men crucified the Son of God. The times were bad when they stoned the apostle Paul, placed him in prison, and finally decapitated him. The times are always bad."

In 1930 I remember people saying, "If we can just get out of these terrible thirties, this deep and awful depression; if we can just outlive such bad times!"

Then came the forties, which were the most terrible years I have ever known, for it was in the forties that we were engaged in the awesome Second World War.

THE TIMES ARE NEVER RIGHT

The times are always bad. They are never propitious for the gospel. It is never easy for ministers of Christ and for the church of our Lord. We must attack, we must confront, we must march. A propitious time never comes, but in this hour, whatever it is, we have to move, we have to march, we have to go on. If we wait for better times, we will wait for a lifetime. The sands of our strength will gradually ebb.

It is like Ecclesiastes 11:4, "He that observeth the wind shall not sow; and he that regardeth the clouds shall not reap." The time to do for God is now, no matter whether the times are favorable or not.

Year after year of the terrible war between the states, Abraham Lincoln sought a man to lead the Union Army who could march, who could win. One after another failed. Finally, he invited Ulysses S. Grant to be the leader of the forces. Of course, he won the war.

Lincoln invited Grant to lead the forces because he would fight, confront, and march.

One day Grant was planning an attack, and one of his generals came to him and said: "General Grant, it is raining. You cannot attack in the rain."

Grant replied: "My general, it is raining on the enemy, also."

It never is auspicious for us to march and to fight. The time to do it is now, whatever the time. The time to go forward is this moment, whatever the moment. We have just now, and that is all.

Leonidas, the noble hero of the Spartans who defended the pass at Thermopylae, was in battle against thousands of invading Persians. One of his men said to him, "General, when the Persians shoot their arrows, there are so many of them, that they darken the sky."

Leonidas replied, "Fine, then we shall fight in the shade."

He had a little army of 6,000 Greeks, and he could have stayed off the Persian host indefinitely, but a traitor had shown the Persian army a secret path over and beyond the cliffs. When Leonidas saw that he was enveloped on both sides and had no opportunity for victory, he dismissed all of the other Greeks except his 300 Spartans. By law, they could not flee before an enemy. So Leonidas and his 300 Spartans fought and died at Thermopylae. After the battle was over, the Amphityonic Council inscribed the following epitaph where the 300 Spartans and their leader Leonidas laid down their lives: "Stranger, report thy word, we pray, to the Spartans, that lying here in this spot we remain, faithfully keeping their laws." That is great! God likewise told us to be faithful unto death; that is, "be thou faithful if it costs you your life, and I will give you the crown of glory." The time to march is now.

THE SPIRIT OF IMMEDIACY

A church that lives in the city must sense the immediacy and the necessity of the hour. We have now, and that is all. We have this moment, but no promise of any other. What we do for God, we must do now, in our time, in our day, in our generation, in this moment.

I well remember a committee meeting in a church that I pastored in a small city. We were talking about a building program to take care of our young people. The members of the committee said: "We cannot enter a building program now. Maybe some other day, maybe some other year, but not now."

One of the finest businessmen in the community and dearest fellow helpers that a minister could ever have, spoke and said: "But, my brethren, I have a young teen-age boy, and if we put this off, my boy will be grown and gone. If we do anything to help my boy, we must do it now."

I realize that the father had his own boy in his heart and mind, but what he was thinking and saying is everlastingly right. Youngsters are youngsters for just awhile. Boys are boys for just a day. Turn your head and look at them again, and they will be grown. Close your eyes and look at them once more, and they will be out into the world. What we do, we must do now. The ministries that we have before God, we must offer and dedicate to Jesus on their behalf now. Tomorrow is too late.

A fellow worker in a church once told me a story about the day of Pearl Harbor. He said: "I was visiting in a poor part of town. As I was walking across the Katy Railroad track, I saw a dirty, unkempt youngster smoking a cigarette. I stopped and began talking to the lad. I said, 'You are so young to be smoking.'

The boy replied, 'Mister, I have been smoking since I was four years old'."

The godly deacon and Sunday school superintendent began to talk to the boy, telling him the good things down at the church, the wonderful activities in the Sunday school, and all of the other things that go with the beauty of the Christian life. He said: "Won't you come? We would love to have you attend. "

The dirty urchin replied, "Yes, mister, I will."

He attended the church, was converted, and was baptized. He became a marvelous teen-age Christian. As a teen-ager in Pearl Harbor, he was one of the first to be killed.

Are you not glad that it was not some other day, some other hour, some other time? It might have been too late. When the awful day came, the boy was saved, he was a Christian, and he was prepared to meet his Lord.

Such is our assignment, our great mandate from heaven. Not some other time, some other day, some other propitious moment, but we are to witness, testify, and plead for Jesus now. We are to point the way to glory, preach the gospel, and plead with people in Christ's stead, "Be ye reconciled to God." Give Him your life, your soul, and trust Him for every tomorrow. See if God does not gloriously remember you in every sweet and precious way.

There is no life like the Christian life. There is no abounding pilgrimage like the Christian pilgrimage. It is deep, it is rich, it is precious, it is beautiful, it is everything that God Himself could bestow upon us in this life, and there is heaven to come!

43

Apollos, Brilliant Alexandrian

And a certain Jew named Apollos, born at Alexandria, an eloquent man, and mighty in the scriptures, came to Ephesus.

This man was instructed in the way of the Lord; and being fervent in the spirit, he spake and taught diligently the things of the Lord, knowing only the baptism of John.

And he began to speak boldly in the synagogue: whom when Aquila and Priscilla had heard, they took him unto them, and expounded unto him the way of God more perfectly.

And when he was disposed to pass into Achaia, the brethren wrote, exhorting the disciples to receive him: who, when he was come, helped them much which had believed through grace:

For he mightily convinced the Jews, and that publicly, shewing by the scriptures that Jesus was Christ. (Acts 18:24-28)

In the first part of Acts 18 we have record of Paul on his second missionary journey going from Corinth to Ephesus, the great Greek city in the Roman province of Asia. In Ephesus he left Aquila and Priscilla, then went down to the city of Jerusalem and again to Antioch. On his third missionary journey he came to Ephesus. When he left Aquila and Priscilla at Ephesus, they begged him to remain, but he said, "I will return again if God wills."

Between the visits of Paul to Ephesus, between his second and third missionary journeys, the Alexandrian, Apollos, came to Ephesus.

Apollos impressed Dr. Luke mightily. You will not find in the Scriptures a more ardent presentation, deeper in respect and admiration, than the way in which the beloved physician presents Apollos. He is described by Luke as an "eloquent man, mighty in the Scriptures, instructed in the way of the Lord, fervent in spirit, and speaking diligently of the things of the Lord Jesus" (cf. vv. 24-25).

There are two men in all history I would love to have heard preach. One is Isaiah, the court preacher in Jerusalem. He belonged to the royal family, and when he preached, he rose from one flight of glorious rhetoric and oratory to another. His perorations were incomparable. Living 750 years before Christ, he spoke of the cross as though he stood on Golgotha himself. I would love to have heard Isaiah, the court preacher.

The second man I would have loved to have heard preach is Apollos. The Epistle to the Hebrews is a homiletical sermon, and whoever delivered it, if it was not Apollos, was a man like him. The author used the Alexandrian text of the Septuagint and he followed glorious flights of oratory as one would find in the finest of Alexandrian rhetoricians.

The Bible says he was an Alexandrian. In the decay of Athens, Alexandria became the center of the cultural and intellectual life of the civilized world, and remained so for centuries. It was founded by Alexander the Great in 332 B.C., but even Alexander never dreamed of the glory and the grandeur that would become synonymous with the city called by his name.

The greatest library the world has ever known was in Alexandria. A great catastrophe overwhelmed the human race when Omar, the Muslim caliph, burned that library in the seventh century A.D. The caliph said: "If what is in that library is not in the Koran, it is not needed. If it is in the Koran, it is not needed," and he burned the library to the ground.

The greatest version of the Scriptures, and the most influential translation ever made in human speech, was made in Alexandria. It is called the Greek Septuagint, the translation by Alexandrian scholars from Hebrew into Greek. The Greek Septuagint was the Bible of the apostles, of the first Christian missionaries and evangelists.

The greatest geometrician and mathematician was an Alexandrian. His name was Euclid, and the Euclidian geometry textbook has been used in colleges and universities for two thousand years, remaining the textbook in many schools to this present day. It is almost symbolic that the Pharos, the lighthouse, one of the Seven Wonders of the World, shined in the harbor of Alexandria.

It was in Alexandria that Greek Hellenistic philosophy had its last and final development, Neoplatonism, whose proponents were the incomparable Greek scholars, Plotinus and Porphyry.

In Alexandria lived the greatest of the Greek Christian fathers, Origen, and the orthodox champion of the faith, Athanasius.

In Alexandria lived the great Jewish philosopher Philo, a contemporary of our Lord. He took Greek philosophy and amalgamated it with the revelation of God in the Old Testament. He did it by allegory. The Alexandrian method of interpretation, preaching, and teaching by allegory is common today.

For example, Philo would take the story of the Garden of Eden in Genesis and would make it conform to Greek philosophy by saying the Garden of Eden was the picture of a man's mind. The trees in the garden were the thousands of thoughts in the human mind. The trees of Life were the thoughts of holiness and godliness. The trees of the knowledge of evil were the evil thoughts in our minds. The serpent represented the lusts of the flesh, carnality, which bring us down to the dust of the ground. The four rivers in the garden represented the four cardinal Greek virtues—prudence, temperance, fortitude, and justice. When Philo was through with the Bible, it sounded like the Timaeus of Plato himself.

All of this leads us to an interesting comparison between the education of Paul of Tarsus and Apollos of Alexandria.

The Education of the Two Men

Paul was educated not only in the Greek schools in Tarsus, but also at the feet of Gamaliel in Jerusalem. He was educated as a strict Pharisee; that is, he was taught all the tradition of the elders, later written down in what we know as the Talmud. He was learned in all of the casuistry and disputations of the Jewish schools of Hillel and Shammai. He studied in Hebrew and he spoke in Aramaic. He was learned in all the rabbinical lores that make for the background of a traditional Judaistic rabbi.

Apollos was educated in an altogether different world, in a world of rhetoric, oratory, and peroration. His teacher was Philo and others who belonged to the school of Philo. The language in which he worked was Greek. The text of the Bible that he used was the Greek Septuagint.

When Apollos came to Ephesus and began to speak boldly for the Lord, Acts 18:25 relates that he knew only the baptism of John; that is, he knew only what John the Baptist knew. This means that he knew the life of Christ, on the other side of the Crucifixion. But he did not know of the Resurrection, the Ascension, the intercession in heaven, the session in glory, and the outpouring of the Holy Spirit at Pentecost. All of the postcrucifixion life of our Lord was unknown to this eloquent preacher, Apollos. This meant he preached Jesus as a great ethical leader; that is, he preached the Jesus of the Sermon on the Mount. He preached the Jesus of righteousness, the Jesus of reformation. Apollos mightily declaimed upon repentance and its sign of immersion in water.

Reformation is a typical explanation and presentation of what one would find in practically all of the modern pulpits of Christianity today. It is the preaching of a faith that is limited by a Jesus of the Sermon on the Mount, a faith of righteousness and justice, all of which is fine. But there is more to the Christian message than just the Jesus of the Sermon on the Mount! What we need is the forgiveness of our sins. We need justification before God. We who face death need Someone who can deliver us from the victory of the grave. That is the preaching of the full gospel of the Son of God. He is not only the Jesus of the Sermon on the Mount, but He is also the Jesus of the atoning blood, the Jesus of the triumphant resurrection, the Jesus of the ascension into heaven, the Jesus who is interceding at the right hand of God. He is the Jesus who is coming again to be King and Victor over all the earth.

When Apollos came to Ephesus and spoke so eloquently and fervently in the synagogue, Aquila and Priscilla who were listening, invited him to dinner and spoke to him of the full message of the atoning grace of the Lord Jesus.

A former dear friend was Preacher E. F. Halleck. I went to be a pastor at Chickasha, Oklahoma, and in the same Chickashaw Association belonged the First Baptist Church of Norman where the University of Oklahoma is located. Preacher Halleck was my predecessor, my senior in the association for seventeen years. He was pastor of the First Church in Noman, Oklahoma, for forty-eight years, and died only recently.

Prior to his Norman pastorate, he was pastor of the First Baptist Church in Pittsburg, Kansas. He was a preacher of the Jesus of the Sermon on the Mount. He was a preacher of Jesus as a great ethical teacher. He was a liberal and a modernist. One Sunday morning at the 11:00 hour, when he had finished his message, he went down to the front of the church and told the people he had been marvelously converted. He had found the Lord as the Savior of his soul in His atoning blood on the cross, and he asked to be received for baptism.

Thereafter, Preacher Halleck was a different kind of man and a different kind of preacher, a great man of God, the one whom I knew as my friend in the beginning days of my pastoral ministry.

That is what happened to the Alexandrian named Apollos. As Aquila and Priscilla listened to him and invited him home with them, they began to speak to him about the Lord with tact and timidity. You see, they were tentmakers, just humble, menial artisans who worked with their hands, but this Alexandrian was eloquent, learned, and brilliant.

THE NOBLE CHARACTER OF APOLLOS

Now we will look at the character of Apollos. First, he was noble. He was a great man because he was also humble and teachable. He could have said to the tentmakers, "What, you who know nothing except to cut cloth and to sew pieces of fabric together, you hope to teach me the way of the Lord?"

Not so, this mighty man of the Word, this eloquent man of Alexandria listened humbly to the tentmakers and came into the full knowledge of the Lord through their witness and understanding. Apollos was a great man.

He gained his secular education in the schools of Alexandria under brilliant teachers like Philo. He gained his religion, his faith, from humble people like Aquila and Priscilla, who made tents.

Apollos came to Corinth to the church the apostle Paul had established, and the inevitable happened. You may already know what it was before I describe it. When Apollos, that learned orator began to speak of the mighty Word of God and the power of the Lord Jesus, he simply swept the church off its feet. They had never heard oratory, rhetoric, or preaching like that. When we read the Book of Hebrews, we know a little about it. The church at Corinth was mightily impressed by the preaching of Apollos. Even Paul, the founder of the church, never preached like that, nor did any man whom the congregation had ever heard.

Something happened in Corinth which one would expect. Some of the listeners said, "We are followers of Apollos." Others said, "No, we are going to stay by Paul, our father and our founder." Others said:

"Neither one of them is an apostle. We are going to stay by Simon Peter." Still others said, "We are going to follow Christ."
In 1 Corinthians 1:12 we read:

> Now this I say, that every one of you saith, I am of Paul; and I of Apollos; and I of Cephas; and I of Christ.

In 1 Corinthians 3 Paul said again:

> For ye are yet carnal: for whereas there is among you envying, and strife, and divisions, are ye not carnal, and walk as men?
> For while one saith, I am of Paul; and another I am of Apollos; are ye not carnal?
> Who then is Paul, and who is Apollos, but ministers by whom ye believed even as the Lord gave to every man?
> I have planted, Apollos watered; but God gave the increase. (vv. 3-6).

In that same third chapter, verse 22 tells us:

> Whether Paul, or Apollos, or Cephas, or the world, or life, or death, or things present, or things to come; all are yours;
> And ye are Christ's; and Christ is God's.

We are told in 1 Corinthians 4:

> And these things, brethren, I have in a figure transferred to myself and to Apollos for your sakes; that ye might learn in us not to think of men above that which is written, that no one of you be puffed up for one against another (v. 6).

Friction developed in Corinth due to the brilliance of the eloquent preaching in Apollos. The church divided over it, some of them staying with Paul, some of them staying with Apollos.

What if Apollos had said: "Think of it. As great as the mighty apostle Paul is, they are choosing me above him. They think I am a greater preacher than he." How easy it would have been for Apollos to have been lifted up and proud in his spirit, to have furthered the spirit of division in the church. Many denominations have come into existence because of the personal ambition of men in the church. They could have had a Pauline church denomination in Corinth or an Apollos denomination and church in Corinth. But look at Apollos. When we read 1 Corinthians 16:12 we see Apollos as he is in his soul and in his heart:

> As touching our brother Apollos, I greatly desired him to come unto you with the brethren: but his will was not at all [*pantos ouk*, "absolutely not"] to come.

Look at those two men. Apollos was saying, "I am not going back to

Corinth to be party to a division, Paul, between you and me. They are pitting me against you; they are trying to make an Apollos Party and a Pauline Party. Paul, I will walk by your side. I will be with you, and if there is to be any party at all, it will all be you. There is not going to be a division between us."

Paul replies to Apollos: "Apollos, I am not envious of your great abilities, your eloquent oratory, and your mighty preaching. I urge you to go, to return, to preach to them the gospel of Christ." That is the Spirit of the Lord.

THE NOBLEST OF ALL CHARACTER IN THE CHURCH

Envy and personal ambition always hurt the church. Look at a tragic development that took place in Sweden. Before Bishop Helander's trial was concluded, Swedish papers quoted the dean of Halmstad, Knut Norborg, who confessed that guilt for the state of affairs disclosed lay on the entire church. Both in the election of bishops and in the selection of pastors, said Dean Norborg, there had too often been "slander and intrigue, quarreling between factions, half-truths and lies, careerism, and everything else mixed into a beautiful witch's brew."

But the destruction caused by ambition is not confined to episcopally-organized churches. It plays havoc in every kind of church, including those that boast of their democratic and equalitarian nature. There is no conceivable kind of church organization, ranging all the way from the tight discipline of monastic orders and the Salvation Army to the loose associations of "full gospel" tabernacles, where the corrosion of ambition is not a constant threat. Nor, as long as the Christian ministry remains in mortal—and therefore sinning—hands, can the destruction caused by the seductions of ambition be wholly escaped.

Envy and pride are great sins in the ministry and in the church. Personal ambition is green-eyed and monstrous. How triumphant for the minister to overcome it!

In the city of London lived a marvelous preacher named F. B. Meyer. One day a youth, nineteen years of age, came to the city and preached like an archangel. Immediately thousands waited upon him. A hall could not be found big enough to hold the uncounted thousands who waited on the ministry of that lad, Charles Haddon Spurgeon.

F. B. Meyer said: "When I looked at the immediate, world-famed glory of young Charles Haddon Spurgeon, I was filled with envy and personal consternation. I took it to the Lord. I got down on my knees before God and I promised God I was going to pray for that young rising star. Every day I prayed for that young and brilliant orator. The day soon came when every time Spurgeon won a victory, I rejoiced as though I had had a part in it myself, for I had prayed for him and held him up before the Lord. When God blessed him, it was an answer to my prayers, and I rejoiced in the favor of Jesus upon him."

How noble for a man to stand beside another brother and rejoice in the grace gifts God has bestowed upon him!

> If the wide world stood row on row,
> And stones at you began to throw,
> I'd boldly out with them to fight,
> Saying they were wrong—and you were right.
>
> If every bird on every tree
> With note as loud as loud could be,
> Sang endlessly in your dispraise,
> One graceless thought it would not raise.
>
> If all the great, and wise, and good,
> Upon your sins in judgment stood—
> They'd simply waste their valued breath,
> For I'm your friend through Life and Death.
>
> If I were wrong, and they were right,
> I'd not believe (for all their might),
> Not even if all they said were true,
> For you love me and I love you.

We are together in the Lord. For the grace gifts God has given to you, I praise Him as you magnify the name of the Lord with them. I love you, I pray for you, and if any seed or root of bitterness ever enters my heart in envy, may God take it away, for I want to walk by your side. May the Lord be magnified in all of our differing gifts!

Did you know that the story of Apollos closes in that note of love and concern? After Paul was delivered from the Mamertine Dungeon, he wrote to Titus, saying in one of his last words:

> Bring Zenas the lawyer and Apollos on their journey diligently, that nothing be wanting unto them (Titus 3:13).

Paul and Apollos, refusing to be divided by ambition, envy, or the plaudits of the world, were together in the Lord. "I am with you,

Apollos," said Paul. "I am with you, Paul," said Apollos. "We will walk in the goodness of the Lord together." That is great! That will make a great church, a great denomination, and a great kingdom. It will bless you, me, and the people of God forever.

This is just another way of saying that it is grand to be a Christian. It is the most beautiful life to live known to man, the foundation upon which to build your house and home. It is the glory in which to rear your children in the love and nurture of the Lord. It is the most immovable foundation of strength upon which to erect your business and your life. It is the way to live and the way to die. It is the way to look up to the glory that God has in store for those who love Him!

44

Lettering In

And when he was disposed to pass into Achaia, the brethren wrote, exhorting the disciples to receive him: who, when he was come, helped them much which had believed through grace. (Acts 18:27)

In Acts 18:24 we read a story of the writing of a letter from Ephesus to Corinth concerning Apollos, the brilliant and eloquent Alexandrian, who was taught full in the way of the Lord. The brethren at Ephesus wrote this letter to the church at Corinth, telling them that Apollos was a fellow Christian and disciple, and they were to receive him as such. The letter written from one church to another stated, "We commend to you this child of God." This is similar to what we send today when a person joins another church by letter.

The development of joining a church by letter in our modern Christian communion is sometimes amazing to me. While holding a revival meeting in one of the large cities of the heartland of America on a Sunday morning, I had given the invitation and a woman in the congregation developed deepening interest. As the moments passed, the pastor went back and spoke to her. Then the family gathered round. Then friends joined the family. The choir sang the invitation again. The pastor pleaded with the woman. Her family and friends also pleaded with her. Finally, she responded and came down to the front.

Standing in the pulpit, I thought, "What a glorious and incomparable victory, for the Lord has brought to pass a great spiritual triumph!"

So we were seated, and the harvest that God had given to us that hour was introduced to the congregation. When the pastor came to that woman, I thought he was going to announce some wonderful and marvelous spiritual epoch. The pastor introduced her and stated that she had transferred her letter from one church in the city to that church, and that was it.

I can well remember my heart sinking as I sat in the pulpit. So that is a marvelous and spiritual triumph! She moved her letter from one part of town to another after long praying and pleading.

According to the Scriptures, there is a biblical basis for the joining of a church by letter. Apollos did that when he moved from the city of Ephesus to the city of Corinth. The congregation at Ephesus wrote a letter and commended him to the brethren of Achaia, Corinth being the capital city.

Another instance of a letter is mentioned when Paul wrote to the church at Rome. Phoebe had in her hand the theological treatise which we call "The Epistle to the Romans." Paul wrote a letter, saying in chapter 16:

> I commend unto you Phoebe, our sister, which is a servant, [a deaconess] of the church which is at Cenchrea [the port city on the southern side of Corinth]:
> That ye receive her in the Lord as becometh saints, and that ye assist her in whatsoever business she hath need of you: for she hath been a succourer of many, and of myself also. (vv. 1-2).

Following is part of a letter that Paul wrote to Colossae from a Roman dungeon, addressed to Philemon, concerning a Christian convert:

> Paul, a prisoner of Jesus Christ, and Timothy our brother, unto Philemon our dearly beloved, and fellow-labourer,
> And to our beloved Apphia [the wife of Philemon], and Archippus our fellow-soldier, and to the church in thy house.
> I beseech thee for my son Onesimus, whom I have begotten in my bonds:
> Which in time past was to thee unprofitable, to thee and to me:
> Whom I have sent again: thou therefore receive him, that is, mine own bowels [of my very heart] (Philemon 1-2, 10-12).

In the Scriptures we find abounding testimony to the practice of writing a letter when a person would move from one city to another, as Onesimus was sent by Paul from Rome to the city of Colossae.

It Is a Modern Practice to Leave Our Religion Back Home

The practice of leaving our church membership somewhere far away is a modern and monstrous development.

One time I pleaded with a family: "Your children have been saved, they are going to be baptized, and they are going to belong to the family of God. You come also and move your letter, move your membership with us."

They replied to me: "No, because some day we may go back home where we came from."

I asked, "How long has it been since you have been back home and how long has it been that you lived here?"

They answered, "Sixteen years!" Sixteen years they had been planning to go back home, and they left their church membership there.

This is not an isolated incident but is a normal pattern in so much of our Christian life.

In a revival meeting I held in one of the great cities on the eastern seaboard, the people took a census of the city. At that time there were more than 25,000 Baptists in that city whose membership was in some other town, in some other place.

I held a revival meeting in one of the great cities in mid-America, and in the census of that city there were more than 30,000 Baptists who had left their membership back home.

I have been in California many times, and again there are uncounted thousands of Baptists who have left their membership back east.

There is a scriptural reason for a church letter. It is right that one church write to another church commending a family or a fellow Christian to a new congregation.

There is also a methodological reason for it. The church back home has a church roll, too, and the clerk keeps the names of those who have been baptized, who love the Lord, and who are present in that congregation. Then when they move to another city and another congregation, it is good that the church clerk send a letter to that church to say that this is a family they are dismissing from the congregation and church roll, and they may add it to their church there.

All that is good, but how could it ever be thought that religion is a matter of paper, or writing a letter? My religion goes with me wherever I am.

Look at the passage Paul wrote in 2 Corinthians 3. He says:

> Do we begin again to commend ourselves? or need we, as some others, epistles of commendation to you, or letters of commendation from you?
> Ye are our epistle written in our hearts, known and read of all men:

Forasmuch as ye are manifestly declared to be the epistle of Christ ministered by us, written not with ink, but with the Spirit of the living God; not in tables of stone, but in fleshly tables of the heart (vv. 1-3).

When I move, I take my religion with me, whatever kind it is, and it is never communicated or carried by a piece of paper.

WHEREVER A MAN MOVES, HE SHOULD MOVE HIS LETTER INTO THE CHURCH

I have four reasons why I think that as soon as we come into another city and find our way to the brethren who love God in that area, we ought to identify ourselves with the people of God.

First, I need to do it for my own soul's sake. When I go to church, there is the bread of life to feed my soul, there is the water of life, the exposition of God's Holy Word from which I drink, and there is the sweet fellowship of the praises of Jesus as we sing together, as we pray together, as we listen to the expounding of the Word of God together. It blesses my soul and my life to identify myself with the people of the Lord. When I do not, I starve my soul, my heart atrophies, and I grow cold and indifferent.

A pastor visited a man who had moved to the city but was not in the church. It was a cold, winter day, and when the pastor visited, he sat down by the man's side before a big fire. As they sat there, the pastor took the long poker and pulled out of those burning coals a burning ember, dragging it out on the hearth. The one ember alone soon became cold, died, and ceased to flame and to burn. Without the pastor saying a word, the man turned toward him and said: "Preacher, I see. I will be there next Sunday."

We are that way. Alone, somehow we grow cold and indifferent. All of us conjoined make a fire, a blaze, a burning in the presence of the Lord. We need encouragement. The world is so much against us. Temptation, coldness, and indifference simply slay us. We need the encouragement of one another. We need the encouragement of the church. Often we fall into such deep problems and spiritual confrontations. We need what the church has to offer our trembling hearts.

That is why the church was organized, why it was built, why Christ gave it to us, that we might encourage each other in the faith in the pilgrim way. I need to put my life in the church; I need it for my soul's sake.

Second, I need to put my life in the church for the sake of the people of God, for the pastor, for those who march, worship, and glorify God by his side, because they need encouragement. When I join myself to them, the pastor is encouraged, the deacons are encouraged, the Sunday school leadership is encouraged, the Training Union leadership is encouraged, the choir, the whole vast multifaceted ministries of the Lord are all encouraged when I respond with my life.

Did you ever think why the Lord asked us to publicly confess our faith in Him? Why could a man not do it privately? Throughout the story of the Bible, God has asked that we publicly avow our faith. On the dark Passover night, the Israelites were to take the blood of the lamb, and with a hyssop, sprinkle it in the form of a cross on the front door of the house at the top of the door on the lintel and on the doorposts on either side. Why could they not have sprinkled that blood on the closet or in the kitchen door at the back? Because God says His people are to be publicly identified, publicly committed. The blood is to be on the front door of the house.

When you read the New Testament, listen to the words of Jesus in Matthew 10:

> Whosoever therefore shall confess me before men, him will I confess before my Father which is in heaven.
>
> But whosoever shall deny me before men, him will I also deny before my Father which is in heaven (vv. 32-33).

That is the universal appeal, demand, and mandate of God. I am publicly to identify myself with the Lord and His people. Why? I think the answer consists of two things: One, I need it. When I publicly testify for the Lord, stand up for Jesus, I am strengthened in the faith. Again, when I publicly commit my life to Christ, I encourage the pastor, the church, and the people of the Lord.

There is one experience in my life I would give anything in the earth if I could go back and change.

One Sunday I was standing in Hyde Park in London, a day in which thousands of people mill around and listen to speakers. A humble pastor had come to that place in Hyde Park, and standing on each side of him were deacons. He was saying the sweetest things about Jesus anyone could imagine. He was telling the people how much Jesus had meant to him and what the Lord could mean to them.

In the crowd were sons of Belial, bestial, uncouth, unnatural, inhuman beings. They spoke violently against the pastor. I was amazed and astonished. One of them especially, I remember, walked up to the pastor, pointed his finger at him, and then pointed to the crowd, saying: "Jesus Christ, if I could get my hands on You, I would crucify You again today. As You were crucified two thousand years ago, so we would murder You today."

Do you know what? I stood there through all of that and never said a word. That is why I would to God I could go back through the years and stand in that place. This time I would make my way up to the pastor and stand by his side, and when that blasphemy was uttered, I would lift up my hand today and say: "Men and women, I am from America. I am a visitor, and maybe I have no right to speak, but I want you to know that as a visitor and as an American, I am a Christian. I have found refuge, peace, hope, and promise in Jesus as my Savior."

I would to God I had done it. That is why the Lord says we are to confess our faith publicly before the people of God and the whole world.

Third, we should respond to the invitation and put our lives in the church because the golden moments of opportunity so quickly flee away. We have them just now and they are gone forever.

In a meeting I held in one of the great cities of the South, the warm fires of the meeting began to burn when a woman came forward in the service. I do not think I have ever seen a woman cry and sob more heartbrokenly than that dear woman.

After the service was over, I said to the pastor, "What was the burden in the heart of that dear and blessed woman that she cried so piteously?"

The pastor replied: "It would be hard for you to understand such a burden of heart unless you had fallen into the same tragic mistake that has overwhelmed her. She belonged to a little country church in Georgia which had a family cemetery beside it. Later, she and her husband moved to the city of Atlanta where two sons were born to them. As the days passed, the two boys grew to the age of accountability. They responded to the invitation of the pastor to give their hearts to the Lord. The little boys went to the mother and said, "Mother, we want to be baptized, we want to belong to the church, we want you to come with us.'

"The mother replied, 'Children, I could not leave the church in the country where my mother and father are buried, where I was baptized.'

"The little boy said, 'O Mother, we are going to be Christians now, we want to be baptized, and we want you to come with us.'

"The mother said, 'No, I could not leave the church at home.'

"So the days passed, and days have a habit of growing into months. Months have a habit of growing into years. In the providence of God, the two little boys grew up and became two of the leading businessmen in the city of Atlanta.

"As the days passed, down the aisle that mother came, placing her life in that church and asking prayer for her two sons. The pastor said that the mother went to those two boys and pleaded with them, but the boys smiled and said, 'Mother, we understand, but we have found another life.'"

The pastor said, "I went to each of those big businessmen and pleaded with them about Jesus. They smiled and said, 'Pastor, we understand, but we have our own lives now and we have found our own way. God bless you in your way, but we are going ours.' That is why that mother cries."

> Oh, there is a time we know not when,
> A place, we know not where,
> That marks the destiny of men,
> To glory or despair.

The time is now. Those golden moments may never come back.

Fourth, we should place our lives in the church with the people of God for Jesus' sake. We owe it to Him. God bless me as I seek to witness and testify to His loving grace where I live.

A man went to a person who was so indifferent and said, "Do you know that Jesus died for you?"

The man tartly replied: "Listen, I have been told that stuff all my life. Yes, I know He died for me."

The man said to him, "Do you thank Him?"

Those words were as an arrow through his soul. The next service he went down the aisle at the church, took the pastor by the hand, and said to him that unusual word, "Pastor, I have come forward to thank Jesus for dying for me."

Lord, if I had a forever, I could not count the blessings You have poured out upon me. If I had an eternity, I could not adequately repay the depth of my gratitude for Your dying for me. Lord, I want to be counted among those who say, "Thank You, Jesus." I want to be numbered with those who praise Thy name. Count me in, Lord. I believe. Here I am; here I come!